AF740437

LEGAL WALES: ITS PAST, ITS FUTURE

161 177560 0

Two week loan

Please return on or before the last date stamped below.
Charges are made for late return.

WITHDRAWN

IS 239/0799

INFORMATION SERVICES PO BOX 430, CARDIFF CF10 3XT

CYMDEITHAS HANES CYFRAITH CYMRU

THE WELSH LEGAL HISTORY SOCIETY

Cyfrol I : Volume I

LEGAL WALES : ITS PAST, ITS FUTURE

Essays dedicated to Professor Dafydd Jenkins on his ninetieth birthday

Edited by

Thomas Glyn Watkin
Professor of Law
University of Wales, Cardiff

CAERDYDD – CARDIFF
CYMDEITHAS HANES CYFRAITH CYMRU
THE WELSH LEGAL HISTORY SOCIETY
2001

WG
11
.L

CARDIFF UNIVERSITY
-1 MAY 2003
PRIFYSGOL CAERDYDD

Cyhoeddwyd gan
CYMDEITHAS HANES CYFRAITH CYMRU

Published by
THE WELSH LEGAL HISTORY SOCIETY

© The Contributors, 2001.

British Library Cataloguing in Publication Data. A catalogue record for this book is available from the British Library

ISBN 0-9541637-0-2

All rights reserved. No part of this publication may be reproduced or transmitted in any form by any means, electronic, mechanical, photocopying, recording or otherwise, or stored in any restricted system of any nature without the written permission of the copyright holder, application for which should be addressed to the distributor. Such written permission must also be obtained before any part of this publication is stored in a retrieval system of any nature.

Printed in Wales by Infographics, Ltd., Cowbridge

Distributed by

Cymdeithas Hanes Cyfraith Cymru
Ysgol y Gyfraith, Prifysgol Cymru, Caerdydd, CF10 3XJ.

The Welsh Legal History Society
Cardiff Law School, University of Wales, Cardiff, CF10 3XJ.

CONTENTS

LIST OF CONTRIBUTORS

The Venerable Anthony Crockett is the Archdeacon of Carmarthen

Brian Hutton is the former Secretary and Deputy Librarian of the National Library of Scotland

David J. Ibbetson is Regius Professor of Civil Law in the University of Cambridge and a Fellow of Corpus Christi College

Richard W. Ireland is a Senior Lecturer in Law at the University of Wales, Aberystwyth

David Lambert is currently Legal Adviser to the Presiding Officer of the National Assembly for Wales

Dr. Christopher McNall is a Lecturer in Law at the University of Wales, Cardiff

The Honourable Mr. Justice Thomas is Presiding Judge on the Wales and Chester Circuit

Thomas Glyn Watkin is Professor of Law and Director of the Centre for Civil Law Studies at the University of Wales, Cardiff

PREFACE

Legal Wales : Its, Past, Its Future is a celebration volume. It celebrates, firstly, the foundation of the Welsh Legal History Society, *Cymdeithas Hanes Cyfraith Cymru*, and it does so by publishing the first collection of its proceedings. Six of the eight papers contained in the volume are based on lectures delivered to the Society by members at the three meetings held during the first fifteen months of the Society's existence. These include the Society's inaugural lecture at Cardiff in May 1999 given by Professor David Ibbetson, the text of which has also been published in the *Transactions of the Honourable Society of Cymmrodorion* for the year 2000. Also included are the papers given by Dr. Christopher McNall, the Venerable Anthony Crockett and Mr. Richard Ireland at the National Library of Wales in November of the same year, and those given by Mr. Brian Hutton and myself at the Welsh Legal History sessions which concluded the Fourteenth British Legal History Conference at the University of Wales, Aberystwyth in July 2001. The other two contributions are a specially-written review of the beginnings of the National Assembly by Mr. David Lambert, and the text of our President, Mr. Justice Thomas', powerful and thought-provoking Lord Morris of Borth-y-Gest Lecture given at the University of Wales, Swansea in October 2000.

Secondly, the volume celebrates the rich and diverse history of law in Wales, and does so at a very significant moment in the nation's legal history. Over the last two millennia, Wales has experienced infusions of legal culture from various sources – the civil law of ancient Rome, the canon law of the Christian Church, the customs of its own native rulers and peoples, the common law of neighbouring England. On the threshold of the third Christian millennium, the creation of the National Assembly marks the start of yet another chapter in that story. The essays in the first half of this volume examine a variety of topics from Wales' legal past: the impact of the Edwardian conquest upon the native laws and their administration; the influence of competing legal cultures upon legal development in Wales; the contribution of eminent Welsh lawyers to British and world jurisprudence, and the tenacity of Welsh standards and perspectives in the face of legislation and judicature largely controlled by Westminster. The essays in the second half of the volume shift our gaze from that past to the present and the future, setting out the opportunities and challenges which face Legal Wales in the wake of devolution, and in the context of what can be learned from the lessons of the relatively recent past.

Finally, the volume celebrates the ninetieth birthday on St. David's Day, 2001 of Wales' most distinguished legal historian, Professor Dafydd Jenkins. The contribution which Professor Jenkins has made to the development of Welsh, and indeed British and European, legal history over a period of almost seventy years has been formidable. The founding father of the British Legal History Conferences and the *doyen* of the Colloquia and Seminars on Welsh Mediaeval law held under the auspices of the University of Wales' Board of Celtic Studies, has not only himself edited legal texts, such as *Llyfr Colan* and *Damweiniau Colan*, written textbooks, such as *Cyfraith Hywel*, and numerous articles in both scholarly and popular journals, he has also inspired and been the inspiration of many other scholars and students to emulate his example and take up the task of unravelling the strands of Wales' legal past, and always with an eye to the importance of that legal heritage to the future of the nation. Several contributors acknowledge their debt to him in what they have written. I happily do so here, and it has been of immense importance to this Society that at its birth it had not only Dafydd's encouragement and support, but also his blessing. We all hope that he finds pleasure in its dedication to him and much of interest in its contents. It is a matter of regret that this first volume does not contain a contribution written in Welsh, a deficiency which we hope to rectify in future publications.

As editor of this first of the Society's volumes, there are some notable expressions of thanks that I am both bound and privileged to make. At the time of writing this Preface, the Society has 150 members, all of whom have by their willingness to join made possible the success of this venture. The energy and enthusiasm of our President, Sir John Thomas, has been a key factor in driving the enterprise forward, and thanks are also due to him not only for allowing us to publish the text of his Lord Morris of Borth-y-Gest lecture but also for donating the honorarium arising therefrom to the Society. I should also like to thank the Society's committee, Mr. Michael Jones, Dr. Peter Roberts and Mr. Richard Ireland for their support in many and various ways, and in particular to Mr. Richard Ireland for organizing both of the Society's meetings at Aberystwyth. I am indebted to my personal assistant at Cardiff Law School, Miss Linda Mackleworth, for her help with many of the routine daily tasks which fall to the Secretary and Treasurer. Finally, I should like to thank all of the contributors to this volume for their willingness to give papers to the Society and prepare them for publication, and also for the efficient and timely manner in which they submitted their final copy so as to make this volume's publication both possible and punctual.

Thomas Glyn Watkin
Cardiff
October, 2001

THE COMMOTE AND COUNTY COURTS OF WALES, 1277–1350

Christopher McNall*

THE English administrative settlement of Wales, instituted in the wake of Edward I's military victory over the princely house of Gwynedd in 1283, has attracted considerable comment from historians.[1] However, relatively little attention has been paid to the impact of the imposition, central to this settlement, of an English legal order upon the laws and legal institutions of the conquered territories.[2]

At the Conquest, the Welsh long had been possessed of their own system of laws - the *cyfraith*, traditionally attributed to Prince Hywel Dda (Howell the Good), and originating as early as the tenth century. In its most developed form, this law,[3] to be found in three distinct Codes - associated with Gwynedd (Latinised as 'Venedotia'), Dyfed ('Dimetia'), and Gwent ('Gwentia') - supplemented by a sizeable body of miscellaneous provisions, contains much of refinement and sophistication; indeed, the overall tenor of this corpus was assessed by Maitland as 'lawyer-made law, glossators' law, text-writers' law',[4] which may perhaps be taken as a high measure of approval. Such a description is merited by a system of pleading bristling with complexity[5] and substantive provisions which appear startlingly advanced even to modern

---

* Cardiff Law School. Some of this material was presented as papers to the Welsh Legal History Society and the Oxford Celtic Seminar, and I am very grateful for the feedback garnered on those occasions, as well as to Paul Brand and David Ibbetson for their detailed comments.

1 E.g. R.R.Davies, *Conquest, Co-existence and Change: Wales 1063-1415* (Oxford and Cardiff, 1987) 360-370.

2 A conspicuous exception is Llinos Beverley Smith's landmark study, 'The Statute of Wales, 1284' (1980) 10 *Welsh Historical Review* 127-154.

3 The edition cited in this study is *The Ancient Laws and Institutes of Wales,* ed. Aneurin Owen (quarto edition, two volumes, London, 1841) [ALIW].

4 F.W.Maitland, *The Laws of Wales - The Kindred and the Blood Feud,* in Collected Papers, ed. H.A.L. Fisher, vol 1, 202 (Cambridge, 1911).

5 See T.M.O. Charles-Edwards, 'Cynghawsedd: Counting and Pleading in Medieval Welsh Law' (1986) 33 *Bulletin of the Board of Celtic Studies* 188-198; A.R.Wiliam, 'Llyfr Cynghawsedd (Book of Pleadings)' (1988) *Bulletin of the Board of Celtic Studies* 73-85.

eyes (for instance, the principles said to have been applicable to pre-natal injury).[6]

This is some of the background against which the principal vehicle and cornerstone[7] of the Edwardian legal settlement, the Statute of Wales,[8] described by Pollock and Maitland as 'the most comprehensive code that any English legislator issued during the middle ages',[9] was promulgated by the King and Council at Rhuddlan in March 1284. After reciting the annexation of Welsh lands to the English crown, the statute's preamble observes that, once the Welsh laws and customs diligently had been gone over before the King and his nobles, some were abolished, some retained, and some corrected.[10] A number of examples of the integration of Welsh legal practice into the framework of the new dispensation show the retention to have been genuine;[11] for instance, it was ordained that if a defendant, summoned at three successive sittings of the county court, failed to appear, the court, at its discretion, could award damages to the plaintiff, and the defendant, 'according to Welsh law and custom',[12] was to incur a penalty payable to the King. This rule is at variance with the English law administered in England,

---

[6] ALIW vol 1 p 201 leges 1 and 2 (Gwynedd Code).

[7] E.g. Michael Prestwich, *Edward I* (London, 1988), 206: the statute was 'a most statesmanlike attempt to resolve many of the problems posed as a result of the ... conquest'.

[8] *Statutes of the Realm* (Record Commissioners, London, 1810) vol 1, 55-68.

[9] Sir Frederick Pollock and F.W.Maitland, *The History of English law before the time of Edward the First* (first edition, Cambridge, 1895) vol 1, 220-221.

[10] ... leges et consuetudines parcium illarum hactenus usitatas coram nobis et perceribus regni nostri fecimus recitari quibus diligenter auditis et plenius intellectis quasdam ipsarum de consilio precerum predictorum delivimus quasdam permisimus et quasdam correximus.

[11] Although this has not been unchallenged. For instance, R.R.Davies has written that 'The Statute of Wales shows a large measure of intolerance of native customs and scant respect for the way of compromise' (*The Law of the March,* (1970-71) 5 *Welsh History Review* 1 at 28).

[12] 'secundum legem et consuetudinem Wallensicam'. The custom seems to have been ALIW vol 1 p 471 point 112 (Dyfed Code). A 1281 inquiry into Welsh laws provides evidence for this custom in the Cardiganshire commotes of Mefenydd, Anhuniog and Yr Creuddyn (*Calendar of various Chancery rolls* (London, 1912) 207-208 (evidence of Howel, son of William); 209 (testimonies of Griffin Person and David ab Griffin).

[13] Pollock and Maitland, *op.cit.,* vol 2, 591-595.

in which neither judgement could be entered, nor damages awarded, against a defendant until he happened to put in an appearance.[13]

The statute goes on to divide the conquered territories into six counties.[14] Each was to have a county court, and, with an attention to detail typical of Edwardian legislation, the statute lays down the manner in which county courts were to be held, and delineates their jurisdiction. Presided over by the sheriff, the county court was to convene once a month. The sitting was to begin with statements, sworn by juries assembled from each locality, of serious criminal offences and deaths within their respective districts, to be followed by private prosecutions of the more serious criminal offences: wounding, 'mayhem', rape, arson, and robbery. The county court also was to have jurisdiction over all pleas of trespass in which the damages claimed did not exceed forty shillings, replevin, debts of less than forty shillings, and other contractual claims. Upon making a civil claim, the plaintiff was to provide pledges for prosecution, and the defendant was to be summoned to the next county court. All these provisions accord with contemporary English practice.[15]

Financial abstracts of the business of some Welsh county courts have survived for scattered years from the beginning of the fourteenth century, and these allow the actual range of business to be investigated. The earliest abstract details the pleas and perquisites of the Carmarthenshire county courts for the year beginning at Michaelmas 1301.[16] The plural is used because the organisation of jurisdiction in Carmarthenshire during this period was unusual; with separate county courts for the Englishry and the Welshry, Carmarthenshire was, in effect, a 'double county'.[17] It is not clear whether the division in Carmarthenshire was effected along geographical lines, or according to the ethnic background of the parties to any particular

---

[14] Anglesey, Caernarvon, Merioneth, Flint, Carmarthen, and Llanbadarn with Cardigan.

[15] The principal study is Robert C. Palmer, *The County Courts of Medieval England 1150-1350* (Princeton, 1982).

[16] Public Record Office SC 2/215/32.

[17] *A History of Carmarthenshire,* ed. Sir John E.Lloyd (Cardiff, 1935) Chapter 3 (D.L.Evans).

[18] Originally, in English law, a render to a lord of the best live beast, but commuted

claim. Only Welsh names appear on the roll of the Welshry court, whilst the Englishry court (again, judging solely from the names) appears to have had only English as plaintiffs, although there do seem to have been Welsh defendants. This suggests either that there were no Welsh living in the Englishry, or that any resident Welsh were not permitted to sue there. Whatever the truth of the matter, the Welshry court is by far the busier of the two - about 180 items are recorded for the year, bringing in the decent total of just under forty pounds. This is in stark comparison with only nine suits in the Englishry court, none of which appears to have been contentious, and which generated only about one-thirtieth of that sum. In asking how this disparity can be accounted for, it seems that the Welsh not only were more populous than the English, but also were subjected more stringently than their English neighbours to certain feudal-like dues (for instance, heriots)[18] which, payable in court, would have left their mark on the roll. For the sake of completeness, a third court - that of the Hundred of Carmarthen[19] - must be mentioned.[20] Judging from the fact that all but one of the names mentioned in the account of its business are English, the Hundred court seems to have been exclusively a court of the Englishry. However, even if the Hundred Court was siphoning business exclusively away from the Englishry county court, it still only managed to generate the paltry income of just over fifty shillings. Accordingly, whichever way it is looked at, there was far more litigation, generating far more revenue, in the Welshry than the Englishry,[21] and this picture stands several decades later.[22]

The account of the Welshry court is simply a long list of names and sums, most accompanied with a caption noting the reason for its having been

---

at an early period to a monetary payment.

[19] Recorded as having sat seventeen times during 1301-2.

[20] For a record of it, see SC 2/215/32 m 4.

[21] This is also on all fours with the evidence of the business of other Englishry courts, for instance Beaumaris town court generated just over £2 in pleas and perquisites in 1307-8 (SC 2/215/1), and Conway town court only 10 shillings and six pence between Michaelmas 1301 and Michaelmas 1302 (SC 2/215/48).

[22] E.g. For five courts held in Carmarthenshire between October 1338 and January 1339, the Englishry generated £1-11-8, and the Welshry £3-9-6: SC 2/215/22, mm 1, 2.

[23] For instance, 'under' (*sub quo*) the sheriff of Merioneth were to be the cantred of

extracted. Paltry though this information is, it does nevertheless point towards a good range of civil and criminal business. On the civil side, a range of pleas falling within those legal categories which the statute of Wales had assigned to the newly-established county courts is encountered; for instance, claims of trespass (of which there are four, bringing in amercements of between ten pence and two shillings and sixpence) and debt (for instance, arising from the sale of livestock). The matters addressed by the Welshry court's criminal jurisdiction appear to have been of a fairly venial cast; principally, petty theft and brawls. The highest fine imposed, even when blood is said to have been drawn, is only seven shillings and sixpence.

However, the county was not the root administrative division of post-Conquest Wales. At levels below the county, the statute of Wales preserves the basic pre-conquest Welsh administrative units, the cantreds and commotes (*cwmwd*);[23] furthermore, the statute provides that there were to be 'commote bailiffs' who 'faithfully were to do and discharge their offices and diligently attend to them, according to what shall be given them in charge by the justices and sheriffs'.[24] The commote resembles the English Hundred, and, accordingly, its retention can be seen as providing an element of continuity between the pre- and post- Conquest legal orders. The policy of the 1284 statute in this respect seems to have been foreshadowed by the treatment of five Cardiganshire commotes taken by the English in the war of 1277.[25] A surviving account roll for a three-year period beginning in December 1277[26] returned by the reeves (*prepositi*) of several lands belonging to the manor of Llanbadarn Fawr[27] evinces a pre-1284 Edwardian policy of retention of the commote and its internal administrative structure; the account of the commote of Mefenydd is stated to have been returned by the reeve, one Madoc Ychcchan (sic), 'by the view and witness' (*per visum*

Meirionydd, and the commotes of Ardudwy, Penllyn, and Edeirnion, 'with their metes and bounds'.

[24] Sint eciam ballivi commotorum qui officia sua fideliter faciant et exequantur et eisdem diligenter intendant secundum quod justiciarii et vicecomites eis iniungant.

[25] Geneu'r Glyn, Anhuniog, Perfedd, Mefenydd, and Yr Creuddyn. See A.H.Williams, *An Introduction to the History of Wales:The Middle Ages* (Cardiff, 1948) 135 n 2.

[26] SC 6/1158/1.

[27] Just inland from Aberystwyth.

et testimonium) of Howel ap Gwilym, the *rhaglaw*, or steward, of that commote. The same is seen in the commote of Geneu'r Glyn: Madoc is named as the reeve, but the account is by the view and witness of another *rhaglaw*, one Griffin ap Madoc. Not only has the commote been preserved as the basic accounting unit, but also the local administration, in the person of the principal administrative office associated with the commote, the *rhaglaw*, appears to have remained in Welsh hands. The retention is more than simply in name: the accounts include an item for the maintenance of the *rhaglaw*'s horse and manservant[28] - a customary payment exigible at Welsh law.[29]

The commotes are known to have functioned as judicial units before the Conquest[30] but little is known about this aspect of them. The Welsh laws provide[31] that every commote was to have a judge (*ynad* or *brawdwr*)[32] - perhaps an officially-appointed professional,[33] responsible for holding a commote court, and for keeping a written record (the court book, or *llyfr llys*[34]). It should, however, be noted that this picture might not have held true everywhere; for instance, it seems to be at variance with the supposed

---

[28] 'pro sustentacione unius garcionis et equi Raglow': SC 6/1158/1 m 1.

[29] The grant of the shrievalties of Cardiganshire and Carmarthenshire to Bogo de Knovill in June 1279 is recited in a 1281 letter to the Barons of the Exchequer recorded on the Close Roll (*Calendar of the Close Rolls*, 1279-1288, 101). Knovill was to be given allowance in his farm of the offices not only for *gwesdva* (entertainment dues), but also for the maintenance of horses belonging to himself and the *rhaglaw*.

[30] E.g. ALIW vol 2 p 545 lex 176.

[31] ALIW vol 1 p 146 lex 13 (Gwynedd Code); p 469 lex 110 (Dyfed Code); vol 2 pp 27 lex 10; 213 lex 7.

[32] R.R.Davies, 'The Administration of Law in Medieval Wales: The Role of the Ynad Cwmwd (Judex Patrie)' in *Lawyers and Laymen: Studies in the History of Law presented to Professor Dafydd Jenkins* (ed. T.M.Charles-Edwards, M.E.Owen and D.B.Walters, Cardiff, 1986) 258-273. Davies' conclusions (at 265 et seq) relate, however, only to the north-eastern Marcher lordships of Denbigh and Dyffryn Clwyd (for which, also see Davies' *The Law of the March, op.cit.*). The office is also touched upon in David Stephenson, *Thirteenth Century Welsh Law Courts: Some Notes on Procedure and Personnel* (Aberystwyth, 1980).

[33] The opinion of R.R.Davies is that the position of the *ynad* in North Wales 'approximated to that of an expert arbitrator' (The Administration of Law, *op.cit.supra*, 262-263).

[34] ALIW vol 2 p 561 lex 231.

practice in the Cardiganshire commotes acquired by Edward I in 1277. At a 1281 inquiry into legal practice in them, several witnesses state that all pleas moved in those commotes were to be determined by twelve men chosen by the King's bailiff, and without any *ynad*.[35] That there were functioning commote courts before 1284 seems clear enough, although no *llyfrau llys* seem to have survived; account rolls of the Cardiganshire commotes of the later 1270s show the courts to have generated almost as much income as rents. For instance, in the year beginning at Christmas 1277, the commote of Mefenydd produced rents of about £21, but the pleas and perquisites of the commote were accounted at almost £17.[36] In subsequent years, the pleas were worth about £14 and £10.[37] The same picture holds across the Cardiganshire commotes: in Perfedd, the 'fines, pleas, perquisites, heriots, reliefs, and lerewites" came to over £6, compared to just under £10 by way of rent.[38]

The evidence in the statute of Wales for the retention of the judicial functions of the commotes is, admittedly, slender - the statute makes no explicit mention of commote courts. However, it does provide, at the end of the long section detailing the matters to be inquired of at the sheriff's twice-yearly tourn, that the commote bailiffs were 'henceforward to hold their commotes, and to do and administer justice there between litigants." It is submitted that to have invested the commote bailiffs with this power would have been meaningless unless there was some forum in which it could be exercised. Furthermore, the statute provides that pleas of debt for less than forty shillings were to be brought in the county court, 'and likewise in the commotes',[39] which appears to recognise some degree of judicative competence in the commotes. It can be argued that the casual - even offhand - way in which this is said, looking almost as if it was tacked on as an after-

---

[35] *Calendar of various Chancery rolls* 206-207. R.R.Davies has observed that 'there can be no doubt' that 'local *ynaid* of the professonal variety were unknown' in west and south Wales (The Administration of Law, *op.cit .supra,* 264) .
[36] SC 6/1158/1 m 1.
[37] *Ibid.*
[38] SC 6/1158/1 m 3d.
[39] ... set placita de debito que summa .xl. s non attingunt in comitatu placitetur et in

thought, suggests that it was almost so obvious as not to need saying. The limitation imposed by the statute upon the jurisdiction of the county court when it came to hearing pleas of trespass has already been adverted to; that is, the county court was to have no jurisdiction where the damages claimed exceeded forty shillings.[40] However, in relation to trespass, the statute makes no mention of the commote. Assuming the disparity of treatment between debt and trespass to be other than an accident of drafting, one explanation which presents itself is that the 'forty shilling rule',[41] as it has come to be known, was still, in 1284, in a state of instability or flux in association with the action of debt in the county court.[42] Hence, express mention of the impact of the forty shilling rule upon proceedings in the commote court would have been needed simply as a means of heading-off potential misunderstanding: in short, forty shillings was the limit in the county in debt, and the county limit applied to the commote too. That is, the forty shilling jurisdictional limit could not be evaded through the expedient of bringing debt in the commote rather than the county. By way of contrast, the position in the action of trespass was already settled - forty shillings was the limit in local courts;[43] accordingly, there would have been no need to say that this applied in the commote as well. Thus, commote courts seem to have survived as judicial entities, and, as such, present an exception to what seems to have been a general policy that pre-Conquest legal institutions were not to be incorporated into the post-Conquest legal order; such a policy is deducible from the administration's firm rebuffal of pleas from Welsh lords - even those known to have been in favour with the English - that their pre-Conquest seigniorial courts be restored to them.[44]

However, it is one matter to postulate the survival of the commote court,

---

commotis similiter.

[40] Trespass for more than forty shillings was to be pleaded before the Justice of Wales.

[41] J.S.Beckerman, 'The forty shilling jurisdictional limit in medieval English personal actions' in *Legal History Studies 1972*, ed. Dafydd Jenkins (Cardiff, 1975)

[42] Palmer, *The County Courts of Medieval England*, 251 et seq.

[43] Palmer, *op.cit.*, 235.

[44] E.g. *Registrum vulgariter nuncupatum, 'The Record of Caernarvon'* (ed. Sir Henry

and quite another to delineate its post-Conquest form. The first question, and a difficult one at that, goes to the identity of the person exercising judicial authority in the commote court. Although the Welsh laws provided for the office of 'commote judge', the statute mentions no such official, and, as already has been noted, some commotes may not have had a judge in the professional sense. Bearing in mind the provisions of the statute, it has to be considered whether the 'commote bailiff' was contemplated as possessed of a judicial function. In the Welsh laws, the commote bailiff is the *rhingyll*, who appears in a number of guises but generally as an official associated with the administration of justice - a beadle, usher,[45] or an itinerant bailiff executing summons[46] - rather than a judge. Indeed, the Dyfed Code goes so far as expressly to distinguish the *rhingyll* from the judge.[47] The sole evidence in the Welsh laws that the *rhingyll* could fulfil a judicial role is a provision that the *rhingyll* was one of the four officers who could dispose of any plaint,[48] although the trustworthiness of this list might well be doubted since, in one version of it, the fourth officer so qualified is named as the *afforthor* (a corruption of *porthor*), or porter.[49] However, David Stephenson, in his study of the governance of pre-Conquest Gwynedd[50] charts the development of the *rhingyll* from a 'factotum' of the commote, to the steward of the commote's *llys*, or hall. In such a light, it would be less surprising to encounter the *rhingyll* as a more senior and responsible official.

Assessment of the activity of commote courts under English rule is

---

Ellis, London, 1838) 215 (Petition of Tudor ap Gronow, 1305).

45 In the Dyfed Code (ALIW vol 1 p 405 lex 1), *rhingyll* is translated as 'apparitor' (a servant, attender, or usher). However, Owen states (ALIW vol 2 p 1125) that the translation of *rhingyll* as 'apparitor', 'does not accurately represent the definition of the office'.

46 The illustration of the *rhingyll* in National Library of Wales MS Peniarth 28 f 6v shows him carrying the lance which pertained to his office; *Peniarth 28: Darluniau o lyfr Cyfraith Hywel Dda* (ed. Daniel Huws, National Library of Wales, 1988) nr 7.

47 ALIW vol 1 p 405 lex 1.

48 ALIW vol 2 p 40 lex 2.

49 ALIW vol 2 p 253 lex 34.

50 *The Governance of Gwynedd* (Cardiff, 1984), Chapter 4.

51 E.A.Lewis, 'The Proceedings of the Small Hundred Court of the Commote of

hampered by the small number of commote court rolls which seem to have survived; the earliest located dates from the mid 1320s and is for the so-called *parvum hundredum* or 'small hundred' of the commote of Ardudwy in Merionethshire.[51] However, this - some forty years after the statute - is perhaps too late a point at which this discussion can begin. Notwithstanding the absence of plea rolls, this study proposes to attempt to throw some light on the jurisdiction of commote courts from the estreats of their rolls returned to various offices of the Exchequer, and which finally have come to rest at the Public Record Office.[52] These record the financial receipts of the court, whether arising by way of fines or amercements handed down by it, or sums paid into court to secure its assistance in various ways. As such, estreats were prepared as financial, rather than legal, records. The practice seems to have been for the revenue of each commote to be estreated on a separate membrane; the estreats from each county's several commotes were then stitched together and returned to the Exchequer. By way of illustration, the estreat from Cardiganshire for the year beginning in Michaelmas 1301[53] consists of five membranes, detailing the revenue of courts in five of the nine commotes known to have made up that county.[54] The disappearance of the estreats for the remaining commotes may perhaps be attributed to the vicissitudes of time, although surviving estreat rolls from the 1330s provide a fuller picture; for instance, there are estreats for all the Cardiganshire commotes for the year beginning at Michaelmas 1338,[55] and the same holds broadly true of the other Welsh counties. The principal inhibitor arising in connection with use of the estreats is that the information which they give, on the whole, is sparing; generally, the estreats restrict themselves to the dates and locations of courts, and a note as to the sums involved, each sum

Ardudwy in the County of Merioneth from 8th October 1325 to 18th September 1326' (1928) 4 *Bulletin of the Board of Celtic Studies* 153. The roll is Public Record Office SC 2/225/28.

[52] To be found in SC 2 (Special Collections: Court Rolls), SC 6 (Special Collections: Ministers' and Receivers' Accounts), and LR 11 (Office of the Auditors of Land Revenue and Predecessors: Estreats of Court Rolls).

[53] SC 2/215/16.

[54] See Melville Richards, *Welsh Administrative and Territorial Units: Medieval and Modern* (Cardiff, 1969).

[55] SC 2/215/22.

[56] SC 2/215/16 m 1d (Wednesday at the feast of St Peter ad Vincula, 30 Edward I).

accompanied with a note of the reason for it having been collected. For instance, the estreat of proceedings before the court of the commote of Mefenydd (Cardiganshire) held on August 1st 1302[56] records receipts of 38 shillings arising from 12 transactions: ten amercements - which range from one shilling for 'a trespass done' (*pro transgressione facta*) to 10 shillings 'for *camlwrw*' (a particular form of fine)[57] - and two fines levied from plaintiffs seeking to be put into seisin of land.

However, despite their brevity, the estreats can be put to use in answering questions of a substantive legal nature. In effect, it is proposed that the jurisdiction of the commote courts during the early decades of the fourteenth century can be 'back-engineered' from these documents which detail that aspect of litigation of principal concern to the Crown - namely, the flow of cash into the Royal coffers. One loophole presents itself immediately to this exercise, and, by way of *caveat*, it should be made clear that this objection may be a serious one. This, given the particular nature of the estreats, is that there is no way of knowing with certainty whether these documents enable the full picture of the commote courts' jurisdiction to be drawn; it is possible that pleas may have been brought which were deemed impermissible, and these perhaps would have left no trace on the roll. A further difficulty is that a considerable proportion of the entries on the estreats reveal nothing at all of the substance of the plea: the caption merely says that a plea or plaint had been brought. For instance, in the 1302 Mefenydd estreat is to be found an amercement of twelve pence taken from one David ap Llewelyn 'for a plaint' (*pro querela*)[58] but nothing further is said as to the nature of this plaint. Such entries, of course, are invaluable in assessing the overall weight of business of the courts but this is probably the high-water mark of their usefulness to this study.

Nothing in the set of 1301-2 Cardiganshire estreats[59] suggests that the commote courts, at that time, were anything other than thriving institutions. Courts sat 14 times that year in each of the five commotes for which estreats have survived; this works out at about once every four weeks - a sharp contrast to the provision in the Welsh laws that the commote court could be

[57] See below.
[58] SC 2/215/16 m 1d.
[59] SC 2/215/16.
[60] ALIW vol 2 p 323 lex 6; p 365 lex 1.

held daily.[60] The pattern matches the familiar 28-day cycle which determined the sittings of English county courts.[61] However, we can be reasonably sure that we are dealing here with sittings of commote courts, rather than peripatetic sittings of the county court. The statute of Wales prohibited the county court from sitting on Fridays, Saturdays, or Sundays, but we see sittings in the commotes on all those days.[62] Also, the county court was to sit in different places on successive days, and, although this is the general pattern revealed by the estreat, courts sometimes are recorded as sitting in two commotes on the same day - this happened on almost one in three of the 37 days on which courts in Cardiganshire are recorded to have sat between January and October 1302.[63]

Business at these sittings appears to have been brisk. Between Michaelmas 1301 and Michaelmas 1302, the five Cardiganshire commotes generated an income of just over £90, with totals ranging from about £27 in the commote of Geneu'r Glyn down to a third of that in the commote of Perfedd.[64] These sums, on the whole,[65] are markedly higher than the sums recorded as having been levied from the pleas and perquisites of the commotes in the later 1270s. For instance, in the year between Michaelmas 1278 and Michaelmas 1279, just over £65 was levied from four commotes.[66] At the beginning of the fourteenth century, the money is made up in dribs-and-drabs from a stream of litigants; for instance, the £15-11-4 issuing from

---

[61] E.g. Between Michaelmas 1301 and Michaelmas 1302, the court in Anhuniog ('Hanhunyank') sat on October 11th, November 2nd and 25th, December 21st, January 18th, February 15th, March 15th, April 12th, May 12th, June 7th, July 5th, August 1st and 30th, and October 3rd.

[62] E.g. Mefenydd (Friday, June 1st 1302).

[63] E.g. Perfedd and Geneu'r Glyn on Monday, January 15th 1302, Mefenydd and Yr Creuddyn on the following day.

[64] SC 2/215/16: Mefenydd £19-5-6; Anhuniog £15-11-4; Yr Creuddyn £19-5; Perfedd £9-2; Geneu'r Glyn £27-8-4.

That these figures would not have been out of the ordinary is suggested by the fact that, between Michaelmas 1302 and Michaelmas 1303, Geneu'r Glyn generated £26-0-4 (SC 2/215/20 mm 15-15d).

[65] Perfedd is the exception, although that commote generated only £6-3 in pleas and perquisites between December 1277 and Michaelmas 1278; SC 6/1158/1 m 3d.

[66] SS 6/1158/1: mm 1 (Menenydd, £13-6-4), 2d (Yr Creuddyn, £14-4-10), 3d

the commote of Anhuniog arose from 72 transactions, for the most part bringing in a shilling or two, although there is one unusually large item - twelve individuals who had stolen the toll from a mill were fined just over seventy shillings.[67] There does not seem to have been anything unusual about the Cardiganshire commotes; the evidence from the estreats of the same year's business of the six commotes which made up the *cantred* of Cantref Mawr in Carmarthenshire[68] bears this out; those commotes produced an income of just over £55 from almost 500 transactions.[69]

The estreats can be used to provide a snapshot of the jurisdictional ambit of the commote courts. One important factor which should be borne in mind is that the statute of Wales, besides the express retention of certain distinctive rules of Welsh law (for instance, those relating to partible inheritance)[70] makes the far-reaching concession that the Welsh could continue to use Welsh law for all manner of claims[71] except theft, robbery, arson, and homicides. It should perhaps, then, be of no surprise that the post-Conquest commote courts seem to have been a redoubt of Welsh laws and customs. Two phenomena in the commote estreats are indicative of this.

The first relates to what the estreats refer to as *camlor*, which, it is suggested, is a Latin form of the Welsh *camlwrw*. Under the Welsh laws, *camlwrw* was a fine exactable under three broad heads: disobedience to the King; doing something wrong against the King, and doing something wrong or illegally.[72] The examples of wrongs given by the Welsh laws are manifold;

(Perfedd, £27-8-11), 4 (Geneu'r Glyn, £10-18-4). There is no mention of any courts in the commote of Anhuniog (m 2).

[67] quia furati fuerunt de tollon' de Molend' de lansafret; SC 2/215/16 m 2.

[68] SC 2/215/18.

[69] Mm 1 (Cetheiniog, £10-7-10); 2 (Maenor Deilo, £9-13-4); 3 (Mallaen, £14-7); 4 (Caeo, £12-15-4); 5 (Mab-Elwyn, £4-10); 6 (Mabudryd, £6-5-11). These figures should be set alongside the figures for the income of the Welshry county court mentioned earlier in this study.

[70] Quo ad successionem hereditate partibilis est inter heredes masculos et a tempore cuius non extitit memoria partibil' extitet, dominus Rex non vult quod consuetudo illa abrogetur.

[71] Et quia Wallenses nobis supplicarunt ut eis concedamus quod ... uti possunt lege Wallens' qua uti consueuerunt ... Nos per communi pace et quiete predicti populari nostri Wallensis premissa eis concedimus.

[72] ALIW vol 2, pp 613-617.

taking a lord's timber; breaking up the highway; withholding customary dues; unlawfully bearing arms; approaching judges during their consultations; and making open attacks. Disobedience is described in terms of failing to respond without proper cause to lawful summons; failing to answer suit; or receding from a plaint. Sums captioned as payable by way of *camlwrw* feature prominently in the estreats from the early fourteenth century; for instance, six of the twelve entries arising from the sitting at Mefenydd commote on August 1st 1302 are captioned as being *pro Camlore* - these range from one shilling to half a mark.[73]

The second phenomenon of which repeated mention appears in the estreats, is *leyrwyt. Leger-wíte* was an institution known to English law, described by the *Leges Henrici Primi*, dating from the beginning of the twelfth century, as 'the offence of (or fine payable for) fornication',[74] and lying, alongside fighting, as a minor criminal matter. *Leyrwyt*, thus defined, is a feature - although, it should be said, by no means a prominent one - of English manorial jurisdiction into the fourteenth century; for instance, *leyrwyt*, payable by three women who were 'violated' appears in the rolls of a Lincolnshire manor of Crowle in 1319,[75] and in a Suffolk manor in 1334 in respect of a birth outside marriage.[76] Whatever the meaning of *leyrwyt* in England, it is difficult to know what is meant by the *leyrwyt* to which the estreats refer. It is encountered very frequently (and much more frequently than in English manorial or Hundred court rolls) and the sums payable in connection with it make up a considerable proportion - about a quarter - of the totals levied;[77] indeed, are so prominent that they are the only item separately accounted for. For instance, in the commote of Anhuniog (Cardiganshire) in 1301-1302, the sum of the perquisites of the court *sine leyrwyta* is given as just under £13, while the sum made from *leyrwyt* adds

---

[73] SC 2/215/16 m 1d.

[74] *Leges Henrici Primi* (ed. L.J.Downer, Oxford, 1972), pp 126-7; c.23, 1; 337.

[75] *Select Cases in Manorial Courts* 1250-1350, ed. L.R.Poos and L.Bonfield (1997) 114 Selden Society 130 nr 169.

[76] (1997) 114 Selden Society 136 nr 178.

[77] In Cardiganshire between Michaelmas 1301 and 1302, £73-1-6 arose from pleas and perquisites, and £17-10-8 from leyrwyt.

[78] SC 2/215/16 m 2: Summa perquis' <sine leyr'> (interlined) £12-16, summa <leyr'>

about a further £3 to this;[78] this chimes with the volume of business at Anhuniog during that year - of the 72 items, exactly a quarter relate to *leyrwyt*. However, it is rare for the caption which accompanies the note of the sum to go beyond the bare mention that *leyrwyt* had been paid. In itself, the very absence of detail is perhaps revealing. Entries for *leyrwyt* on the rolls of English manor courts always specify the context in which the fine had arisen; in England, *leyrwyt* connotes a wrong, and the dimensions of the wrong must be laid bare. However, the general silence of the Welsh entries in this respect, together with the prominence assumed by *leyrwyt*, both suggests that what was referred to as *leyrwyt* was understood at large, and was substantively different to its English namesake. It is suggested that Welsh *leyrwyt* encompasses two distinct institutions. The first is *amobr*, or 'maiden fee', described by the Welsh laws as one of the three legal punishments (*cosp*), payable to the King, and lying in a range of circumstances all involving sex: for instance, extra matrimonial co-habitation, prostitution, rape, and conception outside marriage.[79] For instance, in the commote of Yr Creuddyn (Cardiganshire) in 1301 it is recorded that *leyrwyt* of five shillings was payable for one Ena, the daughter of Owain, (*quia*) *pregnans est*.[80] It should be said that some estreats do mention *amobr per se* - for instance, a 1343 entry from Yr Creuddyn that a sum had been payable *pro amobragium*.[81] It is contended that the prominence of *leyrwyt* on the estreats is accounted for by the fact that *leyrwyt*, besides *amobr*, seems also to have included what was known in England as *merchet*, or a fine paid by a tenant to his lord for liberty to give his daughter in marriage, the payment of which commonly was regarded as a distinguishing mark of villeinage.[82] Occasionally, this comes to the surface in the estreat; for instance, in the commote of Anhuniog we read of two shillings payable for the *merch*[83] of one Gryffydd ap Gronon.[84] It is contended that the exaction of *amobr* and *camlwrw* both represent a strong survival of indigenous law in

(interlined) £2-15-4.

[79] ALIW vol 2 pp 610-613; sections 29-32.

[80] SC 2/215/16 m 3.

[81] E.g. SC 2/215/26 m 9.

[82] Pollock and Maitland, *op.cit.*, vol 2, p 543.

[83] Possibly *merchet*, although 'merch' also means 'daughter'.

commote courts.

The commote court during this period, besides administering a continuance of Welsh laws, was also the forum for the range of English personal actions introduced by the statute of Wales: *camlwrw* and *leyrwyt* are seen alongside many entries captioned as arising in respect of trespass (*de transgressio*), covenant (*de conventio*), and debt (*de debito*). Trespass is a particularly prominent plea; of the 111 entries issuing from the commote of Geneu'r Glyn (Cardiganshire) in 1302-1303, 32 relate to pleas of trespass, producing about a sixth of the court's income.[85] The preponderance of trespass pleas on the estreats may well be attributable to the fact that amercements were payable, unlike in pleas of debt or covenant, in respect of all pleas: not only when the defendant lost, but also when the plaintiff lost. Unfortunately, the substance of the trespasses are, for the most part, unspecified. There are six amercements of up to ten shillings for unspecified trespass, and six, all amerced at sixpence (which seems to have been the 'entry level' fine) for trespass 'in the wood' (*in bosco*). In all likelihood, these latter trespass claims would have related to facts no more serious than the two unfortunates amerced ten pence each in Mabudryd (Carmarthenshire) in 1302 'because they collected nuts in the forest'.[86] Probably to be counted alongside this latter, minor, kind of wrongs are those trespasses noted to have been trespasses 'in the corn' (*in blado*) which, it may be supposed, simply involved the defendant, or his animals, straying into the plaintiff's crops.

Although it is well known (for instance from the abundant evidence of the court rolls of the Marcher Lordship of Dyffryn Clwyd in north-east Wales)[87] that Welsh land law did not disappear in 1284,[88] very few entries in the commote estreats relate to real property. Perhaps this is because the commote was not seen as the appropriate forum for such litigation. Even the Welsh laws seem to have circumscribed the jurisdiction of the commote

---

[84] SC 2/215/16 m 2 (1302).

[85] SC 2/215/20 m 15d, producing 72 shillings from a total of £22-8-4.

[86] SC 2/215/18 m 6; quia colligerunt nutes in foresta.

[87] For which, see, generally, R.R.Davies, *The Law of the March*.

[88] E.g. SC 2/216/3 m 5 (Llanerch, October 23rd 1320; in placito inpingnoracionis tirprid). And see, generally, Llinos Beverley Smith, 'Tir prid: Deeds of gage of land in late medieval Wales' (1976-78) 27 *Bulletin of the Board of Celtic Studies* 263; *idem.*, 'The gage and land market in late medieval Wales' (1976) 29 *Economic*

court in matters relating to succession to land, providing that only the simplest claims (namely, where the plaintiff counted on descent from a father or grandfather) could be heard there.[89] The reason given was that a claim outside this limit could only properly be pursued against a whole stock of correlatives (up to sixty co-heritors are mentioned) who might well be resident in a number of different commotes.[90] Accordingly, before 1284, such pleas were to be heard only in the court of the prince. Most of the real property claims heard in the post-Conquest commotes are captioned, without expansion, 'for a plea of land' (*pro placito terre*). This is disappointing, since the land law measures extended to Wales by the 1284 statute are, from a legal point of view, amongst the statute's most interesting features. On the face of it, the introduction of writs of novel disseisin, mort d'ancestor, dower, and entry to the Welsh lands, coupled with the recognition and preservation, in a modified form, of the Welsh custom of partible inheritance between all male heirs[91] would have had a strong and complex impact. The estreats record the involvement of the crown in land transactions at commote level; in Mefenydd in May 1302 we read of one Gruffudd ap Rees who had given the lord prince five shillings to have seisin in the lands of one Ewan, which had escheated through lack of tenants,[92] and in Cetheiniog (Carmarthenshire) in that same year, five shillings were given to pay for the lord's help in obtaining land.[93] The commote court during this period also seems to have been the appropriate forum for juridical procedures touching land; in Geneu'r Glyn (Cardiganshire) in 1302, four defendants are amerced the considerable sum of thirty shillings for having failed to swear (*iurare*) the boundaries of certain lands, and there are also scattered entries relating to fines - generally of only trifling amounts given for livery of seisin.[94]

In respect of the criminal jurisdiction of the commote courts, a difference

---

History Review (2nd series) 537.

[89] ALIW vol 2 p 427 lex 29.

[90] ALIW vol 2 p 431 lex 9.

[91] Quo ad successionem hereditate partibilis est inter heredes masculos et a tempore cuius non extitit memoria partibil' extitet, dominus Rex non vult quod consuetudo illa abrogetur.

[92] Pro defectu tenent'.

[93] SC 2/215/18 m 1; pro auxilio domini habendo ad terram petitam.

[94] E.g. SC 2/215/16 m 3 (Yr Creuddyn, 1302); three shillings pro seisinam habend'.

can be seen between the Cardiganshire and Carmarthenshire commote estreats. For the former, relatively little which we would be inclined to categorise as criminal is seen. However, the criminal jurisdiction of the latter seems to have been quite extensive. In terms of offences against the person, besides the usual clutch of fights, can be seen references to fines for more serious offences. For instance, there are two mentions of rape, one carrying an amercement of a mark, the other of a mere two shillings, in the estreat of the commote of Caeo in 1302.[95] Rape, described as such, is of interest because rape, under the Welsh laws, probably would have fallen within *amobr*. The fact that only a small fine is imposed in these instances perhaps suggests that these are instances falling in fact under the provisions of the Welsh law, which just happen to have been described on these two occasions in Latin.

Some conclusions can be drawn regarding the business of the commote and county courts in Wales at the turn of the fourteenth century. The first is that it would seem that the commote court during this period is perhaps best described as an alternative to the county court - that is, lying alongside, rather than beneath it. This opinion was mooted by Sir Goronwy Edwards some eighty years ago in his edition of Flintshire pleas,[96] and, it is suggested, the commote court records support this hypothesis. Furthermore, there can be little doubt but that the jurisdiction of the commote courts appears largely to have been coterminous with that of the county courts in the realm of the main personal actions introduced by the 1284 statute, namely debt and trespass. The commote courts also seem to have remained the forum for distinctively Welsh legal institutions. Even where the records permit us to compare commote and county court records side-by-side (as in Carmarthenshire), no Welsh law is encountered in the county court even where that county court happens expressly to have been designated for the Welshry. However, when it comes to criminal jurisdiction, the picture may have been different, and, again, comparing the Carmarthenshire Welshry county court with the

[95] SC 2/215/18 m 4; pro raptu facto; pro raptu facto cum uxore Ieuan ap Menyr.
[96] J.Goronwy Edwards, 'Flint Pleas 1283-1285' (1922) 8 *Flintshire Historical Society*.
[97] LR 11/54/786 m 2d.

commote courts suggests that the county, rather than the commote, court was the appropriate forum for criminal causes.

This study has dealt only with the earlier segment of the records, and a few observations are offered about the evolving jurisdiction of the commote courts later into the fourteenth century. The picture revealed by estreats from the later fourteenth century is that, although income from pleas seems to fall away by the 1340s (perhaps pleas eventually were mopped up by the county courts), income from perquisites (such as payments on the marriage of a villein's daughter, or on the alienation of land) remain buoyant, and come to constitute the majority of the court's work. For instance, in the commote of Mabwnion (Cardiganshire) between February and September 1349, all but seven of the seventy entries, and over 95% of the court's revenue, related to heriots.[97]

The principal conclusion of this study is that, despite the Edwardian conquest, the commote court for some years seems to have remained a genuine and viable legal institution; that is to say, litigants were prepared to go there, abide by its judgements, pay the sums demanded of them - in short, to accede to its jurisdiction. Furthermore, it can be argued not only that the jurisdiction of the commote was unsupplanted by the statute of Wales, but also that the 1284 statute seems to have been the mechanism by which commote jurisdiction was bolstered - even if only in the short term. It is already well-known that Welsh law and legal institutions did not die in the conquered lands in 1284,[98] and this study has endeavoured to explore one further aspect of their vitality.

[98] See R.R.Davies, 'The Twilight of Welsh Law, 1284-1536' (1966) 51 *History* 143.

LEGAL CULTURES IN MEDIAEVAL WALES

Thomas Glyn Watkin*

Introduction

DURING the Michaelmas term in the year of Our Lord 1495, a young, newly-appointed serjeant-at-law gave a reading on the statute *Prerogativa Regis* at the Inner Temple. He was probably in his mid-thirties, and was destined to become one of the youngest chief justices in the history of the common law courts, being appointed chief justice of the common pleas at the end of September 1502 in succession to Sir Thomas Wood. At the time of his appointment he was not much more than forty years old if that. Not surprisingly, he was highly regarded for his legal learning, and described as being "the oracle of law in his age". Regrettably, his career was cut short in its prime, for he died in October 1506, not more than 46 years old – some indeed saying that he was not yet forty years old at the time of his death. The lawyer in question was Sir Thomas Frowyk.[1]

In the course of his reading on *Prerogativa Regis* in 1495, Frowyk discussed the law relating to wreck and royal fish. In doing so, he touched upon an issue which is absent from other readings upon the statute, for instance that given during the same term at Lincoln's Inn by Robert Constable. Frowyk mentions the geographical limits of the right to royal fish. He said:

---

* The author would like to thank all those who asked questions and ventured comments on an earlier version of this paper at the Welsh Legal History session of the British Legal History Conference at Aberystwyth early in July, 2001.

[1] *The Dictionary of National Biography* says that he was born at least by 1464 when he is mentioned in his grandmother's will. Professor J.H. Baker, in the *Biographical Dictionary of the Common Law*, ed., A.W.B. Simpson (London, 1984) gives his birth as c. 1460. Fuller, *Worthies*, (1662) says that he died before reaching forty, but this is disproved by the mention in the will. There is no doubt regarding his relative youth on appointment as Chief Justice of the Common Pleas nor of the fact that he died at an early age, albeit Croke's statement in Keilway's Reports that he died "in florida juventute sua" appears generous as a description of early middle age.

> The article says *whales, sturgeon, etc.* These fish the king shall have at common law, because they were royal if they were taken in the parts of England. But if they were taken outside the parts of England, as in the parts of Calais, Normandy, and so forth, the king should not have them; likewise in Wales, where they have various royal lordships, [and it is considered outside] the realm. In these cases whoever finds the fish shall have them to his own use.[2]

Frowyk makes two points about title to royal fish in Wales. Firstly, they are not the king's, but secondly, and perhaps more remarkably, they are not the property of the holders of the various royal lordships either. Rather they go to the person who finds them.[3] Frowyk's answer to the question of who may take the fish in the absence of a royal right to them appears to involve a rule in Wales not unlike the civilian concept of *occupatio*; they belong to the first taker.[4] Not only is the royal claim denied, but the feudal claim is contradicted as well.

Frowyk's comments on the position in Wales, and indeed in Calais and Normandy, is not replicated in either Robert Constable's contemporaneous reading nor his son-in-law, John Spelman's, comments on royal fish in 1521 when reading at Gray's Inn. Frowyk would appear to have had no connection with Wales, being of a London family, and no connection with royal fish either, other than that his mother's maiden name was Sturgeon. His additional knowledge on this somewhat arcane topic therefore appears to

---

[2] J.H.Baker (ed.), *John Spelman's Reading on Quo Warranto*, Selden Society vol. 113 (London, 1997) p. 38:

> Le article est *ballenas, sturgeones*. Ceux [pisses] le roy avera per le comen ley, pur ceo que il fueront royall sils fueront prises in partibus Anglie. Mes [sils furent prises hors dez parties dengleterre], come en les partes de Cales, Normandie, [etc.] le roy navera, et auxi en Gales ou ils ount diverse seignories royalles, [si] le roy [est] hors del royalme <[et] en ceux cases cesti que eux trovera> avera a son use demesne.

[3] One manuscript substitutes "le pernour de tielz pissez eux avera" for "en ceux cases cesti que eux trovera avera", but does not affect the result.

[4] The civil law calls this method of acquiring ownership *occupatio* and categorizes it as arising by natural law:

> Wild beasts, birds, fish, that is, all animals, which live either in the sea, the air, or on the earth, so soon as they are taken by any one, immediately become by the law of nations the property of the captor; for natural reason gives to the first occupant that which had no previous owner. And it is immaterial whether a man takes wild beasts or birds upon his own ground, or on that of another.
>
> Justinian, *Institutes*, II. 1. 12.

confirm the view that he was indeed "the oracle of law in his age". However, his reading it must be remembered came at the end of the first decade of the reign of Henry VII, the first king of the Tudor dynasty, when perhaps a greater awareness of Welsh matters would have been present among the courtiers at Westminster.[5] Not much more than a generation later, the second Tudor sovereign, Henry VIII, would legislate to absorb Wales into the realm of England and thus extend the jurisdiction of the common law to his Welsh subjects with regard to most legal matters affecting their lives.

Frowyk's distinction nevertheless poses some interesting questions with regard to the laws of Wales on the eve of the Union. If the rule regarding royal fish was different in the lordships of Wales, what exactly was the rule and whence did it arise? Given that Frowyk refers to the distinction existing in the royal lordships in those parts, why did the lords not claim such fish as *iura regalia* given their Marcher status? Had they not chosen to do so, or had they tried but failed? Was the legal position with regard to royal fish consistent throughout Wales or did it vary from place to place, from lordship to lordship? Some of these issues will be explored in this paper in the belief that, despite the narrowness of the question, it contains in a microcosm an interesting vantage point upon the diverse legal cultures which competed for dominance in Wales in the four or five centuries separating the Anglo-Norman invasions from the Tudor Union with England.

The Native Welsh Laws

The native laws of Wales are preserved in three main traditions, falling into two linguistic divisions according to whether the text has been preserved in Latin or Welsh. During the nineteenth century, Aneurin Owen in his *Ancient Laws and Institutes of Wales*, classified the surviving legal materials into three versions or *dulliau*, which he believed represented the customs of

[5] The closest connection Frowyk appears to have had with Wales was by acting as an assize judge in the western counties of England. I am grateful to Dr. Paul Brand for the suggestion that he may have had fellow students who were Welsh while he was studying at the Inner Temple. Regrettably, records of admissions to that inn do not commence until 1547.

different parts of the country. The customs of the North, he took to be represented by *Dull Gwynedd*; those of the South-West by *Dull Dyfed*, and those of the South-East by *Dull Gwent*. In English, these versions were somewhat misleadingly rendered as the *Venedotian*, *Dimetian* and *Gwentian Codes* respectively. These versions were compiled no earlier than the twelfth century and mainly during the thirteenth. Although each is described as being rooted in the Law of Hywel Dda, the native Welsh leader of the early tenth century who to some extent unified Wales under his rule, considerable diversification with regard to their content and structure had occurred prior to their compilation in the versions which have survived, a diversification which may have resulted from the partitioning of Wales amongst Hywel's heirs after his death. Twentieth-century scholarship has moved on from Aneurin Owen's classification, while continuing to recognize a relationship between the traditions and the various parts of Wales, although also recognizing that there remained a not inconsiderable degree of mutual influence among the various versions. Today, the law books are treated as falling into the two main linguistic divisions of Latin and Welsh, the five Latin Redactions being known respectively as A, B, C, D and E, while the Welsh texts are now referred to as *Llyfr Cyfnerth*, *Llyfr Iorwerth* and *Llyfr Blegywryd* respectively, these three Welsh versions corresponding to Aneurin Owen's Gwentian, Venedotian and Dimetian Codes. The Cyfnerth tradition is regarded today as being connected with the Mid Wales territory of Maelienydd rather than Gwent, but Iorwerth is still seen as being written from the perspective of the North and Blegywryd from that of Deheubarth in the South-West. *Llyfr Colan* is regarded as being a compressed version of Iorwerth, and Cyfnerth is recognized as being a much looser tradition that the other two.

There are also clear relationships between the Latin Redactions and the Welsh versions. The strongest affinity is between Latin D and Blegywryd; indeed, Blegywryd is regarded as being a Welsh translation of Latin D. Latin A is also connected with the South, but has affinity with the Cyfnerth tradition. Once thought to be the oldest of all the texts in either language, Latin A is now treated as being part of the Cyfnerth group, but that group is still regarded as being the earliest of the surviving traditions. Latin B, C and E are all regarded as having a northern perspective.

All of the extant law books come from parts of Wales which remained predominantly under Welsh native rule at the time of their compilation. No compilation survives from areas which had been acquired by the incoming Anglo-Norman lords.

Royal Fish and Fishing in the Native Welsh Laws

None of the extant traditions has anything to say about certain species of fish being reserved to the ruler, so that there is nothing in the native law books to contradict Frowyk's testimony. What they do discuss is the right of the ruler to whatever the sea casts ashore, describing the sea in this regard as the king's packhorse, that is something which brings him profit. The sea is the first in a list of eight such packhorses which are regularly set out in both the Latin and the Welsh compilations. The others are waste, *desertum*, which included any property without an owner, a foreigner who had left the jurisdiction, and whose goods the king therefore took, a thief whose goods likewise went to the king, a deceased person with no heir whose goods also passed to the ruler, the *ebidew* – a death duty rather like a relief or heriot, the *dirwy* – a fixed fine for certain offences, and the *camlwrw* – a lesser financial penalty for wrongdoing. The sea however always comes first.

According to the extant laws, "It is free for everybody to fish the sea", but "what the sea casts ashore,... belongs to the king" for three days and thereafter may be taken by anyone. "Dead fish in the ocean all belong to the king". In one version, what the sea casts ashore "whether alive or dead, belongs to the king", while another draws a distinction between live and dead fish, classifying them as one of the three things which the king is to have if cast on land by the sea – "dead fish if the king take them before the third flow and the third ebb", whereas "live fish… caught in nets, or wears, or with hooks, belong to their owners [that is, the owners of the nets, wears or hooks], if they be alive".

Writing early in the twentieth century, T.P. Ellis in his *Welsh Tribal Law and Custom*, described the provision giving fish washed ashore to the king as 'peculiar' in that it went against what he regarded as being the general rule that "Fishing was unrestrictedly free to every one in Wales, in the sea or the river". The peculiarity, it is submitted, probably arises from a tension between two principles in this context, one being that fishing was free, while the other was what might be termed the 'packhorse' principle, that whatever the sea carried to land belonged to the king because the sea was the king's packhorse. Dead fish were therefore undoubtedly the king's because it was the sea which transported them; live fish on the other hand might not have been carried thither by the sea, being capable of self-propulsion. Accordingly, they might be taken in the same manner as fish in the ocean and become the property of their captors.

A more interesting conflict of principles is evidenced however by the rules relating to river fishing in the native laws. This conflict casts doubt upon T.P. Ellis' bold assertion quoted above that "Fishing was unrestrictedly free to every one in Wales, in the sea or the river". The law books present a rather different picture.

It is recorded in the texts that "Whoever shall set a net in a river which shall not belong to him, is to have a third of the fish, and the other two parts go to the proprietor of the river". This laconic statement implicitly recognizes three principles, namely that rivers can be privately owned, that the owner of a river has a proprietorial interest in the fish, and that notwithstanding the proprietor's interest, the first taker of the fish also has a claim which needs to be satisfied.[6]

The first principle stands in stark contrast to the civilian notion that rivers were not susceptible to private ownership. This was the position in

---

[6] Latin D states : "Si quis rethe miserit in aquam non suam absque licencia, tercia pars capturi reti et due domino cadent, et regi *camlwrw*". [If anyone sets a net in a river not his own without a licence, a third goes to the owner of the net and two to the owner of the river, and the king gets his *camlwrw*]. Blegywryd follows this: "Y neb a dotto rwyt y mwyn auon ny phieipho, trayan y pyscawt a geiff, a'r deuparth y perchen yr auon", but does not give the king his *camlwrw*, that is payment for an offence or calumny.

Latin A also has the rule about dividing the produce of a net placed in a river without authority : "Si quis rete miserit in aquam sine licencia, rete habebit terciam partem et heres duas". So also does Latin B : "Si quis rete miserit in aquam non suam absque licentia, tercia pars capture reti et due domino aque cedent; et regi *camlwry*", and Latin E follows B : "Si quis rethe miserit in aquam non suam absque licencia, tercia pars capture rethi et due domino aque cedent; et regi *camluru*".

For the Latin Texts, see Hywel D. Emanuel, *The Latin Texts of the Welsh Laws* (Cardiff, 1967), pp. 134 (Latin A), 228 (Latin B), 389 (Latin D), 480 (Latin E)

Roman law both in the time of Gaius and in that of Justinian. It would appear therefore to follow that when parts of Wales were under the dominion of Rome, the rule described by Gaius and Justinian would have operated in those parts. Although the Roman authorities may have allowed the native population in the provinces to live according to their own legal traditions, such allowances were only feasible with regard to those legal relationships which did not involve the Roman authorities. It is hardly credible therefore that local custom could coexist alongside the Roman principle that rivers, the sea and the seashore, to take the three instances pertinent to this discussion, were things *extra commercium*, that is incapable of private ownership as being in the case of rivers the common property of all inhabitants of the State or in the case of the sea and the seashore actually common to all mankind.[7]

Nowhere for where there is evidence in Wales preserves the Roman rule. Latin B and E for the North, Blegywryd and Latin D for the South-west and Latin A for the central south-east all require a licence for a net to be placed in a river, but all except Latin A speak of the offence being committed by a person to whom the river does not belong, *aquam non suam*. Latin A alone treats it as being a matter of licence with no mention of ownership and interestingly carries this terminology through to the sharing, for where the others talk of the owner of the river having two-thirds, *due domino <aque> cadent*, the Welsh *deuparth y perchen yr auon*, Latin A speaks of *heres duas*, albeit the meaning is probably the same.

The rules relating to river fishing in all those parts of Wales for which evidence survives suggest therefore that the Welsh laws had amalgamated two separate viewpoints, the Roman and the feudal, to produce what might be described as a compromise solution, a compromise born of the clash of

---

respectively. For Blegywryd, see Stephen J. Williams and J. Enoch Powell, *Llyfr Blegywryd* (Cardiff, 1961), p. 81.5.

[7] Thus, Justinian's *Institutes*, II. 1. 1–2 :

> By the law of nature these things are common to mankind – the air, running water, the sea, and consequently the shores of the sea. No one, therefore, is forbidden to approach the seashore, provided that he respects habitations, monuments, and buildings, which are not, like the sea, subject only to the law of nations.
>
> All rivers and ports are public; hence the right of fishing in a port, or in rivers, is common to all men.

two legal cultures. T.P. Ellis, writing early in the twentieth century, while noting that in Arfon in north Wales, the fishing in certain rivers was a lordly preserve, nevertheless believed that the compromise solution was, in the south, the result of Norman incursions, incursions which resulted in the native Welsh view that fishing was free, a view that may have stemmed from the Roman occupation, being forced to accommodate to some extent the feudal view that river fishing was the lord's preserve.

There are of course other explanations. One could postulate that the ancient pre-Roman rule was in favour of private ownership and that with the departure of the Romans it partly revived, hence its presence in the unromanized north.[8] However, this is inherently less likely than the view that the claims of private lords in all parts of Wales entered upon the scene with the advent of feudalism. This would accord both with Blackstone's view of how the law in this area developed in England and the evidence with regard to the tensions between the civilian and feudal conceptions in many other parts of Europe which like south Wales had been part of the Roman empire.

Writing in the eighteenth century of the acquisition of property in animals *ferae naturae*, Blackstone considered that :

> it cannot be denied, that by the law of nature every man, from the prince to the peasant, has an equal right of pursuing, and taking to his own use, all such creatures as are *ferae naturae*, and therefore the property of nobody, but liable to be seized by the first occupant. And so it was held by the imperial law, even so late as Justinian's time…
>
> with regard to the rise and original of our present civil prohibitions, it will be found that all forest and game laws were introduced into Europe at the same time, and by the same policy, as gave birth to the feodal system; when those swarms of barbarians issued from their northern hive, and laid the foundations of most of the present kingdoms of Europe, on the ruins of the western empire. For when a conquering general came to settle the oeconomy of a vanquished country, and to part it out among his soldiers or feudatories, who were to render him military service for such donations; it behoved him, in order to secure his new acquisitions, to keep the *rustici* or natives of the country, and all who were not his military tenants, in as low a condition as possible, and especially to prohibit them the use of arms. Nothing could do this more effectually than a

[8] Although there were Roman settlements in northern Wales, in particular military bases, the region did not become romanized in the sense of experiencing a civilian adoption of Roman lifestyles and culture to the same extent as in the south.

> prohibition of hunting and sporting: and therefore it was the policy of the conqueror to reserve this right to himself, and such on whom he should bestow it; which were only his capital feudatories, or greater barons. And accordingly we find, in the feudal constitutions, one and the same law prohibiting the *rustici* in general from carrying arms, and also proscribing the use of nets, snares, or other engines for destroying the game.[9]

Blackstone posits a situation, as in England, where the feudal principle in effect eradicated the civilian approach. Across Europe, however, the story was less straightforward, with resistance to the feudal principle enjoying varied degrees of success.

The feudal conception of property was very different from the Roman. Property which had no owner was regarded as being not open to occupation by the first taker but under the special protection of the territorial lord. This led to a confusion between what was the private property of the ruler and the property he protected as belonging to no one. In Italy, as Calisse described a century ago, it was thus that "over the things withdrawn from private control were created the regalia or royal prerogatives". These became the subject of royal monopolies, or, by concession of the monarch, the monopolies of lesser lords.[10] Waters and woods became royal domain and private individuals were required to abstain from them. Private persons might not fish or hunt in the rivers and woods, so that the regalia became rights of a private character, albeit founded upon reasons of public law.[11]

In Italy, it had already been established in the half millennium following the fall of the western empire, when the Lombards and the Franks exercised political control, that things such as lakes, rivers, ports, bridges and market places, which had been *res publicae* to the Romans, were State property from which the ruler could exact payment from those of his subjects who wished to use them. With feudalism, such property, being under the protection of the ruler, became confused with his own private property, so that hunting in a forest or fishing in a river required the lord's permission. At the Diet of Roncaglia in 1158, the emperor set out the rights which he claimed were

---

[9] Blackstone's *Commentaries* Book II, Ch. 27, pp. 408-414.

[10] See, for instance, C. Calisse, *A History of Italian Law* (Boston, 1928; reprinted New York 1969 [*Continental Legal History Series*, vol. VIII]), p. 675.

[11] See Calisse, *History of Italian Law*, p. 676, 677.

exclusively his: these *regalia* included mints, tolls and customs, markets and castles, grants of safe conduct and protection of merchants, Jews and foreigners, goods confiscated from convicts and the goods of those who died without heirs, lordless estates, the sea-shore, rivers, roads, hunting and fishing, mines, salt beds, treasure trove, the right to practise certain trades and the right to administer justice. This list found its way into the *Libri feudorum* and thus into the body of laws which would form the basis of the *ius commune*, ensuring its continued influence in western Europe, particularly in Germany, until the eighteenth century.

The rulers of Italy however did not have it all their own way. The communes of the twelfth century were not prepared to surrender their claims to communal ownership over many of the rights which the emperor claimed without a struggle. After their victory over the imperial forces at the Battle of Legnano in 1176, they were able to force concessions at the Peace of Constance in 1183. Under its terms, woods, pastures and rivers were restored to communal ownership, and succeeding centuries saw the communes recover their rights over other activities such as hunting and fishing.[12]

Brissaud, writing of France, also noted that the feudal law did not distinguish very clearly between sovereignty and ownership, seeing in the regalia not just a power to police the exploitation of things in common ownership, but an ownership in the lord. Against this was pitted the Roman conception of public ownership, from which followed the right of the first taker to game and fish. Feudal theory saw such wild animals as appurtenances of the waters and forests and thus seigniorial property. The powers of lords to establish fisheries were derived from this view, while the Roman approach conceded to lords only the power to police exploitation in the communal interest, allowing freedom to hunt, fish, etc., subject to such control.[13-14]

In France, the feudal jurists argued that the earth and even the sea belonged to the king, so that important fisheries were often infeudated and

---

[12] See T.G. Watkin, *An Historical Introduction to Modern Civil Law* (London, 1999), pp.220–223.

[13] See J.-B. Brissaud, *A History of French Private Law* (Boston, 1912; reprinted New York 1968 [*Continental Legal History Series*, vol. III]), pp. 279–281.

[14] See Brissaud, *History of French Private Law*, pp. 285–287.

sometimes even maritime fisheries were the subject of grants. However, Brissaud noted that in all these cases, such seigniorial claims were gradually abandoned and the right of fishing declared free to all. This left the overlords' powers as mere rights to police the exploitation of such resources.[15-16]

Much the same was true in Germany, where public rivers could not be the object of private rights, but could be subjected to regulation. The right to fish originally belonged to every member of the folk, while fishing in the open sea was always regarded as free. The right to take clams and other aquatic products was unrestricted.[17]

What is preserved therefore in the native Welsh laws appears to be a record of a significant moment in not only Welsh but European legal development, a moment when two legal cultures strove for dominance in relation to the status of various things and activities. The Welsh solution, as witnessed by the law books of the twelfth and thirteenth centuries, was to effect a compromise, whereby the lord's powers to police activities such as fishing were preserved, but the claims of the first taker and the proprietor of the river to the fish taken in it were compromised. Fishing in the sea and for live fish on the sea-shore remained governed by the civilian approach, while things washed up on the beach were to be the king's, the 'packhorse' principle. Arguably, there is independent evidence from one lordship in south Wales which further substantiates this view of Welsh mediaeval law as a synthesis of different legal cultures.

The Charter Evidence from South Wales

It is against this background that the earliest charter evidence from Wales must be assessed. The charter granted by William, earl of Warwick to the burgesses of Swansea during the twelfth century granted them amongst other things "within Pulkanan and Blakepulle, all the beach upon which to make

---

[15] See Brissaud, *History of French Private Law*, pp. 238–239.
[16] See J.-B. Brissaud, *A History of French Public Law* (Boston, 1915; reprinted New York 1969 [*Continental Legal History Series*, vol. IX]), pp. 478–479.
[17] See R. Huebner, *A History of Germanic Private Law* (Boston, 1913; reprinted New York 1968 [*Continental Legal History Series*, vol. IV]), pp. 282–283; 286-287.

their fisheries". It therefore conceded to them a privilege which would not otherwise be theirs, namely to make fisheries.[18]

The same grant continued by reserving to the lord porpoises or sturgeon taken in such fishery, although the person in whose fishery it was taken was to receive either twelve pence or one load of corn. Porpoise and sturgeon were regalian rights in that such fish were the king's fish, and the earl's claim appears to have reserved to himself what would generally have been royal rights. This royal right was recognized throughout the succeeding centuries in the parts of England as Thomas Frowyk's highly-regarded reading on the statute *Prerogativa Regis* said. However, Frowyk's comments with regard to Wales suggests that the earl's charter reserved to himself privileges which were not only exclusive to the king in England but which by the end of the mediaeval period were settled not to exist for any lord's benefit, not even the king's, in Wales. In Wales, porpoise and sturgeon went to their taker, and this may indicate that William's payment to the burgesses of Swansea for such fish taken in their fisheries was a compromise solution to a dispute as to whether the English regalian right should apply or the Welsh custom. The charter provided a neat solution which gave each party rights based on the charter not on the common law nor the local custom. In Wales generally, and in Gower in particular, other than where, as with the Swansea burgesses, the special provisions of a charter were applicable, the civilian approach of *occupatio* applied even to porpoise and sturgeon, and they became the property of the first taker.

Warwick's claim of the right to take porpoise and sturgeon may have been an attempt by him to assume regalian rights. A century later, Edward I was to attack such assumptions of rights associated with kingship in his *quo warranto* inquiries, which challenged the right of lords to exercise kingly privileges in their territories. Lords were required to establish either that they

---

[18] See *The Charter of Earl William of Warwick for the Burgesses of Sweynesse*, printed in W.H. Jones, *History of Swansea and the Lordship of Gower* (Carmarthen, 1920), p. 154 :

> I have granted to them within Pulkanan and Blakepulle, all the beach upon which to make their fisheries. And if it happen that porpoise or sturgeon be taken in any such fishery, it is mine, and I will give to him whose the fishery is xii pence, or one load of corn. And if the burgesses can take fish in any manner outside the pool, it shall be theirs.

had a royal charter granting them such franchises or else that they had been enjoyed without interruption since before the coronation of Richard I. In the absence of such proof, such privileges were forfeit.

It is noted that when Edward I inquired into the problems of the lordship of Gower, the proceedings bore a close resemblance to proceedings upon a writ of *quo warranto* in the counties of England, and did not possess the undoubted marcher qualities which characterized those relating to neighbouring Glamorgan. The reason for this was that title as a marcher lord was derived from conquest of the land in question rather than grant, and whereas the lords of Glamorgan could base their claims to regality upon lineal descent from the person who had first secured the lordship by conquest, there had been no such continuity of tenure in Gower. The first earl of Warwick had won Gower by conquest, but the third earl had ceded the land to Henry II, and in 1203 King John had granted Gower by charter to William de Braose. It was this discontinuity of title which bedevilled the claim of successive lords of Gower to marcher status,[19] although by and large they were successful in maintaining that claim. It must however be acknowledged that the attacks upon their status and their successful defences

---

[19] See J. Beverley Smith, T.B. Pugh and W.R.B. Robinson, 'The Lordship of Gower and Kilvey' in G. Williams (ed.), *Glamorgan County History, Vol. III The Middle Ages*, (Cardiff, 1971), p. 242 :

> During the course of the litigation over Gower, de Braose inevitably based his defence to a large measure upon King John's charter of 1203 and upon that granted by Edward I in 1304. The fact that his title to the lordship was derived from King John's grant placed de Braose in a position of disadvantage. This gives the proceedings an aspect altogether different from those which had arisen in relation to the lordship of Glamorgan in 1291. Gilbert de Clare (d.1295), earl of Gloucester, based his claim to the regality which he exercised in Glamorgan upon the fact of conquest. He was the lineal descendant of the person who had first secured the lordship by conquest. In Gower there had been, by contrast, no continuity of tenure. The first earl of Warwick had won Gower by conquest; the third earl of Warwick, who died in 1184, was alleged to have ceded Gower to Henry II, and in 1203 King John had granted Gower to the first William de Braose by charter. The proceedings relating to Gower do not possess the undoubted marcher qualities which characterized those relating to Glamorgan, but rather they bear a close resemblance to the proceedings upon the writ of *quo warranto* which were pleaded in the counties of England in the last quarter of the thirteenth century.

of it had more to do with politics and military needs than the finer points of legality.[20] As late as the eighteenth century, the first response of a manorial lord to the lord of Gower's claims to regalities would be to question his marcher status.[21]

Indeed, it is important to note, as one of the most recent writers on the subject has said, that there was no one set of rules or principles which can be identified as the law of the March. Procedures and substantive customs varied from lordship to lordship and from manor to manor within a lordship. One cannot move from saying that a particular lordship was a marcher lordship to definite conclusions about its internal administration or law. Each lordship, sometimes each manor, sometimes each individual part of a manor, was an unit its own right.[22]

---

[20] See B. Morris (ed.), *Gabriel Powell's Survey of the Lordship of Gower* 1764 (Swansea, 2000), p. 2 :

> The all-important claim that Gower was a marcher lordship, bringing to its lord royal rights within its boundaries, was challenged in 1306 during the great lawsuit when his principal tenants complained of William de Breos' oppressions. No conclusion was reached then, because the case was settled when de Breos agreed to grant favourable charters to Swansea and to Gower. The issue arose again in 1369, when the Earl of Warwick (not of the original Warwick family) had briefly reclaimed Gower from the de Mowbrays only to have his claim to marcher lord status immediately disputed by the Prince of Wales' advisors. The case, which turned on legal points which the Warwicks were less able to counter than the de Mowbrays and the de Breoses, went against Warwick, but the prince then regranted marcher status by way of a royal charter, which subsequent lords could point to as their title.

[21] NLW, Penrice and Margam Mss. No. 6538 :

> Henry Duke of Beaufort Complt. And Sr. Edward Mansell Barrt and others Defts.
> Heads of the Defendts. Plea answere or Demurrer as shall be best advised
> Does not know whither the Segniory of Gower was formerly a Ldp. Marcher or no nor whither the then Lords thereof claimed or owned (?) the Royalties and perquisites now sought by Bill…

[22] See Michael Rogers' Introduction to Helen Watt, *Welsh Manors and their Records* (Aberystwyth, 2000) p. 26 :

> The March of Wales was outside the jurisdiction of royal courts in all but exceptional circumstances and each lordship was a self-contained administrative and judicial unit. The laws and procedures used in the numerous courts of the marcher lordships are known together as the Law of the March but in fact there was no rigid or written code of law, uniformly and systematically applied. There were great variations in procedure and custom between different lordships, even

One aspect of this diversity is germane to any assessment of the customs of the lordship of Gower and Kilvey. The lordship was composed of distinct areas known as the Englishry and Welshry, a division present in many lordships, including that of neighbouring Glamorgan. Within the Welshry, the native population lived according to their own customs despite being under the rule of the Norman overlord, often pleading their customs and following their own procedures within his courts.

The absence of any further claim to the regalian right to porpoise and sturgeon within the mediaeval lordship, other than under the terms of the charter, is significant given Edward I's policy. Further, the De Braose charter of Gower in 1306 specifically states in relation to fisheries that: "Qui delfinum piscem, qui wlgaliter 'Porpeys' denominatur, ceperint aut invenint, eum sine alicuijus calumpnia habeant". De Braose has completely abandoned any claim to porpoise and not only does he not claim such fish by regalian right, he concedes such fish to those who take or find them. This accords with the native Welsh laws and with Frowyk's comments on there being no regalian right to such fish in Wales, but rather they became the property of the first taker.[23] The use of the word *calumpnia* recalls the Welsh laws where the fine for fishing with a net in a river without permission was termed *camlwrw*. The royal fish in Gower could be taken without any such offence, albeit that the burgesses of Swansea had agreed to accept payment for their surrender to the lord by the terms of their charter.

---

those which shared a single lord. In the same way, customs could vary between different parts of the same lordship, leading to disputes over the extent of the jurisdiction of different franchises over certain persons or cases. *The Black Book of St. Davids* reveals that customs could vary even within different parts of a single manor. Such variations could apply to procedural details or substantive points of law. These local variations mirrored the variations in customs between different manors in England, but on a substantially greater scale. English settlers were normally subject to a local variant of English Common Law in their own court, often based at a borough. Welsh tenants were subject to a local admixture of traditional Welsh law, local customs, English Common Law, precedent, and seigneurial dictat, influenced on a practical level, by the lord's officials. Courts were held by the lord's steward or his deputy in the lord's name, as were English manorial courts, but the range of issues dealt with was much greater.

[23] See *Charter of Gower 1306* in G.T. Clark, *Cartae et Alia Munimenta quae ad Dominium de Glamorgancia pertinent* (2nd ed., Cardiff, 1910) volume III :

"Qui delfinum piscem, qui wlgaliter 'Porpeys' denominatur, ceperint aut

This interpretation is further supported by the Inspeximus and Recitation by John Mowbray, Lord of Gower dated 16th August 1334, which records a grant made by Henry of Warwick to the abbey of Neath and to the monks thereof of a fishery beneath Pulcanan which Ranulf the Hermit once held, and gives the abbey "libertatem piscandi et pisces capiendi et habendi cujuscunque generis fuerint… ". They may take fish of whatever kind, that is with no restriction regarding fish such as porpoise or sturgeon which in England would be royal and which in Gower had once been claimed by the lord.[24]

This grant goes on to describe the manner in which the "libertatem piscandi et pisces capiendi et habendi" is to be exercised, namely, "cum retibus et aliis ingeniis… Et liberam licenciam construendi et levandi unam gurgitem ex traverso eiusdem aque de Tauwy". As far as the sea shore is concerned, this grant is not of the right to fish, but of the right to fix nets and other devices as well as to build a weir in order to catch fish. It grants rights which were not part of the common right to fish and is in effect an exercise by the lord of his police powers to control the manner in which the common right to fish was exercised.

From the reign of Edward I until the Act of Union of 1536 and beyond, the lords of the manor of Gower had no right to live fish caught on the sea shore, but only a right to police the manner in which the public right of fishing was exercised so as to ensure that it was not improperly exploited. This police power included the right to licence the use of devices such as nets and weirs which encroached upon the public's right to the sea shore. As in the native laws of southern Wales, as witnessed by the Blegywryd and

---

invenint, eum sine alicuijus calumpnia habeant".

[24] See *Inspeximus and Recitation by John Mowbray Lord of Gower 16th August 1334* in Clark, *Cartae*, volume II :

> "unam piscariam desub. Pulcanan quam Ranulfus heremita quondam tenuit. Et libertatem piscandi et pisces capiendi et habendi cujuscunque generis fuerint ubique inter Pulcanan et aquam de Tauwy cum retibus et aliis ingeniis prout melius sibi viderit expedire omni tempore anni. Et liberam licenciam construendi et levandi unam gurgitem ex traverso eiusdem aque de Tauwy a terra eorum apud Glyntauwy que vocatur Enysumwen usque ad firmam et siccam terram de Gouweria. Et quod habeant iidem monachi et eorum successores totam piscacionem ejusdem aque tam ex parte terre mee de Gouweria quam ex parte terre eorum per quadraginta perticatas ex utraque parte terre dicte gurgitis".

Cyfnerth traditions, the lord's permission was needed for such structures or devices. In the north, however, things would appear to have been different. Both Iorwerth and Colan state that whoever owns land adjoining the sea shore also owns that much of the shore as well and may make a wear thereon if they so wish.[25] This is without prejudice to the king's right to what the sea casts ashore, because the sea is the king's packhorse according to Iorwerth, although Colan interestingly says it is the lord's packhorse. The northern tradition does not require the king's or the lord's permission for the building of a fishing wear on the beach. Interestingly, Roman occupation of the north never involved the civilian population adopting Roman ways. One may wonder therefore whether the northern tradition bears witness to the original rule.

In the south, however, freedom to fish on the shore subject to the need for the lord's permission to use devices remained the position after the Act of Union as witnessed in the 1583 Survey of Gower Anglicana, where the tenth article records that: "there are certaine fishings in several members of this lordship, for the which the Lord hath a certaine rent, and that the tenants and inhabitants have liberty to fish freely tyme out of minde, in any other places than such as are allready under rent, as farre as we know".[26] This endorses the view that it is no accident that the Act of Union omits to list fishing as a right appurtenant to the Welsh marcher lordships.[27]

---

[25] "Puybynnac bye yffo tyr eg glan traeth, ef byeuuyd keulet a'r tyr o'r traeth, a gunaet koret arnau os men", ["Whosoever owns land alongside the shore, he owns the same breadth of the shore as of the land, and let him make a weir on it if he wants to".] but without prejudice to the king's right to what the sea casts ashore because the sea is the king's packhorse. See Aled Rhys Wiliam, *Llyfr Iorwerth* (Cardiff, 1960), p. 58, § 88. 1-3; Dafydd Jenkins, *Llyfr Colan* (Cardiff, 1963), 615. English translation from Dafydd Jenkins, *The Law of Hywel Dda* (Llandysul, 1986), p. 112.

[26] See *Survey of Gower Anglicana, 1583* in C. Baker and G.G. Francis (ed.), *Surveys of Gower and Kilvey* (London, 1861–1870) :

> To the Tenth article we say, that there are certaine fishings in several members of this lordship, for the which the Lord hath a certaine rent, and that the tenants and inhabitants have liberty to fish freely tyme out of minde, in any other places than such as are allready under rent, as farre as we know.

[27] See Act for Laws and Justice to be ministered in Wales in like form as it is in this realm, 27 Hy 8, c. 26, 1535, section 30, from Sir Ivor Bowen, *The Statutes of Wales* (London, 1908), pp. 90-91 :

> And it is further enacted by the Authority aforesaid, That all and every lay and

Conclusion

It might appear that this essay focuses upon a very narrow issue, namely the question of to whom what were in the parts of England deemed royal fish pertained if taken in Wales. The answer would appear to have been that given by Thomas Frowyk in his highly-regarded reading at the Inner Temple in 1495. The evidence of the twelfth and thirteenth century Welsh law books and the surviving charter evidence from south Wales are all consistent with his statement.

However, behind this there lies a rich variety of legal doctrines, some civilian, some Anglo-Norman, some possibly native Celtic. To understand the rules set out with regard to this and other issues in the Welsh laws, a knowledge of those laws alone is not enough. The broader historical context

---

> temporal Person and Persons, now being Lords Marchers, and having any Lordships Marchers or Lordships Royal, shall from and after the said Feast of All-Saints have all such Myses and Profits of their Tenants, as they have had or used to have at the first Entry into their Lands in Times past, and also shall have, hold and keep within the Precinct of their Lordships Courts Baron Courts Leets and Law-days, and all and every Thing to the same Courts belonging; and also shall have, within the Precinct of their said Lordships or Law-days, Waife Straise Infanthef Outfanthef Treasuretrove Deodands Goods and Chattels of Felons and of Persons condemned or outlawed of Felony or Murther, or put in Exigent for Felony or Murther, and also Wreck de Mer, Wharfage and Custom of Strangers, as they have had in times past, and as though such Privileges were granted to them by our Sovereign Lord the King by Point of Charter; any Thing in this present Act to the contrary notwithstanding.

It is further submitted that this was still the position during the later seventeenth century as witnessed by the Survey of the Manor of Kilvey conducted on 20

has to be appreciated as does the legal cultures which had existed in different periods within the territory which was to become Wales and indeed the different legal cultures which coexisted within Wales during the Middle Ages. Only by assessing the contribution of the Roman occupation, the canons of the Church, the jurisprudence of the invading Normans and that of the native Welsh can a true picture of the legal state of Wales in the mediaeval period and probably much later be achieved. That the texts from which such a study can usefully be undertaken are now available in a readily-accessible form is due to the labours of many distinguished scholars over the last few centuries. The most recent and by no means least distinguished of that line is Professor Dafydd Jenkins, without whose work neither this essay nor much else in this volume would have been possible to achieve.

September 1686. While the right to fish in the rivers of the manor is expressly reserved to the lord, when the sea shore in mentioned, the lord's rights are to rents for "fishing Weares now upoon the Salt sands". The Survey continues: "no Freehoulder of this Mannor can erect or set up any weares or Engines or device for takeing of Fish without consent of the Lord of the said Mannor… ". Gabriel Powell's survey of Gower and Kilvey as steward for the Duke of Beaufort says much the same concerning Kilvey; having rehearsed the details of the weirs on the sands, it continues: "And no tenant or other person can set up any wears, engines or other devices for the taking fish within the said Manor without the Lord's licence and consent". The distinction between river fishing and fishing on the sea shore is maintained, and the lord has no right to live fish taken on the shore, only a right to police the manner of its taking when the means employed could encroach upon the rights of others regarding the sea shore. See respectively Baker and Francis, *Surveys of Gower and Kilvey* and Morris, *Gabriel Powell's Survey of the Lordship of Gower 1764*, loc. cit., supra, nn. 26 and 20 respectively.

SIR WILLIAM JONES
1746–1794

David J. Ibbetson*

It is both an honour and a pleasure to be invited here this evening to give the inaugural lecture of the Welsh Legal History Society. England got its legal history society, the Selden Society, in 1887, Scotland the Stair Society in 1936, and Ireland its society in 1988. It is fitting that Wales, with its long and impressive tradition of legal history, should join the group, and we all hope that it will have a long and distinguished history.

I should begin with a more than conventional protestation of my own inadequacy for the task in hand. Not simply because I am not Welsh - Sir William Jones, the subject of my lecture and one of the finest of all Welsh lawyers, was himself born in Westminster, educated at Harrow School before going up to University College Oxford, and spent the best part of his career as a judge in India.[1] More importantly, it would take a far greater scholar than I, or, for that matter, than anyone else in this room, to speak with authority about a man whose interests were as far-ranging as Jones. He was not just a lawyer, but a quite extraordinary polymath. Among his writings there are certainly legal works: his book on bailment; his edition of the speeches of the Greek orator Isaeus, together with a commentary on the ancient Greek law of intestate succession and a wide-ranging comparative survey of the same subject; a book on the Mohammedan law of inheritance; and various works on Hindu law. He was better known as an orientalist than lawyer, with a Europe-wide reputation while he was still in his twenties. A brilliant linguist, by a young age he was fluent in most European languages, though I am not sure just how good was his mastery of Welsh. One of his earliest published works was a grammar of the Persian language, one of his greatest

---

* The text of an inaugural lecture given to the Welsh Legal History Society. Apart from the addition of footnote references, no attempt has been made to recraft the paper in preparing it for publication.

[1] Biographical information about Jones, unless otherwise stated, is derived from G. Cannon, *The Life and Mind of Oriental Jones* (Cambridge, 1990). References to his letters are to G. Cannon, ed., *The Letters of Sir William Jones* (Oxford, 1970); references to his works are to the thirteen-volume edition by Lord Teignmouth (London, 1807).

achievements his demonstration of the genetic relationship between Sanskrit, Greek, and Latin. A poet of some ability in his own right, he translated works from Arabic, Persian and Sanskrit into English, and did much to introduce English readers to the splendours of Oriental literature, counterbalancing the prevalent adulation of the Greeks and the Romans. And not just this. He had considerable expertise as a botanist; he did distinguished work on Hindu chronology, linking it in with Greek and Hebrew histories; the game of chess, the subject of one of his first serious poems; the source of the Nile; cures for elephantiasis and other disorders of the blood; and, let it never be forgotten, the comparative morphology of different species of the pangolin. Only a polymath as wide-ranging as Jones himself, if such a person exists, could hope to give a proper assessment of the man. I hope I shall be forgiven, therefore, if I stay more firmly within my own sphere of relative expertise, and concentrate on Jones the lawyer.

But let me begin by giving a thumbnail sketch of Jones's life. He was of impeccably Welsh stock, his grandfather being a farmer on the Isle of Anglesey. Jones's father had raised himself up out of this humble stock and moved to London. He was a very fine mathematician, a Fellow of the Royal Society, and a close associate of Sir Isaac Newton, as also perhaps of William Wotton, the first editor of the mediaeval Welsh laws of Hywel Dda. Curiously, it is Jones the father rather than our Jones whose work became so well-known that his name has been forgotten, so much a part of our everyday life that we forget that it must have had an originator. He introduced into mathematical notation the symbol pi. More to our point, though, through earning his living as a tutor he came into close contact with at least one future Chief Justice, Hardwicke, and one Lord Chancellor, Macclesfield. It was partly through these links that young William, when casting around for a profession, was sucked into the Law.

Jones senior died when William was only a toddler, but he had inherited some of his father's genius. His mother, who brought him up, was in her own way a no less remarkable woman, introducing her precociously talented son to the main works of English literature before he was five years old, and inculcating in him a voracious appetite for reading anything of value that he could lay his hands on. As a schoolboy at Harrow he was thoroughly bookish, reading and discussing before the age of eleven the works of such writers as Joseph Addison and Samuel Johnson. He soon got to grips with

Latin and Greek, picked up a fair handful of modern European languages, taught himself Hebrew so as to be able to read the Old Testament, and began to learn Arabic. By the time he went up to Oxford, he already had the makings of a formidable scholar.

At Oxford he built up his linguistic skills, and his reputation as an orientalist began to flourish. But, as his friends and relatives recognised, however much a career in Oriental scholarship might bring Jones fame it would never bring him fortune. He was encouraged to go into legal practice, where his talents were bound to be more richly rewarded. Hence, in 1770 at the age of 24, he entered the Middle Temple and began to study for the Bar. With his abilities and his connexions he had a good start, and he was soon established as a practitioner on the Welsh circuit. Though his forensic style was over-declamatory, more slavishly modelled on Cicero than the conventions even of the eighteenth century would have approved, he had a reasonable success; but he was hardly destined to become one of the leading advocates of his age. Perhaps, too, he spent rather more time on the pursuit of his oriental studies than was consistent with an orthodox advancement through the legal profession to a position on the Bench. Preferment as a Commissioner in Bankruptcy in 1775 was a mark of approval, but it was a byway in the law rather than the first stepping stone on the road to professional fame.

Jones's eyes were set in a different direction, on the vacant judgeship on the British court in Bengal. Not only would this enable him to make use of his linguistic skills and give him access to a vast range of oriental material compared to that which was available in England, which would enable him to pursue his real interest in Eastern languages and literature; it was, in addition, extremely well paid, and he calculated that he would easily be able to save £4000 annually out of his £6000 salary and within a few years to return to England with sufficient wealth to set himself up as a gentleman, able to devote himself to oriental studies for the rest of his life. It was not to be. India captured him: its language, its law, its literature, its culture. At the same time as fulfilling his judicial duties assiduously, he made a serious study of Sanskrit, essentially inventing the science of comparative linguistics; he translated both legal and literary texts; he almost single-handedly founded the Royal Asiatic Society of Bengal as a channel for bringing south Asian researches to the attention of European scholars, and contributed papers to it on a host of more or less unrelated subjects. In 1794, at the age of forty seven, unremitting overwork and the Indian climate finally caught up with him and he died.

No-one will underestimate Jones's importance as an orientalist, but what of him as a lawyer? In purely conventional professional terms, he was not especially successful. There were many better barristers in the eighteenth century, and although he was clearly a very capable judge the only feature which distinguished him from other British judges in India was his willingness to try to read for himself the Indian legal texts on which he needed to base his judgments rather than relying on the expertise of the court-appointed Pandits, native experts in Indian law. And in terms of legal synthesis, his only real work is his treatise on bailments, published in 1781 shortly before his move to India. Not everybody was impressed by him. Bentham, waspish as ever, described him as 'an industrious man with no sort of genius' who 'went spinning cobwebs out of his own brain and winding them round common law'.[2] Yet, for all this, he remains a central figure both in the eighteenth century Common law and in his influence on the legal history of subsequent centuries. And in his attitude to law and legal history there is much that the present age should respect and remember. Let me try to say why.

Unsurprisingly, Jones did not see law as a crude mechanical skill, a means of earning more than the meagre living that he would have been consigned to as a pure scholar. It was a truly liberal art, alongside other liberal arts. And it was, in some way, symbolically the centre of his world. In an early commonplace book, probably dating from about 1775, he matches a sketch of England surrounded by the other countries of the world with two separate sketches of law at the centre of a wheel, with other arts and sciences radiating like spokes out of this hub - logic, metaphysics, rhetoric, declamation, poetry, exercises (by which he seems to have meant gymnastics and dancing), natural history, anatomy, chemistry, languages, ethics, politics, music, painting, antiquities, history ancient and modern, and mathematics.[3] I don't think he can have been trying to portray law as in any way integral to these other disciplines metaphorically spinning off from it, nor suggesting

---

[2] J. Bowring, ed., *The Works of Jeremy Bentham* (Edinburgh, 1843), vol.10, p.51.
[3] British Library MS Add 8889, f.2v, f.4.

that law was in any way inherently superior to them. But law, on its way at this time to becoming the active hub of his life, was not something different in kind from other disciplines, to be boxed away and kept separate from them. As he would find when he went to India, his theoretical interest in Indian texts and his practical concerns with deciding cases on the basis of native Indian law could run together, culminating in his edition and translation of the Hindu text known as the laws of Manu, the Institutes of Hindu law, and in his beginning to prepare a Digest of Hindu law, consciously modelling himself on the Institutes and Digest of the Emperor Justinian. The true lawyer cannot divorce legal practice from theoretical contemplation of the law.

No less important is Jones's recognition of the importance of legal history. The opening words of the preface of his first book with a legal dimension, his edition of the speeches of Isaeus, put the matter as plainly as could be; they could almost become the motto of a society of legal historians:

> There is no branch of learning, from which a student of the law may receive a more rational pleasure, or which seems more likely to prevent his being disgusted with the dry elements of a very complicated science, than the history of the rules and ordinances, by which nations, eminent for wisdom and illustrious in arts, have regulated their civil polity: nor is this the only fruit that he may expect to reap from a general knowledge of foreign laws both ancient and modern; for, whilst he indulges the liberal curiosity of a scholar in examining the customs and institutions of men, whose works have yielded him the highest delight, and whose actions have raised his admiration, he will feel the satisfaction of a patriot in observing the preference due in most instances to the laws of his own country above those of all other states; or, if his just prospects in life give him hopes of becoming a legislator, he may collect many useful hints for the improvement even of that fabrick which his ancestors have erected with infinite exertions of virtue and genius, but which, like all human systems, will ever advance nearer to perfection and ever fall short of it.[4]

Legal history is enjoyable; it furthers one's sense of patriotism; and it is useful. What more could one ask?

There is no doubting the pleasure that Jones himself got from the study of legal history. Writing to his tutee Lord Althorp from Margate, of all places, in 1774 he eloquently describes the scenery and the delights of sea-bathing,

---

[4] *Works*, vol.9, pp.11-12.

though complaining about the more material and social pleasures offered by the town. The fish, he says, is so much worse than at Weymouth: nothing but a monotonous diet of sole and lobster as compared to the fine dories and red mullet offered by the latter. And much as he would have enjoyed dancing with ladies, he was avoiding the Rooms: the people there, he confides to Althorp with more than a touch of snobbery, were nothing but *gentilshommes bourgeois*. So he made up for this by spending his afternoon re-reading his favourite legal texts.[5] How many of us today would even think of packing Coke and Blackstone in our suitcases? Would any of us actually thumb through them for enjoyment's sake? What greater pleasure could there be, he asks in a letter to the Dutch orientalist Henry Schultens a few weeks later, than the study of native and universal law?[6]

Not merely did Jones read the great legal books. One of his many unfulfilled projects was to edit the classics of the Common law, comparing the printed texts with the manuscripts, and providing them with translations and commentary. Eight volumes were planned: Glanvill in volume one; volumes 2, 3 and 4 for Bracton; the Mirror of Justice in volume 5 and Britton in volume 6. The seventh would contain Fleta and Hengham, and he would finish with Littleton and Fortescue.[7] He got as far as identifying a few relevant manuscripts, and half-prepared an edition and translation of Littleton which is now in the British Library.[8] It was an odd choice of starting-place. Littleton was already translated and blessed with Sir Edward Coke's commentary, and Jones's friend and rival Francis Hargrave was already producing his edition of Coke's version. If only he had started with Bracton or Glanvill! But one of Jones's frustrating weaknesses was to promise more than he would deliver, to put down a half-completed project when another one came his way, or to leap ahead to the conclusion of something without actually doing the work. His half-complete edition of Littleton, for example, comes with a wholly complete manuscript title page - Oxford, at the Clarendon Press, 1776 - together with detailed instructions about the typesetting. We perhaps see something of the same trait in his

[5] *Letters*, vol.1, pp.155-158 (no. 90).

[6] *Letters*, vol.1, p.163 (no. 93): 'Ullamne rem jucundiorem aut nobiliorem esse putemus, quam juris patrii et universi studium [...]?'

[7] British Library MS Add 8889, f.5.

[8] British Library 708 g 22.

father, who on occasion signed himself 'Longitude Jones' in confident, if misplaced, anticipation of his winning the prize offered by the Royal Society for the production of a reliable marine chronometer. Perhaps it is the mark of a genius even to think of such grandiose projects, without the seeds of self-doubt of ordinary mortals. But we may still wish that he had actually gone on and actually done the work. A warning, maybe, for the editorial directors of the Welsh Legal History Society: make sure you get your texts from authors, not just promises of them.

Jones's legal history was not just theoretical or antiquarian. He made good use of it in his understanding of contemporary law, most notably in his treatise on bailments.[9] Here he worked through Bracton, the Year Books and Coke as well as more recent writers and case law, not to mention Roman law, Hebrew law and the laws of a whole host of other nations including - seemingly for the only time in his works - the Welsh laws of Hywel Dda. We might say that history was a part of his whole thinking about law in the same way that historical philology was a part of his whole thinking about language. As a legal practitioner he could temporarily ignore this, just as he could read and speak languages without worrying about their roots, but as soon as it came to theory, or just straightforward scholarship, history was of necessity an integral part of his approach. Like Jones, Frederic William Maitland, the founding spirit of England's Society of Legal Historians, saw legal history not merely as an end in itself, but also as a means to elucidate problems of contemporary English law. Among legal historians today there are those who still try to carry forward the torch for such a historical understanding of contemporary legal institutions. It would be a fitting tribute to Jones if the Welsh Legal History Society were to continue this aspect of his work, too.

But law for Jones was not only a gentlemanly avocation, its history a harmless source of rational pleasure. It also mattered, and mattered deadly seriously, in the political arena. Despite his close friendship with men such as Edmund Burke, his pretensions to social status and advancement, and his natural tendency to gravitate towards people with political power or influence, there was a strong radical streak to Jones. He was deeply conscious of the need for those with power to exercise it properly. There was

---

[9] *Works*, vol.8, p.323-458.

a trust reposed in them, and they should be faithful to that trust. The law was the means whereby their power should be controlled.

In political terms, this meant that Jones was not so much concerned with the existence of strong monarchical government as with the proper functionning of it. In his early years at the bar, for example, he got involved in a case which raised the issue of the lawfulness of impressment, a case which he described as his *prima causa publica pro libertate dicta*.[10] One John Millachip, freeman of London, had been impressed into the Navy. He was released, not without some difficulty, after the City of London had obtained a writ of habeas corpus, only to be seized a second time by a press gang. Significantly, it was not the use of press gangs *per se* that Jones so objected to, but their use without proper parliamentary authority. The American rebellion had to be crushed, and soldiers and sailors were necessary to do this; 'but as there was full time for parliament to have authorized such warrants, there could be no *necessity* for the King alone to issue them *without Parliament*; and that is the single question to be discussed.'[11]

Others of Jones's strongly held political principles stemmed from his belief in the need to impose checks on the exercise of arbitrary power. He had, for example, a firm commitment to the constitutional safeguards afforded by trial by jury. Putting it in modern-day terms, he saw keenly the force of jury nullification; so long as the final decision in a case was left to the jury, it had the power to neutralise any law, however oppressive. Take away the jury, and unbridled power would be that much more difficult to check. In the same way, he recognised that where law broke down force would take over; consequently he opposed the maintenance of a standing army and stood up for the right of the citizen to bear arms.

Jones's radical tendencies led to one of the more curious incidents in his life. It can almost be a seen as set-piece to illustrate his constitutional principles.[12] In 1782, as a result either of a bet or a challenge, perhaps from Benjamin Franklin, that he could not reduce the principles of political

---

[10] *Letters*, vol.1, p.232 (no. 135).

[11] *Letters*, vol.1, p.250 (no. 147).

[12] As well as the discussion in Cannon, *Life and Mind of Oriental Jones*, see M.J. Franklin, *Sir William Jones* (Cardiff, 1995), pp.72-78, and J. Oldham, *The Mansfield Manuscripts* (Chapel Hill, 1992), pp.794-800. The legal proceedings can be followed

morality to a form in which they could be understood by anyone, however uneducated, Jones wrote a brief pamphlet, *A Dialogue between a Scholar and a Peasant*,[13] and caused it to be printed anonymously. His brother-in-law, William Shipley, the Dean of St Asaph, was so impressed by the tract that he caused it to be published in Wrexham, swapping the scholar and the peasant for a gentleman and a farmer. It is not exactly firebrand stuff - the gentleman leads the farmer by the nose into the recognition that, just as the members of a club would not tolerate one of its members arrogating to himself the power to make rules affecting all of them, so it was intolerable that political government should not be properly representative; and since rightfulness demanded that the unenfranchised masses might take steps to protect their interests by armed force if necessary, it followed that they might each keep a musket by his bedside and practise its use every morning. Thomas Fitzmaurice, Sheriff of Flint and brother of the Marquis of Lansdowne, a man who had crossed swords with Shipley before, objected to the language of the pamphlet, and took steps to initiate proceedings against him. Reading between the lines, it looks as if Fitzmaurice drew the work to the attention of the King's ministers, and to the King himself, but they laughed down the suggestion that a prosecution be brought. He therefore triggered the proceedings himself. Jones, meanwhile, had been appointed to the Bench in Bengal. He made no secret of his authorship of the Dialogue, producing the decidedly odd state of affairs of a trial for sedition based on something openly and admittedly written by a man now travelling out to take up office as a judge. There is some suggestion that he may have been bundled off to India more than a little precipitately - in one of his letters written just before sailing he refers to being hurried beyond description as a result of things having happened in such a rush,[14] and in another written a couple of weeks later he tells of the Admiralty being so anxious that the boat should sail, and their orders so peremptory, that it departed as soon as there was a slight breeze.[15] Jones does seem to have been astonishingly complacent about Shipley's prosecution. Writing to Lord Ashburton while still at sea, he

in T.B. Howell, *A Complete Collection of State Trials* (London, 1814), vol.21, cols.847-1046.

[13] *Works*, vol.8, pp.525-537.

[14] *Letters*, vol.2, p.612 (no. 360).

[15] *Letters*, vol.2, p.615 (no. 363).

describes the journey and the climate, only mentioning the trial as an afterthought:

> The grand jury of Denbighshire, have found, I understand, the bill against the Dean of St Asaph, for publishing my dialogue; but as an indictment for a theoretical essay on government was I believe never before known, I have no apprehension for the consequences.[16]

One might have expected, perhaps, a whiff of concern that his wife's brother was in the dock on a serious charge, maybe a hint of embarrassment that it was Jones's own pamphlet that Shipley was being prosecuted for, at the very least a recognition that some might raise doubts about his fitness to sit on the bench. The Attorney-General, Lloyd Kenyon, who was also Chief Justice of Chester, was one such person. Remarking that it was not for him to say whether Jones's position should be reviewed, he thought that it ought to be soberly and seriously considered by the proper authorities. India, he says, was a country to which it would be unwise to send a seditious man.[17] Shipley's counsel, Thomas Erskine, turned the point to the advantage of the defence. Was it really likely that the acknowledged author of a seditious pamphlet would have been appointed to judicial office in a place like India?[18]

Indirectly, and utterly unwittingly, Shipley's Case marks one of Jones's most important contributions to late eighteenth-century English law. It provided Erskine with the opportunity to deliver one of his great set-piece speeches, arguing that the jury should have a hand in determining whether or not the publication in question was a libel and not leave the whole question to the court as a matter of law. His eloquence failed to persuade the King's Bench, but it was not expected that it would: Lord Mansfield's court was strongly trenched in its view that the question of libel or no libel was purely a matter for the judges to decide.[19] More importantly, it was consciously designed to influence parliament in what we see now as the run-up to Fox's Libel Act, and in this it did succeed. In the event Jones's complacency may have been well justified. After the jury had solemnly determined that Shipley

---

[16] *Letters*, vol.2, pp.615-616 (no. 363).
[17] *State Trials*, vol.21, col.869.
[18] *State Trials*, vol.21, col.860.
[19] Oldham, *Mansfield Manuscripts*, 782-805

had in fact published the pamphlet, a fact that was not remotely in dispute, after some memorably intemperate exchanges between Mr Justice Buller, the trial judge, and Thomas Erskine,[20] and after argument that the unsatisfactory nature of the jury's verdict necessitated a new trial, the King's Bench almost cursorily held that the pamphlet was not in fact seditious at all and Shipley was duly acquitted. A report of trial, containing the full text of the unoffending pamphlet, was rapidly written up and circulated. It was soon translated into Welsh, versified, and incorporated into a marginally ribald playlet to be performed around the villages of North Wales. Thus it was that Jones's little jeu d'esprit was finally given far more publicity that it ever deserved, and his ideas transmitted to a far wider audience than would ever have occurred without the prosecution. Utterly unintentionally, we are told, Jones had become the author of the first political tract in Welsh.[21]

We must not let our enthusiasm for the more technical points of legal history blind ourselves to this sort of incident. It is an important point for a legal history society actively to remember, and for its works actively to memorialise, just how many of the basic constitutional principles that we take for granted today were established through the efforts of courageous lawyers in earlier centuries.

Yet Jones remains a slippery customer. At the same time as publicly - rather too publicly - espousing radical political views in England and Wales, he was quite happy to contemplate the strict enforcement of the laws in India. Thus we have starkly paradoxical sentiments expressed in a letter written while travelling to take up his judicial position in Bengal: he sticks firmly by the views in favour of individual freedom expressed in his Dialogue; indeed, he will go through life with the persuasion that they are just and rational; 'though I shall certainly not preach them to the Indians, who must and will be governed by absolute power.'[22]

None the less, in reality, when sitting as a judge Jones's application of

---

[20] *State Trials*, vol.21, cols.950-955, esp. at col.951:

> *Buller*: Sit down, sir. Remember your duty, or I shall be obliged to proceed in another manner.
>
> *Erskine*: Your lordship may proceed in what manner you think fit. I know my duty as well as your lordship knows yours. I shall not alter my conduct.

[21] Franklin, *Sir William Jones*, 78.

[22] *Letters*, vol.2, p.616 (no. 363).

the law did not involve too substantial a departure from his English principles. Strict enforcement of the law emphatically did not mean the approval of abuses of power. We learn from William Hickey's memoirs of a case in India in which an action was brought against a constable for false imprisonment after he had, allegedly mendaciously, procured a warrant and arrested two men.[23] Jones was, we are told, eloquent in his violent denunciation of the acts of the constable, sticking to his guns despite the other judges of the court favouring the constable's plea of justification. In point of pure law there was a good deal to be said for the unliberal view of the majority, but the report of the case shows that Jones was prepared to give weight to a very technical argument that the defendant had not acted in absolute conformity with the power given to him by the warrant and so could justify the giving of judgment for the plaintiffs.[24] At a rhetorical level, though, Jones needed no such argument. William Hickey gives a good view of his indignation:

> Throughout his public life he had been a strenuous advocate for the rights of Britons and the liberty of the subject, and trusted his principles would remain the same to the last hour of his existence; that if such persons as the defendant were permitted to act in the shameful way he had done with impunity there was no saying to what extent the evil might not be carried. No man would be secure either in person or property if such a wretch, such an abandoned, unprincipled profligate was allowed to range uncontrolled over Calcutta under the mask of being a public peace officer…[25]

And so on in this vein. He was no less firm in his opposition to the introduction of summary trials in India for petty larceny and other misdemeanours: take one such step and you were on the slippery slope to try even the most serious of felonies without a jury[26]. The principle was clear for English law - a passage from Sir Matthew Hale proved it - and it should apply equally to all subjects of the British crown, 'for a different faith or complexion can make no difference in justice or right'.

The ambiguity inherent in Jones's political principles and their

[23] A. Spencer, ed., *Memoirs of William Hickey* (London, 1913), vol.3, pp.247-258.
[24] National Library of Wales MS 8476D, esp. at p.47.
[25] *Memoirs of William Hickey*, vol.3, pp.253-254.
[26] *Works*, vol.7, pp.69-70.

application is reflected in an implicit uncertainty within his whole understanding of the nature of law. It has been said that a serious lawyer needs a properly thought out theoretical stance towards the law, something that can provide a coherent framework for legal decisions and concrete analysis. If so, Jones must have been a very serious lawyer indeed: we can discern in his writings a commitment to at least three different, mutually incompatible, legal theories. He provides an admirable illustration of the tensions playing around within Common law thought at the time when theoretical considerations were beginning to transform it from its mediaeval fixation with the forms of action to a more coherent structure based on abstract legal conceptions and categories. More negatively, perhaps, we might say that Jones was a very clever man who could think himself into several different positions without ever committing himself to any one of them, and without ever feeling the need to develop any new theory of his own.

Despite his protestations to the contrary, there was a strong streak of the positivist in him. He admired Blackstone enormously, but did not at all like the main thrust of his definition of law in terms of rules prescribed by a superior power. 'On another occasion you shall know how widely I differ from Blackstone', he wrote to Viscount Althorp in 1779[27]. He was especially dismissive of such an approach when it came to constitutional law, for if it were accepted it meant that the constitution could be changed by statute in a snap of the fingers, in practical terms at the whim of a few self-interested individuals[28]. But in his first major speech after his arrival in India, his charge to the Calcutta Grand Jury in 1783, he takes a far more Blackstonian tack:

> The use of law, as a science, is to prevent mere discretionary power under the colour of equity; and it is the duty of a judge to pronounce his decisions, not simply according to his own opinion of justice and right, but according to prescribed rules. It must be hoped, that his own reason generally approves those rules; but it is the judgement of the law, not his own, which he delivers. Were judges to decide by their bare opinions of right and wrong, opinions always unknown, often capricious, sometimes improperly biassed, to what an arbitrary

[27] *Letters*, vol.1, p.333 (no. 187).
[28] *Letters*, vol.2, p.553 (no. 322).
[29] *Works*, vol.7, pp.4-5.

> tribunal would men be subject! In how dreadful a state of slavery would they live![29]

And he was perfectly happy to defend the statutory creation of the British court in Bengal, as clear a constitutional change as could be imagined:

> Legislative provisions have not the individual for their object, but the species; and are not made for the convenience of the day, but for the regulation of ages.[30]

There are different ways of reading this apparent volte-face. An obvious possibility is that Jones, having just seen his tract on government prosecuted for sedition, was going out of his way to be utterly orthodox to satisfy the British authorities of his suitability for judicial office. Or, perhaps, we are not comparing like with like: the speculative thinker writing tracts about law might believe one thing, but the judge charged with applying the law might do something rather different. And, certainly, if we look at Jones's own judicial work there is not the slightest hint that he approached the task with different preconceptions from those of the other judges on the Bengal bench or from judges in England. Jones the jurist and Blackstone the professor might have disagreed profoundly, but Mr Justice Jones and Mr Justice Blackstone saw completely eye to eye. Whatever the explanation, and sheer inconsistency may be as likely an answer as any, there is no suggestion that Jones felt remotely uncomfortable with adopting a straightforwardly positivist stance so far as his *practice* as a lawyer was concerned.

It was rather different when he was *thinking* about law. Here Jones seems to have been pulled towards Rousseau and Montesquieu, stressing the relationship between a system of law and the people governed by it. This fitted with his firm political belief, expressed in the Dialogue between a Scholar and a Peasant, that legal rules should be made by the people themselves or their properly elected representatives, and not by a self-serving minority. His own definition of law, given as an alternative to Blackstone's positivism, mirrors this: not so much rules prescribed by a superior power, but 'the Will of the whole community'.[31] All this seems pure Rousseau, though - just as with his disapproval of Blackstone - Jones may have had a

---

[30] *Works*, vol.7, p.3.

[31] *Letters*, vol.1, p.334 (no. 187).

certain ambivalence towards him. 'I do not admire him so much as I did,' he wrote in 1772, 'for I have lately read some of his tracts, which are wonderfully absurd.'[32] We do not know which these tracts were – Jones is writing in the context of his essays on music, of which he approved whole-heartedly - but at the very least we can say that Jones was not a slavish follower of Rousseau's every word. Later on, especially after his move to India, his thinking moved much more in the direction of the version of the theory espoused by Montesquieu, towards a belief that law should reflect the culture, in the broadest possible sense, of the people falling under the law. 'Any system of judicature affecting the natives of Bengal and not having for its basis the old Mogul constitution,' he advised Edmund Burke, 'would be dangerous and impracticable.'[33] And, however good the Common law, it would have been unjust to impose this on the Indians: 'A system of liberty forced upon a people invincibly attached to opposite habits would in truth be a cruel tyranny.'[34] The theoretical base of this was finally made explicit in his edition of the Laws of Manu, the 'Institutes' of Indian law:

> It is a maxim in the science of legislation and government, that Laws are of no avail without manners, or, to explain the sentence more fully, that the best intended legislative provisions would have no beneficial effect even at first, and none at all in a short course of time, unless they were congenial to the disposition and habits, to the religious prejudices, and approved immemorial usages of the people, for whom they were enacted.[35]

Such an approach was easier to square with the position of the British administration in India than were his earlier more explicitly Rousseau-esque views. It was one thing to say that the laws imposed by the British legislature and applied by the British courts should reflect the immemorial usages of the Indian peoples, but it would have been quite another to have said that the Indians should be able to determine for themselves what their own laws should be.

All the same, there was a drawback to Jones's approach. If the law applied by the British judges was to be in conformity with Indian legal

---

[32] *Letters*, vol.1, p.114 (no. 62).
[33] *Letters*, vol.2, p.643n.
[34] *Ibid.*
[35] *Works*, vol.7, p.75.

traditions, the British judges would have to have some way of discovering what they were. One route was to rely on native experts, Hindu pandits and Islamic maulvis, but this was not ideal: sensitive adjudication demanded more than just applying paper rules identified ad hoc by experts such as these. The alternative was for the British judges themselves to become masters of the materials they were to apply. Jones had the linguistic skills to have some hope of getting on top of the texts himself, but he recognised that it would be unreasonable to suppose that every British judge would be able to do so. Hence he got down to making a translation of what he perceived to be the necessary sources himself, consciously aping the sources of Roman law: the laws of Manu became the Institutes of Hindu law; and his last work, completed and published posthumously was entitled a Digest of Hindu law, as if a compilation of the best bits selected from the classical Indian writers.

But even with this there was still a problem, this time one that Jones could not overcome. As Montesquieu perhaps recognised, cultural relativism not only affected laws but also lawyers, so that the individual studying legal institutions in different societies would tend to be struck by the superiority of those found in his own. Jones, unfortunately, was no exception to this. There was an obvious complacency in the way in which he believed in the perfection of the Common law: not merely the jury system, but also the English rules of evidence, the excellent logic of the rules of special pleading, and the practice of having two or more advocates arguing on the same side - for were it not for this how would young barristers get enough work?[36] He maintained this belief after his move to Bengal, repeatedly refracting Indian law through European eyes. However much he was concerned to establish what the relevant 'rules' of Hindu or Islamic law were, he never questioned the appropriateness of English procedures. However skilled he was as a linguist, in translating Indian legal terms he perhaps unconsciously adopted a thoroughly European conceptual vocabulary, too frequently mapping Indian words onto inappropriate English counterparts. And however much he immersed himself in Indian culture, he never rid himself of a pathological

[36] *Works*, vol.9, p.58.

suspicion of native pandits and maulvis, whom he thought to be untrustworthy, partial and open to corruption.[37]

At heart, we may suspect that for all this adoption of Montesquieu's ideas Jones was at heart a believer in the third principal theory of the eighteenth century, natural law. Natural law may well have been especially congenial to Jones in so far as it provided a legal parallel for his linguistic and philological thought. Just as languages - Latin, Greek, Sanskrit - were related in terms of their fundamental principles, so legal institutions could be seen to be similar in their basic ideas. This is all stated more or less explicitly in his early work on intestate succession in Ancient Greece, his edition of the speeches of Isaeus.[38] The perspicuous student, he writes in the preface, cannot fail to be struck by the striking uniformity among all nations in the fundamental principles of the subject. 'Being clearly deduced from natural reason' they are 'equally diffused over all mankind, and are not subject to alteration by any change of place or time.'[39] Differences there are too; but these are the result of progressive legislative tinkering through the ages. The role of natural law may be marginally less explicit in his treatise on bailment,[40] but it is absolutely fundamental both to the structure of the book and to the particular rules which he deduces. His whole aim, avowedly, is to synthesise rational general principles out of the positive laws of different states. Most important of these, for him, were English law, which on this subject was in a terrible mess, and Roman law. Interpreting the English texts with a degree of imagination that is not always absolutely convincing, he demonstrates that its rules harmonised exactly with Roman law. Bolstering this up with citations to Greek law, Jewish law, the law of Turkey, the mediaeval Welsh law-books, classical Indian law, the contemporary laws of Germany, Spain, France, Italy and Holland, the barbarian laws of the Visigoths and Bavarians, and capitularies of the Emperor Charlemagne, he was able to synthesise the general principles which he said underlay the laws of all nations. It is at this point, and at this point alone, that his natural-law

---

37 Ibbetson, 'Sir William Jones as a Comparative Lawyer', in A. Murray, ed., *Sir William Jones, 1746-1794* (Oxford, 1998), pp.19-42.

38 *Works*, vol.9, pp.1-362.

39 *Works*, vol.9, p.12.

40 *Works*, vol.8, pp.325-456.

credentials come up to the surface, when he quotes the first and greatest of all of the Natural lawyers, Hugo Grotius: 'All of these agree with the Roman laws, though they are not derived from them but from the principles of natural equity'[41].

The Treatise on Bailments undoubtedly constituted Jones's most important direct contribution to English law. Despite its heavy Romanisation, its derivation of rules from what we might regard as something of a mish-mash of different legal systems, and its foundation in a Natural law theory which even at the time at which Jones was writing was falling out of fashion and coming to be regarded as intellectually unsound, his version of the law of bailment, and particularly of the duty of the bailee, was enthusiastically taken up by lawyers and adopted as English law almost without demur. Chief Justice Parker, of the Massachussetts Supreme Court, summed up the common perception of Jones's work half a century later:

> ... a profound and brilliant treatise ... in which, with a wonderful mixture of learned research and classical illustration, he has analyzed the complicated contract of bailment; and applied the principles of moral philosophy, the doctrines of the civil law, and the usages of all nations, ancient and modern, to the different branches of this diversified subject, so as to leave little room for speculation, except as to the application of his rules to particular cases, as they arise.[42]

Joseph Story was a shade more critical, arguing that his judgement had been clouded and his reasoning obscured by his refraction of the Common law through Roman law categories.[43] But Jones's style was very readable, his learning obvious and seductively persuasive, his analysis and conclusions highly plausible, and his arguments sufficiently well grounded in English case-law that only a scholar as capable and committed as Story would make the effort to burrow beneath them. It is, perhaps, only in the fairly recent past that Jones's analysis of the specific duties of different kinds of bailee has come to be superseded in England by a general test of reasonable care in all

---

[41] *Works*, vol.8, p.445 (quoting Grotius, *De Iure Belli ac Pacis*, 2.12.13).
[42] *Foster* v. *Essex Bank* (1821) 17 Mass. 479, 499
[43] J. Story, *Commentaries on the Law of Bailments* (London, 1839), p.xxiii.
[44] J. Oldham, 'The Survival of Sir William Jones in American Jurisprudence', in G. Cannon and J. Brine, eds., *Objects of Enquiry* (New York, 1995), pp.92-101.

the circumstances; and in the United States his work continues to be cited for a variety of different purposes.[44] Moreover, by a slightly curious route, Jones's formulation of the basic liability of the bailee in terms of the breach of a duty to take the care that would have been taken by a reasonable man, was quickly integrated into English law as a general metwand for legal liability; so that by the middle of the nineteenth century it had been transmuted from a test specific to the law of bailment to the fundamental statement of the Common law tort of negligence.

The Treatise on Bailment exercised a profound influence on English law, even outside its narrow subject area. What if Jones had written other books of the same type, elucidating other branches of the law? He claimed at one stage to have in hand the production of a vast legal work;[45] though this, I fear, is another of those boasts that was some little distance from the truth. But he certainly envisaged writing a comprehensive series of monographs on the model of his treatise on bailment,[46] and if he had done so we can be quite certain that it would have reoriented English law into quite a different form from that which it actually took. At the very least, it would have reformulated other areas of Common law in a more romanised, more European, mould; it could well have broken down the artificial barrier between law and equity; it might even have brought the Common law to such a stage of abstract development that it could have been swept along by the nineteenth-century continental enthusiasm for codification.

Counterfactual history can be fun, but it does have to be taken with a pinch of salt. Jones did not write his series of monographs; the Common law did not, or at least did not obviously, turn its face towards Europe; and codification seems as far off as it ever was. Jones's potential influence on the whole structure of the law was never quite actualised.

But let me stick with the theme for a few moments, because what Jones did not do for law and legal history is perhaps just as important as what he did. Had he lived longer - and we have to remember that he was only forty seven when he died - he might have set in motion the science of comparative legal history to put alongside the science of comparative philology, whose foundations he laid towards the end of his life. All the building blocks were

---

[45] *Letters*, vol.1, p.243 (no. 144).

[46] *Works*, vol.8, pp.454-455.

in place. He had a familiarity with a whole range of legal systems, and a substantial expertise in several important ones: English law, Roman law, Hindu law, and Islamic law. His book on bailment had shown that he could get to the essence of legal institutions without losing sight of their details. There was an unresolved tension in his thinking about law, between his inclination towards natural law with its tendency to smooth over distinctions between systems and his recognition that different laws were appropriate to different societies; and already in his edition of Isaeus he was grasping at the basic idea that legal systems could start from an identical base and then diverge through progressive legislative changes. He did, it is true, need to move away from the dead-end idea that the starting point was something deducible by natural reason and that it was only or primarily legislation that brought about legal change; but it would not have been a big step to move from recognising that some languages were genetically related to each other while other languages belonged to different families to postulating that legal systems too were more closely or less closely related. Jones, no doubt, would not have got it all right, any more than he did with linguistics, where he excluded slavic languages from the Indo-European stock but included Chinese. But we may be sure that he would have begun to map out the territory for a discipline that still, over two hundred years later, has yet to get properly off the ground.

This brings me back once again, and for the final time, to the Welsh Legal History Society. It does not need me to tell the present audience of the long and distinguished history of Welsh law, and I have no doubt that the Society's publications will contribute richly to the study of that history, both in deepening our understanding of it and making it more accessible to lawyers and scholars in Wales and elsewhere. But may I also harbour the hope that its work, true to the example set by William Jones, will always keep in sight the comparative dimension: the distinctive character of Celtic legal thought, the nature of the links between Welsh law and what we might call Germanic systems in the early Middle Ages, the seepage of legal ideas from Wales into England, and, of course, the contributions of Welsh lawyers like Jones to the understanding of legal systems both far-flung and near at hand. For, as Jones himself points out in a passage I quoted earlier, it is through a sensitivity to this comparative dimension that the true qualities of one's own legal system are brought into sharp relief, through this that the scholar will feel 'the satisfaction of a patriot in observing the preference due in most instances to the laws of his own country above those of all other states.'

Jones the lawyer, Jones the historian, Jones the Cymrodor, Jones the editor and translator of texts, Jones the founder and supporter of learned societies. 'Oriental Jones' he may have become, but he would have been wholeheartedly behind the formation of a Welsh Legal History Society. He would have joined enthusiastically, though his annual subscription might not always have been paid on time; he would have been a passionate supporter, though he might not always have been able to attend its meetings; he would have promised to edit texts, though they might never have appeared. But we should remember too that there was another side to Jones, the Jones who enjoyed good food and good company, who despite his workaholic excesses gave the finest dinners in Calcutta. 'Leave year-books and parchments to grey-bearded sages',[47] he wrote in one of his poems. Let us leave the business side of forming the society, and go to celebrate its existence in the way that Jones would most have approved.

[47] 'Written for a Fete Champetre in Wales', in *The Poetical Works of Sir William Jones* (London, 1807), vol.1, p.284.

PUTTING ONESELF ON WHOSE COUNTRY? CARMARTHENSHIRE JURIES IN THE MID-NINETEENTH CENTURY

Richard W. Ireland

Prologue

IT is now many years since I had the dream I am about to recount, though I will never forget it. I was about to start teaching a course on medieval legal history at Aberystwyth at the time. It was an exciting period for me for I felt that at last, after a year of giving lectures on such topics as the law relating to cheques (my knowledge of which, like Bede's sparrow flying through the mead-hall[1], came from nowhere, flapped briefly and then returned into darkness forever) I was about to teach "my" subject. Then I had the dream. In it I emerged from the main lecture theatre having addressed the class on some weighty medieval issue. Outside on the steps stood the unmistakeable bearded figure of Dafydd Jenkins. He was shaking his head slowly from side to side. "Rubbish" he said, "Complete rubbish".

Dafydd Jenkins was a hard act to follow within the Aberystwyth Law Department, as my subconscious so graphically reminded me that night. I was, moreover, perhaps not the right person to try. Dafydd was, is, Welsh, a proud Cambridge graduate, eminent, elegant and imposing. I was, am, English, went to "the other place" and, well, none of the rest. I was frightened of him. Yet over the last quarter of a century the fear evaporated, to be replaced by rather different sentiments. The paper which follows is one which I associate particularly with Dafydd. I gave a first version of it to the Fourteenth British Legal History Conference held in Edinburgh in 1999. I well remember walking back with Dafydd from the city centre to the Hall of Residence in which we were both staying. It was not a short walk and the irony of the fact that I was troubled by a sore hip joint and was struggling to keep pace with a man considerably my senior was not lost on me. Thereafter, over a drink, I was comprehensively "out-anecdoted" in a most convivial evening. It is right too, I think, that the text should appear in a publication of

[1] Bede *Historia ecclesiastica gentis Anglorum* ii,13.

this Society. I travelled down with Dafydd for the Inaugural meeting in Cardiff. On our return, as the car flashed past Pont Abraham Services in the early hours of the morning my intellect seemed to have gone the way of my hip joint. Not so with Jenkins! "Let Helen hold Blackacre", I remember him beginning a critical exegesis on the law of obligations. He is still a hard act to follow, but while my respect for him remains the fear has given way to friendship and affection. It is with these sentiments that this paper is presented.

Introduction

I feel rather sorry for Talfourd J, though such sympathy for members of the nineteenth century judiciary is not a frequent response which I encounter in my researches into the administration of the criminal law. Thomas Noon Talfourd was a scholar and a member of a powerful literary circle[2]. The author of *Ion* and *The Athenian Captive* was a friend (and subsequent executor and editor) of Charles Lamb and knew Leigh Hunt, Wordsworth, Coleridge and, though he was rather more diffident about it, of the society painter and possible serial murderer Thomas Wainewright[3]. He was MP for Reading, which town he praised extravagantly in his poetry ("the cradle and the home of generous thought[4]") and made his legal reputation as the motor for change in the law of copyright which resulted in the Copyright Act 1842[5]. He died whilst charging the Grand Jury at Stafford in 1854. It was not, I suspect, the first time that a jury had taken his breath away.

---

[2] For Talfourd see E. Foss *A Bibliographical Dictionary of the Judges of England* (London,1870) pp.648-9, *Dictionary of National Biography* vol XIX (London,1909) pp.343-6, A.W.B. Simpson (ed.) *Bibliographical Dictionary of the Common Law* pp.500-1.

[3] For Talfourd and Wainewright see A.Motion *Wainewright the Poisoner* (London,2000) p.118.

[4] The author had a Welsh connection. The volume of his poetry which I used in the National Library of Wales bears an autograph inscription from Talfourd to "William Jones of Glandwr".

[5] See C.Seville *Literary Copyright Reform in Early Victorian England* (Cambridge,1999), which explores Talfourd's role.

In July 1851 Talfourd presided over his first[6] Assize in Carmarthenshire. He arrived in the county town at 6pm on a Saturday in "very unfavourable"[7] weather. He was met by the javelin men who had fortified themselves by partaking of a "handsome dessert and wine" at the Ivy Bush. Things did not start well however as the Commission did not arrive until the North Mail came in and Sir Thomas had to wait for two hours before events could officially begin. On the next day he will no doubt have been captivated by the preaching of the Assize sermon by Archdeacon Bevan at St Peter's church which took as its text "If thine eye offend thee, pluck it out". Talfourd opened the judicial business of the Assizes by congratulating both the Grand Juries (for Carmarthen, as we shall see was blessed with two) on an absence of crime in their jurisdictions. Criminal behaviour was, he said, often occasioned by a lack of education or by drink. I wonder if he had cause to remember the implied compliment to the learning and sobriety of the society of West Wales on his way home.

The criminal business of Assize was proceeding when Talfourd had his first surprise. During a recess one of the jurors, David Thomas the publican of the White Horse in St Clears, went home, having arranged for someone else to take his place. Talfourd was bemused "This is something novel. I am not aware that he has power to make any such arrangement"[8]. Thomas was fined £5 and the business continued. A number of cases had been decided before Samuel Jones was arraigned and, the trial having concluded, the jury was asked, under a procedure which had been introduced by statute in1827 [9] to prove an earlier conviction from Neath. "We know nothing about that at Neath" they say, provoking laughter in the courtroom. The judge explained the factual nature of the inquiry. "We know nothing of the Neath business" asserted the jury before finally agreeing that the earlier conviction was proven[10].

---

[6] *Carmarthen Journal* 13/June/1851.

[7] The details are taken from the *Carmarthen Journal* 25/July/1851.

[8] *Ibid.*

[9] 7&8 George IV, s11.

[10] *Carmarthen Journal* 25/July/1851. Although the press report and the laughter in court suggest this was a simple misunderstanding of the jury's role in that they were not being asked as to whether the earlier conviction was correct in fact the jury's position is entirely defensible. The Act requires that there be "Proof of the Identity of

Then Morgan Thomas, a drover, was tried for forgery. The prosecution opened its case and evidence had been begun to be given when Talfourd stopped the proceedings and asked if the jury understood English. Several members replied in the negative. Perhaps choosing to ignore the worrying implications which such an answer might have for the business already transacted the judge had an interpreter sworn and continued with the trial[11]. The case against the defendant was a very strong one and Talfourd's summing up was strongly in favour of conviction. The jury acquitted. The newspaper account reports an interesting exchange: "His Lordship: "Gentlemen is that really your verdict?". The Jury replied in the affirmative. The Judge: "Very well"[12].

Perhaps Talfourd was relieved when the County business was concluded, for another jury was empanelled to try the prisoners from the Borough. It was they who heard the evidence against John Davies, tried for obtaining by false

---

the Person of the Offender", though it does not specify how, or to whose satisfaction, that proof should be made. The jury, in "knowing nothing" of the Neath proceedings presumably knew nothing as to whether the person named in the certificate of previous conviction was the same man who stood before them. As we shall see personal knowledge might be a matter of some import to the jury at this time. As will become apparent newspaper reports have been used extensively within this paper as evidence of activity in court and for direct quotation of speech. Clearly however such sources are not beyond question as to their authenticity. Not only may newspapers work to a political and editorial agenda (The *Carmarthen Journal* and *The Welshman* were politically opposed) but also the mechanics of transcription argue against the creation of an exact *verbatim* record, as differences between different newspapers' accounts of the same proceedings demonstrate. Nonetheless I have no reason to suppose misrepresentation in the reporting of the factual results of the cases, whilst I suspect -but cannot of course prove- that the essence of transactions in the courtroom is likely to be sufficiently accurate to qualify as useful evidence. Though I have enjoyed making use of "direct" quotation from individuals in reports, I cannot claim to be sure that they represent precisely the words spoken.

[11] In the trial of William Perkyns for embezzlement on Assize at Cardigan in 1876 the judge, who had been moved to laughter by the antics of the jury, swore in an interpreter at the conclusion of a case after the jury had failed to reach a verdict and had his notes translated for the benefit of the jurors who did not understand English. Despite a summing up "strongly against the prisoner" the jury eventually returned a verdict of not guilty. See the *Cardigan and Tivy-Side Advertiser* 14/July/1876. I am grateful to the staff at Ceredigion Archives for this reference.

[12] *Carmarthen Journal* 25/July/1851.

pretences. He was convicted after a long retirement by the jury, who however recommended the prisoner for mercy. Again the newspaper report suggests that the judge was rather unprepared for this turn of events: "His Lordship: "On what grounds Gentlemen?" The foreman "Because, my Lord of the great intricacy of the case" (roars of laughter followed this announcement). His Lordship: "Gentlemen, let me ask you whether you all understand the nature of the case". The Jury: "Yes my Lord"[13].

Whether Talfourd discussed these matters on his return to the dinner tables of literary London is unknown. He had at least had the satisfaction before witnessing the events of the courtroom of being able to congratulate the Grand Juries on the absence of crime to be tried. Such sentiments had been expressed by other judges who had been on the Circuit. Indeed it was a commonplace in the nineteenth century, with Wales – Gwlad y menyg gwynion ("Land of White Gloves") – known by the token given to those who presided over its crimeless "maiden" Assizes[14]. In such a degree of order, as Baron Pigott, told the Court in Carmarthen in 1866, the Welsh were superior to their Eastern neighbours: "I wish the English counties could boast of the same minimum of crime as you have in Wales"[15]. Not all however were convinced that the Grand Jury was performing its duties with the utmost diligence. A discordant note in the chorus of praise apparently came from Brett LJ addressing the Grand Juries of Cardiganshire and Pembrokeshire in the 1880s: "Gentlemen," he said "I would willingly congratulate you on the non-existence of crime in your several counties IF it did not exist, but as I believe it does exist, though by some means it is not brought before me, my congratulations must assume a modified form"[16].

---

[13] *Ibid.*

[14] See D.Jones *Crime in Nineteenth Century Wales* (Cardiff,1992) ch.1. For an example of the practice see the presentation of gloves to Crompton J. there being no prisoners from Carmarthen Borough, *Camarthen Journal* 23/July/1852.

[15] *Carmarthen Journal* 20/July/1866.

[16] Quoted in Jones *Crime in Nineteenth Century Wales* p.3. Like Jones (see his footnote 9) I have some difficulties with the quotation, my own being that it, by his account, was addressed in the same terms to both Grand Juries. I do not doubt its substance however.

The aim of this paper is to investigate jury behaviour in an area of Wales in the mid-nineteenth century. The survey concentrates in particular upon the County of Carmarthenshire and its boroughs between around 1845 and 1875 and forms part of a continuing investigation of the treatment of crime and disorder within that area and period. The analysis offered here does however draw on evidence from outside the county and reference will be made in particular to events in neighbouring Cardiganshire. The validity of the conclusions which may be drawn from this analysis for other areas of Wales and beyond is a matter which awaits the historians of those other areas, but for my own part I suspect that at least some of the findings may have resonance in other counties. The picture presented here is of competing models of law enforcement in collision: an asocial legal model which looks to the establishment of guilt of an individual offence by an individual offender within the courtroom and a rather differently contextualized view of the legal system which finds expression in the contribution of lay participants in the legal process. It is, I think, improbable that such models should have come into conflict only in one county or even (though in the piece which follows I will address specific issues which undoubtedly give a specifically Welsh dimension to that conflict) entirely to Wales. Such speculation however is not my current concern[17].

I have stated that this paper is concerned with jury behaviour, but a problem immediately arises. Which jury are we to look at? I have already mentioned both Grand and Petty juries, and County and Borough juries, but even this oversimplifies[18]. I have looked at the behaviour of 8 different juries

---

[17] Note the perceptive comments of T.A. Green discussing the English jury in *Verdict According to Conscience* (Chicago,1985). Having ascribed the decline of "jury equity" to changes in policing and punishment regimes in the nineteenth century Green remarks: "Reform of the law of sanctions had an immediate impact on jury behaviour in many trials for felony. Parliament had largely removed the need for massive and daily jury-based intervention on behalf of criminal defendants…..Jury-based intervention did not end in the middle of the nineteenth century. It remains a pervasive and vital aspect of the (so-called) fact-finding process even in lesser felonies where life is not at stake. In that setting, however, it has not always been noticed" (p.363).

[18] The Grand Jury, an institution effectively abolished in 1933, was responsible for determining whether the indictment should proceed to trial before the Petty (or trial)

having different social compositions – from the Justices of the Peace, Members of Parliament and members of the leading gentry families of the County Grand Jury at Assize, their rather inferior landholding counterparts at the County Quarter Sessions, the manufacturers and newspaper proprietors of the Borough Grand Jury at Assize and the ironmongers and confectioners of the Borough Grand Jury at Quarter Sessions and the respective petty jurymen. These latter were comprised to an overwhelming degree of farmers within the County, though the identities of Borough petty jurors remain elusive[19]. Clearly then "the jury" was an institution which in its particular

---

Jury. For details of procedure see D.Bentley *English Criminal Justice in the Nineteenth Century* (London,1998).

[19] Jury qualification for County Quarter Sessions Grand juries and County trial juries was settled by the Juries Act 1825 (6 Geo.IV c.50) s.1 which lays down the property qualification for such bodies as, in brief, £10 a year in freehold land and/or rents or £20 worth of property under a long lease. For Wales the qualification was three fifths of this amount. This differential was removed, and qualifications further amended in an Act of 1870 (33&34 Vict. c.77, s.7). Assize Grand Jurors are not mentioned in the 1825 Act specifically, their elevated composition being apparently a matter of settled custom at this time. Qualification for Borough Grand and Petty juries at Quarter Sessions are fixed by the Municipal Corporations Act 1835 (5&6 Will.IV c.76, s.121) and dependent simply on the status as burgess. Carmarthen Borough's rights under its Charter to jurisdiction over felony which was tried before Assizes (taking this role at the demise of Great Sessions in 1830) necessitated an Assize Grand Jury, but the 1835 Act does not regulate this. To discover the types of individuals actually on the juries involves a little cross referencing. Grand Juries (Assize and Quarter Sessions, County and Borough) are listed in *The Carmarthen Journal* in its reports of sittings and the names can be checked against Census data. Petty jury lists do not appear. For Quarter Sessions (but not Assizes) the list of those summoned appear (though not invariably) in bundles of Quarter Sessions papers. Rarely the clerk has ticked those who actually serve. The preponderance of farmers on trial juries which is anecdotally mentioned in newspaper references (and which I take to be applicable to Assizes also) is confirmed in this source. For example, for the Easter Quarter Sessions 1841 all 35 names on the list were farmers (Carmarthen Record Office-hereafter CRO -QS Box 2), in July 1846 52 out of a total of 60 are so described (CRO QS Box 6) Not much changed after the 1870 Act, in January 1871 32 out of 36 on the list are farmers, in October 1871 35 out of 36 (both CRO QS Box 14). The most elusive individuals are the Borough trial jurors, I have found no names for these at Assize or Quarter Sessions. It is possible that they represented a greater social mix because of the relatively small number of persons entitled to sit. The report which preceded the 1835 Act and which revealed significant political manipulation of the Carmarthen jury

manifestations was comprised of a range of property holders, its composition more clearly marked by those it excluded than those it included. It might be thought dangerous to ascribe any element of shared community mentality to such a diversity of persons. Indeed I will in the ensuing discussion distinguish at times between the sentiments which might inform the different juries. Yet I will also propose that there are important links, cemented by experience, between factors which influenced the operation of the different juries as well as important differences.

The Petty Jury and the "Perverse" Verdict.

Throughout the nineteenth century Welsh trial juries had a reputation for the perversity of their verdicts. Anecdotal evidence as to this general reputation is seen in a number of sources, whether dating from the early or later decades. So, for example, evidence brought before the Select Committee on the Administration of Justice in Wales 1817-21 spoke of jurymen determining their verdicts before hearing the evidence, whilst the 1829 Commissioners on the Superior Courts of Common Law saw the partiality of jurors as a major deficiency in the operation of the moribund Court of Great Sessions[20]. Half a century later the same sentiments are still current. In 1877 an article in the *Cornhill Magazine* makes the first reference I have come across to the story of the eminent Welsh judge remarking as his hounds overtook a hare "By G-d, A Cardiganshire jury can't save her now!"[21] The author of the piece remarks that "A man who is tried [in Wales] by a jury of his neighbours has always a splendid chance of escape, but if some of them

---

stated that "one or two of the labouring class" were known to have served. (*First Report of the Commissioners to Inquire into Municipal Corporations in England and Wales*, 1835, *Parliamentary Papers*, vol.xxiii, p.213). Information after 1835 has, if it survives anywhere, eluded me. I am confident however that separate trial juries for the Borough continued to sit during the whole period covered by this paper.

[20] See G.Parry *A Guide to the Records of the Great Sessions in Wales* (Aberystwyth,1995) pp.xxix-xxxii.

[21] "F.P.C." "The Celt of Wales and the Celt of Ireland" (1877) *Cornhill Magazine* p.674. Whilst preparing this article to be sent off I came upon a splendid anecdote related by Lord Hooson and quoted in the obituary of Roderic Bowen Q.C. (*The*

happen to be also his fellow chapel-goers of the same denomination, his acquittal may, it is feared, be predicted with approximate certainty"[22]. It may be remarked in passing that this anecdote appears in an article entitled *The Celt of Wales and the Celt of Ireland*, for on other occasions when Welshmen do the "right" thing in respect of law and order they are classed by their contemporaries with the English, when the "wrong" they may find themselves grouped with the Irish[23]. Comments from observers as to the Welsh juries' lack of impartiality could be multiplied, but whilst they speak of a powerful impression, important in itself, they are no proof that Welsh juries are more likely to act contrary to evidence than any other. Ideally the researcher would be able to prove the point statistically.

I cannot do this. I have subjected Carmarthenshire's acquittal rates in respect of felony prosecutions to computer analysis and will refer to the results later, but even if I had a suitable control sample against which to judge the findings the difficulty, at this distance of time and without the benefit of listening to the evidence, of identifying "perverse" verdicts would

---

Independent 24/July/2001). On the first visit of Lord Parker L.C.J. to Wales Bowen is said to have remarked: "You are about to meet a Welsh jury for the first time. Beware. Welsh juries are against sin-but not dogmatically so".

[22] *Ibid.*

[23] See the expressed intention of the Home Secretary, James Graham, during the Rebecca disturbances that Wales should not become "a second Ireland", quoted in D.Jones "Rebecca,Crime and Policing: A Turning-Point in Nineteenth Century Attitudes" (1990) *Trafodion Anrhydeddus Gymdeithas y Cymmrodorion* p.105. Lewis Morris (infra note 36) subsequently claimed that if not for governmental concessions after Rebecca Camarthenshire and Cardiganshire would have been left "at the level of Tipperary and Westmeath". See also the comments of the *Carmarthen Journal*, following the lack of an arrest for the murder of Ruth Jones: "It is said of the *Irish* peasantry that their assistance is much more easily procured *against* the law than for it; and Mrs S.C.Hall in her "Stories of the Irish Peasantry", states, that in Ireland, "hundreds of sober honest (?) men will absolutely *know* where a villain is concealed, and yet suffer him to escape and commit more crimes, because their prejudices will not suffer them to *inform*." It is apprehended that our humbler countrymen are not quite free of similar "prejudices"; and the publication of a Welsh translation, or adaptation, of Mrs Hall's short tale of "Do you think I'd inform" would be a work of great benefit to the Welsh peasantry" *Carmarthen Journal* 12/September/1851(italics original).

make me very wary of statistical analysis. Whilst the electronic manipulation of archival evidence has done much to enable us make sense of quantities of that evidence, it is of limited value in the determination of its quality and the human processes which it records. Anyone who would pretend otherwise would deserve to be considered as the legal-historical equivalent of a snake oil salesman!

Yet having worked with the records for some years I have no doubt that there is substance in the unease of contemporaries in relation to the capacity of Carmarthenshire's juries to surprise those who had heard the trials upon which they sat. It is not only in the cases that went before Talfourd J. that press reports of criminal trials record the surprise of the judge or indeed of the whole court. Insofar as we are able to attempt to reconstruct the state of the evidence (and we must be very cautious indeed if we attempt to do so) against the accused, we are perhaps able to comprehend an element of astonishment. Esther Anthony, tried for larceny before Quarter Sessions in 1851, had the evidence of two witnesses against her. Her alibi having been disproved she put in no other defence. "After a brief summing up by the learned Chairman," the *Carmarthen Journal* relates, "the jury to the astonishment of the whole court, returned a verdict of *Not Guilty*. Another specimen of the intelligence of a Welsh Jury!"[24]. In 1853 two policemen and a railway inspector testified that Elizabeth Henfield, a 13 year old, took coal from the railway. The prosecutors obviously knew that it would be difficult to obtain a conviction, the youth of the offender and the impersonality of the company which was the victim making such a difficulty predictable, and the court was reassured in advance that only a token sentence was sought. Henfield was acquitted. The Chairman of the Sessions offered the defendant some advice which seems to indicate that the physical requirement of the offence, at any rate, had been satisfied. "I hope", he admonished, "that this will be a warning to you and that in future you will not attempt to take anything that does not belong to you, whether in sport or earnest"[25].

---

[24] *Carmarthen Journal* 7/March/1851.

[25] *Carmarthen Journal* 1/July/1853. It is of course possible that the defendant was found by the jury to have lacked the necessary *mens rea*, the reference to "sport" perhaps suggesting this. It is also possible, as the prosecutors seem to have feared, that they did not dwell too long upon such legal subtleties. For a similar attempt to

Sometimes it is the lack of surprise at acquittal which is the telling detail. Thomas Davies, the farmer tried in 1866 for an unnatural offence with a heifer (he is unforgettably listed in the Felons' Register, which carries a photograph of his lugubrious countenance, in the box reserved for the description of his complexion. Amongst the many descriptions of individuals as "pallid" or "fair" Davies's "cadaverous" adds a rare Gothic touch[26].). Davies would not be convicted of this offence. As we will see, none of those charged with it before a jury ever were in the evidence assembled for this paper. *The Welshman* newspaper knew as much, observing with a knowing smile that "perhaps the strongest evidence in favour of the prisoner was given by his sister who stated that on the day in question (a Sunday) she saw her brother read the Pilgrim's Progress. What jury could withstand such evidence?"[27].

While the vast majority of "perverse" verdicts are acquittals this is not universally so. The choice of the jury to reach its verdict independently of the evidence could operate against the prisoner on occasion. In 1853 John Harries, a quack doctor, was found guilty of theft despite the Chairman of the Quarter Sessions issuing the instruction that there was "insufficient evidence to convict". Rather apologetically, I think, he sentenced the luckless Harries to one day's imprisonment.[28]

Perversity, Independence and Exclusion

Why were Welsh juries, even to an age not entirely unaccustomed to the practice of "jury equity" regarded as so notably unreliable? One solution which found favour at the time was quite straightforward: ignorance. We have seen that the county petty jurors were farmers, those of the Borough probably even less genteel. If this were not bad enough for a society for

---

cast acquittal as an admonition see the trial of William and Mary Ann Fagan for theft before Crompton J. on Assize: "His Lordship in discharging the prisoners said they had met with a merciful jury, and he hoped they would take the warning given them." (*Carmarthen Journal* 23/July/1852).

[26] CRO *Felons' Register* (Acc.4916-hereafter F.R.) no.1133.

[27] *Welshman* 9/March/1866

[28] *Carmarthen Journal* 1/July/1853.

whom the tilling of the field was an antiquated if necessary means of earning a living, its ancient practices ripe for improvement by science and by estate-owners but still less exciting than manufacture, then the fact that the property qualification for Welsh farmers was less than for their English equivalents was bound to arouse suspicion. It was, of course, difficult to believe that a poor man might be clever. The differential property qualification was abolished in 1870 and it is possible that discontent with Welsh verdicts lay behind the change. This is however difficult to establish as the Bill was barely debated in its passage, though the "little dissatisfaction" which judges had voiced on the matter was put directly to one of the two Welsh witnesses to the Select Committee to which the Bill was referred. William John, the Town Clerk of Haverfordwest, in reply, said that he thought the difference in qualification was not material to the issue. I am inclined to agree with him[29]. We have seen that the ensuing Act did not alter the balance of professions of County jurymen, nor did it render the "reliability" of their verdicts immediately unimpeachable.

It was true that Counsel knew that farmers were very knowledgeable about certain matters, as the provision of details in the courtroom which might require some agricultural knowledge indicates[30]. But they could also apparently be prejudiced. In the case of William Jones in July 1871 his Counsel argued of the defendant, accused of theft, that "if the prisoner had not borne the character of an honest man he would not have been able to get a farm" The jury were called upon to deliver an "honest verdict". *The Welshman* newspaper laconically reported the subsequent acquittal under the headline "A Dishonest Verdict"[31]. Such behaviour could be lampooned by those who had, or aspired to, the intellectual prowess which these men so clearly lacked. A press report of 1851 mocks the jury foreman for not

---

[29] See the *Select Committee on The Juries Bill* (1870,vi, Parliamentary Papers) p.103ff.

[30] See the trial of David and Ann Davies for theft of wool *Carmarthen Journal* 1/July/1853. The jury's knowledge of the "semi-civilized" people of Llangeler was also invoked in this case.

[31] *Welshman* 7/July/1871. But compare the trial of Margaret Evans accused of stealing milk where the defendant's counsel unsuccessfully tried to refute the evidence having presciently observed that "the Jury as farmers would no doubt wish to protect the interests of farmers" *Carmarthen Journal* 24/October/1851.

understanding how one transported previously could still be in the country (a question which may have baffled some learned researchers of our own day) and describes him, in terms which indicate that his only relation to advanced knowledge could be as its object not its subject, as having "a countenance which might have been a beautiful study for Lavater"[32]. However, these men, though they may not have been learned, were not necessarily stupid. We are not obliged to, and I certainly do not, accept their verdicts as evidence of rustic imbecility.

They did on occasion display one specific educational failing – they might not, as we have seen, speak English, the language of the courtroom. The 1851 case with which we started is by no means unusual, indeed the *Carmarthen Journal* had drawn attention to the problem more generally earlier in that year[33]. In evidence to the Commissioners on the State of Education in Wales in 1847 the magistrates clerk at Lampeter had revealed that even a Grand Jury at Cardigan had needed him to translate into Welsh for them[34]. Amongst petty jurors the lack of comprehension of English was a much more common event. It is no wonder that evidence might be misunderstood or minds made up in advance of hearing that evidence when it was given in a foreign language. It is true that translators would be provided by the court where a need was seen to arise, though I believe that their task was generally -though apparently not exclusively, as our first case shows—conceived of primarily as being to translate evidence from Welsh to English, not *vice versa*. That case also shows that they were not always requested, a circumstance probably indicative of a reluctance, evident from

---

[32] *Carmarthen Journal* 10/January/1851. The newspaper might have been a little more circumspect in its endorsement of physiognomy. On August 13th 1847 it had reported that Mr Jefferson of Montreal had delivered an "admirable" lecture on the subject in Laugharne. The issue of September 3rd carries the story of the lecturer fleeing without paying his bills!

[33] "Some of the jury…who are placed in the box frequently are unable to understand a word of English. It is true both the prisoners and the jury have the advantage of an interpreter, but as the trials are conducted in the English language, the whole of the jury ought to be familiar with that language", *Carmarthen Journal* 11/July/1851.

[34] See the comments of Mr Williams in the *Report of the Commissioners on the State of Education in Wales* (1847, *Parliamentary Papers* vol. xxvii Part II) p.61. He relates further that a juryman had once asked him "what was the nature of an action in which he had given his verdict", *ibid.*

other sources, to own up to not speaking English[35]. Yet ignorance of that tongue within Carmarthenshire at this time is unsurprising.. At mid century the county's jury roll contained approximately 2,500 persons. According to the best figures we have, derived from Ravenstein's survey of 1871, some 94% of Carmarthenshire's population was Welsh speaking of whom approximately one third spoke only Welsh. English was not the principal language of the locality[36]. Nor was any linguistic discrimination of the kind revealed to the Select Committee in 1870 as routine in Pembrokeshire, where jurors were not summoned from the Welsh speaking part of the County unless they were known to speak English, possible within a County which knew no such geographical division.[37]

In 1871 a remarkable letter from Lewis Morris of Rolls Chambers[38] appeared in *The Times* and was reprinted for domestic consumption in *The Welshman*. "Of any twelve common jurors in Mid Wales", asserted the author, "from one half to three quarters are absolutely ignorant, for speaking purposes, of more English than the monosyllables Yes And No. They, or some of them, can understand a little, but a very little, more of the colloquialisms in everyday use, such as relate to the price of food or other necessary matters. The foreman, probably, has as much knowledge as will enable him, if you speak very slowly and with a strong Welsh accent, and use none but the commonest words, to follow a very brief and very clear explanation of the facts". Having gone on to describe the employment of "indifferent" translators in trials, Morris concludes: "And at the end of it all the poor puzzled peasants put their heads together and come to a thoroughly independent decision, which very likely goes the round of the papers as an "Extraordinary Verdict of a Welsh Jury".[39] Interestingly, in the light of what

---

[35] See D.Parry-Jones *Welsh Country Upbinging* (London, 2nd ed. 1949) p.103.

[36] See D.Jones *Statistical Evidence relating to the Welsh Language 1801-1911* (Cardiff,1998) pp.212, 223.

[37] See the evidence of William John, Town Clerk of Haverfordwest to the *Select Committee on the Juries Bill* (1870 *Parliamentary Papers*,vi) pp.103ff.

[38] I suspect that this was Lewis Morris the author. It is, I think, improbable that it was his father of the same name, who was the rather more distinguished lawyer. Both were practitioners at this point, the father was on the bench. Both were from Carmarthen.

[39] *Welshman* 24/November/1871

will be stated shortly about the role of the Grand Jury, Morris was of the opinion that this state of affairs presented no great problem for Assize cases since they were so few in number in Wales, but related his observations as to possible remedy only to the ongoing debate about the County Court.[40]

Sometimes in a court where jury, witnesses and defendant all spoke Welsh it was the legal personnel who were very much the outsiders. As Mark Ellis Jones suggests in relation to earlier Great Sessions cases of this character: "In a sense….the interpreter was sworn in mainly for the benefit of the judge and counsel".[41] Sometimes too it seems that defendants would know this. In 1866 Evan Jones, charged with bigamy addressed the jury directly in Welsh assuring them that the charge had been contrived against him by his brother. Bigamy being a crime which was, as the judiciary were well aware, susceptible of easy documentary proof, a fact which served to outflank the jury's tendency towards independent decision making. Jones, like almost all the other persons prosecuted for this offence in the sample studied, was convicted.[42]

---

[40] Sometimes the results of the linguistic complication are particularly interesting. Bridget Dowd, an Irishwoman tried by Quarter Sessions in 1853 for theft could speak only Irish and many of the jurors could speak no English. Two translators are used to remedy the mutual incomprehensions and the trial concluded in three languages. I cannot resist mentioning here the proceedings against Julia Gautiere in respect of the theft of shoes in 1851. Taken for a Frenchwoman she is offered the ancient privilege of a jury *de medietate linguae*, an institution preserved by s.47 of the 1825 Juries Act (see Bentley *English Criminal Justice* p.90). In her next appearance in a newspaper report she is described as representing herself as Swiss. She was, in fact, Irish. The prosecutrix having failed to appear she never stood trial in any language, *Carmarthen Journal* 4/July/1851, 5/September/1851, 10/October/1851.

[41] See M.Ellis Jones ""The Confusion of Babel"? The Welsh Language, Law Courts and Legislation in the Nineteenth Century" in G.Jenkins (ed) *The Welsh Language and its Social Domains 1801-1911* (Cardiff,2000) p.589.Note also the case discussed by T.G.Davies , *Who can Expect Health?* (Neath,n.d.) p.100 where the evidence of an English speaking doctor was preferred to that of a Welsh speaking one who had examined a monoglot defendant in a case of fitness to plead.

[42] F.R. no.1140, see *Carmarthen Journal* 20/July/1866. Compare F.R. nos. 144, 480, 776, 783, 892 (acquiited),1176, 1316.

Not surprisingly opinion as to the appropriate remedy for this mutual incomprehension was divided. The Education Commissioners in 1847 predictably stated that it lay though Welsh learning English. The Welsh language periodical *Seren Gomer*, which has been active in the campaign for linguistic pluralism in the arguments surrounding the County Courts Act of 1846, disagreed strongly, expressing outrage at the report of the dismissal of monoglot Cardiganshire Assize jurors in 1847 and carrying an impassioned cry for Welsh speaking judges.[43]

Whilst I have so far concentrated particularly upon the issue of language, the distinction between the law and the jurors is, I think, not simply linguistic but more broadly cultural. It was, apparently, in English that the defendant John Hughes, a solicitor's clerk, made his direct appeal to the jury in a case of embezzlement before the Borough Quarter Sessions in October 1865, reminding them that he was "a native of the town and of respectable parents", who were known to the jury members. He was acquitted, but probably remained in court long enough to catch the laconic observation of the Deputy Recorder: "Well gentlemen, that is your verdict and not mine".[44] Issues of community, of locality may also have been in operation.

The Assize in particular might be seen as rather more than a trial of individuals but also a moral audit of the countryside. The Welsh still felt the outrage which the observations on morality introduced into the Report by the Education Commissioners in 1847 had produced. Ieuan Gwynedd Jones has examined the role of *Brad y Llyfrau Gleision*, the "Treachery of the Blue Books", in the development of Welsh political consciousness in the nineteenth century.[45] I think that the reaction may have extended also into an attitude toward the law, particularly perhaps law as exemplified by Assize judges perceived as outsiders by virtue of residence, language and religion.

---

[43] See *Seren Gomer* 1847, p.126. For the County Courts argument see for example the petition reproduced in *Seren Gomer* for 1845, p.61. The debate is considered in Ellis-Jones,"Confusion of Babel"p.593 et seq.

[44] *Carmarthen Journal* 20/October/1865.

[45] I.G.Jones *Mid-Victorian Wales* (Cardiff,1992) Ch. 5. "The politicization of the people of Wales grew out of, and was nurtured by, the cultural gap between, on the one hand, what the Blue Books reported and, on the other, the reality as perceived by the communities themselves" (p.104)

In short I propose that it is possible to see a connection between the blue books and the white gloves.

I have noted in an earlier paper how difficult it was to secure convictions within Carmarthenshire within the period here discussed not only for infanticide but also in respect of other offences related to childbirth, even those where the legal penalty was not so grave as it was for child destruction.[46] I would tentatively suggest, though the point is not without difficulty,[47] that this pattern extended beyond those offences to a wider set of those which we might broadly describe as those connected with "morality" in a sexual or domestic sense – bestiality (to which reference was made earlier),[48] rape and indecent assault,[49] and, to an extent, intrafamilial violence.[50] Such offences, as *Seren Gomer* admitted in relation to

---

[46] R.W.Ireland " "Perhaps My Mother Murdered Me": Child Death and the Law in Victorian Carmarthenshire" in C.Brooks and M.Lobban (eds) *Communities and Courts in Britain 1150-1900* (London,1997) p.229 *et seq.*

[47] It would be possible to go into further details of the cases discussed below, in particular to analyze the characteristics of particular defendants, but I have not done so for the purposes of this paper.

[48] See F.R. nos.333 (no bill), 378 (discharged without trial), 1130 (no bill), 1133 (discharged without trial), 1357 (acquitted). But note that before 1861 this was a capital offence and thereafter subject to a minimum of 10 years' imprisonment (24&25 Vict c.100 s61). The cases could, I concede, represent instances of traditional "jury equity". The last three postdate the Act. Evidential issues may also have proved difficult in such cases.

[49] I have taken these offences together since the indictments tend to be rather elastic (see *infra*, note 60). See F.R. nos. 120 (rape-no bill), 173 (carnal knowledge of a child-discharged without trial), 335 (assault with intent to rape-convicted of common assault), 342 (rape-no bill), 444 (assault with intent to rape-no bill), 733 (assault with intent to rape-convicted), 744 (assault and rape-discharged without trial), 796 (attempted rape-convicted of indecent assault), 803 (assault with intent to rape-acquitted), 938 (assault with intent to rape-acquitted), 974 (assaulting child with intent to rape-acquitted), 986 (assault and rape-discharged before trial), 1094 (indecent assault on a child-acquitted),1209 (three defendants, "violent and indecent assault"-all acquitted). Note the problems of evidence, in particular where child victims were involved. And see, for example the comments on the cases tried at petty sessions of Henry Morris (*Carmarthen Journal* 29/August/1851) and John Roberts (*Carmarthen Journal* 23/December/1853).

[50] Most domestic violence was tried, if at all, summarily. What I have in mind are cases such as F.R. nos.258 (attempting to strangle wife-discharged without trial), 527

infanticide, could be seen as bringing shame not simply upon the individual but upon the parish as a whole and, though the journal did not itself pursue the point, by extension upon Wales itself. The glee with which the same periodical seizes upon instances of shocking crimes in England, such as an instance of incest in Hull, indicates that the criticisms of the Education Commissioners still smarted amongst those who wrote, and probably those who read, such material. I am far from suggesting that every jury acquittal can be construed as an act of political nationalism. Rather I believe that older, less legalistic conceptions of order (which included a sense that dirty washing, even very dirty washing, need not necessarily be aired in public) of a kind once to be found more generally in England too persisted in areas insulated, albeit of course not wholly so, by topography and language from the inexorable encroachment of Victorian uniformity and legal individualism. Yet by the same token I am persuaded that the sense of grievance and of a sense that Welsh people had not only been misrepresented but misunderstood by English officialdom was hardly conducive to a rapid and total surrender of traditional practice to the representatives of the Common (*sic*) Law.

Grand Juries: Class and Community

Yet in the areas of "morals offences" there may have been a reluctance not only among petty jurors to convict but also among Grand Juries to sanction prosecution in the first place, by returning as "True Bills" the allegations laid before them. Surely it cannot be argued that the prejudices of the farmers who might distrust the intrusions of the legal system were shared by elements within the local gentry who were (for Justices of the Peace featured prominently on County Grand Jury lists[51]) its agents? The particular social condition of petty jurymen has certainly been considered in some studies of

---

(murder of wife-convicted of manslaughter, apparently to the consternation of the judge, who remarked; "a nicer shade of distinction between this case and murder is scarcely possible", *Welshman* 16/March/1855), 785 (manslaughter of wife-acquitted), 964 (assaulting wife-tried by petty sessions, insane), 1166 (attempting to poison husband-acquitted).

[51] They acted, it need hardly be said, in a judicial capacity at both petty and-significantly in the context of this discussion-Quarter Sessions.

jury activity which consider the role of wealth and class in jury composition.[52] Yet there are, I suggest, instances of actions by Grand Juries every bit as wilfully "perverse" as those of their socially inferior countrymen.[53] In the Borough Quarter Sessions for January 1851 Mary Thomas, who "could not speak the English Language very fluently" was before the court on a count of larceny of a coat. The Recorder pointed out as the indictment was proposed that the defendant had given a false account of how she came by the coat and having reminded the Grand Jury that they were not trying the case (for their task was only to judge whether there was sufficient evidence for the trial to proceed) he pointed out that there was "not the slightest difficulty in the case". The Jury returned "No Bill".[54] They did so too in the case of Ellen Donoghue in 1869 on a count of concealment of birth. The body of a child, wrapped in a carpet, was found buried in the field next to her house on the day that Donoghue left the locality. Medical examination revealed, and the defendant did not deny, that she had just given birth. The Grand Jury's inscrutable pronouncement ensured that the case would never be heard.[55] Why such a reluctance to prosecute? It is perhaps significant that it was the Grand Jury who received the praise for the conduct of the population they oversaw when the legal audit of morality was played out at Assize (at least when Brett LJ was not the auditor).[56] But again I think that narrow self-interest was unlikely to be the only motive for an at times

[52] So, despite their concentration upon evidence from England at an earlier period than that discussed here, the reader is referred to P.J.R. King "Illiterate Plebeians, Easily Misled: Jury Composition, Experience and Behavior in Essex 1735-1815 (p.254) and D.Hay "The Class Composition of the Palladium of Liberty; Trial Jurors in the Eighteenth Century" (p.305), both in J.S.Cockburn and T.A.Green (eds.) *Twelve Good Men and True: The Criminal Trial Jury in England 1200-1800* (Princeton,1988).

[53] There is local evidence of poor attendance of Grand Jurymen, even at Assize. See for example the comments of Blackburn J. in 1865 (Carmarthen Journal 17/March/1865).

[54] *Carmarthen Journal* 10/January/1851. Note the earlier comments about the relative social position of Borough as opposed to County Grand Jurymen.

[55] *Carmarthen Journal*, 4/June/1869. See Ireland "Perhaps My Mother" p.237.

[56] See for example the praise given to the County Grand Jury by Crompton J viewing the light Assize Calendar: "It showed that the efforts of the wise and good amongst them of late were really taking effect and bringing forth fruit", *Carmarthen Journal* 23/July/1852

exaggerated conception of the requirements of a *prima facie* case. A knowledge, based upon experience, of the futility of sanctioning a prosecution doomed to failure may certainly have played a role. Whilst it might be impossible to predict the outcome of every case, the Grand Jury who viewed Ellen Donoghue's appearance in court might be forgiven for assuming that no conviction would be forthcoming in a trial of that nature. If the legal historian at a distance of almost a century and a half can predict what the petty jury would decide, I am pretty sure that those who sat in the same courtroom could do so, and the temptation to put an early and covert end to proceedings rather than have the embarrassment of an acquittal after the evidence had been adduced in court may have been considerable. Judges too may have shared in the complicity. At the Spring Assizes in 1851 Vaughan Williams J, a native of Carmarthenshire who had learned his trade as recorder of Kidwelly, had suggested that the cases of rape and of bestiality which appeared in the calendar should not be brought to trial "unless necessary", in order to avoid the publicity "which promotes such crimes", although such a sentiment, at least in respect of the latter offence, appears not to have been restricted to proceedings in Wales.[57] Yet I think that these are not the only considerations which might inform the Grand Juries' decisions. Whilst wealth and status might distance the gentleman who perused the indictment from the farmer who determined guilt, experience beyond that gained within the courtroom might unite them.[58] Grand Juries were not

---

[57] *Carmarthen Journal* 21/March/1851. No Bill was found against either David Davies (bestiality) or David Thomas (rape). The suggestion that such a comment was general in respect of bestiality cases is derived from comments by Blackburn J. on Assize, *Carmarthen Journal* 9/March/1866. Note also the comment of Crompton J to the Grand Jury in a case of perjury in 1854 when counselling caution in the indictment unless there is a likelihood of conviction, "since a number of persons escaping conviction on such a charge has a most mischievous result upon the community" (*Carmarthen Journal* 24/March/1854). Whether or not the comments were specific to the locality I cannot say, but I am reminded of a comment by the Rev.D.Edwardes about perjury: "Small nationalities, small sects, the oppressed party are rarely conspicuous for truthfulness" *Reminiscences* (Shrewsbury,1914) p.14.

[58] Compare T.A.Green in *Twelve Good Men* at p.386 on the trial jury: "It will not do to define the jury solely in terms of the class ties of its members, or of their politics in the simple sense of their conscious identification with, or rejection of, authority. We need to know to know the constraints within which juries acted, even when they

isolated from their countrymen in small face-to-face communities. Serving on the Borough Quarter Sessions Grand Jury in January 1851 was Charles Hill, who lived in the same street, Lammas Street, as the notorious Mary Ann Thomas, a "nymph of the pave" second only in celebrity in Carmarthen to Ann Awbery, who herself lived just around the corner in Goose Street. Stephen Awbery (possibly a relative of Ann's), another member of this jury, could probably look out of his bedroom window in Spilman Street directly onto the crowded and turbulent lodging houses of Dan y Bank.[59] Moreover Grand Jurymen could expect to be approached directly by those who had an interest in a case, such behaviour apparently being common in cases of indecent assault (the rarity of prosecutions for which we have noted earlier, and an offence which allowed of an easy manipulation in the form of the indictment) even into the twentieth century.[60] The crowds that surrounded the courtroom through which the jury men travelled were also capable of conveying ideas that went beyond the rules of evidence.

---

were not cognizant of those constraints, and we need to know the psychology that jurors typically possessed when reaching determinations of life and death, even when they were unaware of those feelings". An appreciation of such complexities is, I maintain necessary, *mutandis mutatis*, in the analysis of the behaviour of both Grand and petty juries.

[59] Residence details are taken from the 1851 census, the Grand jury lists appear in *Carmarthen Journal* 10/January/1851. Much more could be written about Mary Ann Thomas and Ann Awbery. The latter was committed to gaol in 1851 for what the Mayor declared to be her fourteenth time. Mr Alderman Morris suggested it was closer to her hundred an fourteenth! (*Carmarthen Journal* 18/July/1851). Again the position of Assize Grand Jurymen is not exactly comparable, but similar considerations may, I feel, apply.

[60] In 1902 the *Carmarthen Weekly Reporter* stated that when "respectable" persons were charged with indecent assault "every man on the Grand Jury is seen before the trial comes on". An instructive case is that of Henry Davies, alias Jones in 1851. He was indicted for indecent assault although originally he had been charged with "a more serious offence" (presumably rape). The Grand Jury found a True Bill only for common assault, *Carmarthen Journal* 10/January/1851. It was not however only in cases of this nature that the Grand Jury might be briefed in advance. At the trial of Jeffrey Davies in 1861 who confessed to the theft of a watch his father's claim that the defendant was " not in his senses", "and this circumstance seemed to be well known to some of the Grand Jury", *Carmarthen Journal* 11/January/1861. For other such "medical" instances see my comments on the cases of Eugene Buckley and of Frances Anne Jones from 1846 in R.W.Ireland "Eugene Buckley and the Diagnosis of

Another factor may be of importance too. Juries knew that a failure to indict or an acquittal need not be the end of the matter. The extra-legal consequences of offending might be more potent than the activities in the courtroom with older notions of compromise and of stigma brought into play. In one 1870s sheep stealing case the jury acquitted the defendant but it was stated that "all the blotting paper in the kingdom would not wipe the stain from his character".[61] Counsel knew it too, the distinction between legal and social punishment being adverted to in an address to the jury in the case of seventy year old Owen Jones (previously acquitted in Pembrokeshire and Cardiganshire) in 1853: "They (the jury) could not remove the stigma that would *ever* attach to the grey-headed old prisoner for being suspected of such an offence, but they could throw open the prison doors to him and restore him to the bosom of his family" (my italics). He was, of course, acquitted.[62]

As was indicated earlier a statistical analysis of indictment and prosecution records, even though possible, must be approached with considerable caution. At first sight then it seems to run counter to the hypotheses about language and community expressed above to learn that a minority of those cases of felony in the period between 1844 and 1871 which resulted in acquittal, only around 46%, apparently involved defendants born within Carmarthenshire. A very similar proportion of those against whom Grand Juries failed to find a true bill (around 45%) were "natives" of the county. Quite apart from the technical pitfalls which inhere in this analysis,[63] the proportion of occasions upon which "outsiders" were remanded for felony to the gaol (the sample upon which the statistical survey is based) would seem surprisingly high, accounting for (excepting for a moment the technical problems in arriving at this figure) some 57% of remands for

---

Insanity in the Early Victorian Prison" (1993) *Llafur* p.15.

[61] I fear that I have been unable, in producing these footnotes, to find the source of this quotation in wading through the masses of material I used in preparing this paper. I promise that I didn't make it up!

[62] *Carmarthen Journal* 23/March/1853

[63] The figures are taken from computer analysis of the 1448 entries in the Register of Felons (for the details see R.W.Ireland and C.Breay "Hard Labour on a Hard Disk": Carmarthen's Register of Felons on Computer" (1993) xxix *The Carmarthenshire Antiquary* p. 61). There are a number of difficulties in the analysis. Firstly the cases represent instances of (generally but not invariably!) custodial remands, not individuals, *i.e.* the same person may appear more than once on different occasions.

felony. In a county the Census return for which in 1851 suggested that 88% of the recorded population were born within the boundaries, a proportion which had dropped only to 85% in 1881, the high representation of "strangers" is compatible with a number of explanations.[64] One of these which may have merit is that the remanded "native" population was already a class which had undergone a more rigorous selection procedure before the decision to remand, leaving a comparison of the jury dispositions of the two groups based on unmatched samples. In any event I stress that it is no part of my contention that local people were not prosecuted or convicted by Carmarthenshire juries, for indeed the corollary to the above indications that sometimes the verdict was more likely to be general to the offender rather than specific to the offence easily accommodates conviction as well as acquittal in particular cases. Rather I think that it is important to recognize that juries were dealing not with statistical aggregates, but with individual cases. In at least some of these, I have no doubt, factors of language and of locality of the kind discussed above, played a part in the construction of the jury's decision. Nothing that I have seen on my computer screen has led me seriously to doubt that.

Secondly I have not investigated within the overall totals the class of persons discharged off remand before trial. Thirdly not all entries include details of place of birth. Fourthly where these are given they often depend on the assertion of the prisoner, who may have good reason not to tell the truth. Finally the question of birth county is not necessarily determinative of community or linguistic cohesion-a drover from Cardiganshire might be a well known "local" figure. In preparing this paper I undertook an analysis of the last residence of the remands as well as their place of birth. In addition to the difficulties outlined above I realized that without any clear indication by those making the record of the qualification for "residence" the figures may beg many questions. It would seem that temporary residence in a lodging house might not qualify, as the details of F.R. no 780 Mary McDermott, recorded as of "no settled home" indicate (see the discussion of her case in R.W.Ireland "Confinement with Hard Labour: Motherhood and Penal Practice in a Victorian Gaol" (1997) 18 *Welsh History Review* p.631), but no clear indication as to positive qualification is apparent. For what the figures are worth they read as follows (all percentages are approximate): Total of remands whose last residence is given as Carmarthenshire-63%, percentage of those acquitted recorded as having last residence in Carmarthenshire-74%, percentage of those against whom "No Bill" was found recorded as having last residence in Carmarthenshire-71%

[64] D.Jones *Statistical Evidence* p.149.

Conclusion

Previous studies have, I suggest, tended to look at jury behaviour too narrowly. Often the acquittal against evidence is seen as being related entirely to the severity of anticipated punishment in a classic instance of "pious perjury". This is clearly important, but I think that the focus may narrow our perspective, one of the many evils of the prevalent fault of taking serious crime as the focus of criminal justice history. Traditional explanations of this kind struggle, I think, to explain the intriguing paradox of farm servants who felt sufficient shame to conceal their pregnancies from the farmers who employed them, only to be routinely acquitted at trial on indictments for concealment of birth by groups of similar farmers.[65] I think jury activity is better seen as part of a wider approach to law and dispute settlement prevalent in rural Wales exemplified by the recollections of D.Parry-Jones in respect of the shooting of a woman by her rejected lover:

> There was a trial, but the court never knew half of what the unsworn juries discussed in the fields. They could tell you how the murderer ran; at what time and at what farm he re-appeared to establish an alibi; who was with him; who met him in his flight to take his gun, and who made the bullet. They related enough, were it related in a proper place, to hang two or three men. But the trial was in an alien tongue and men became mute as they thought of it. Were it a trial in their own tongue where they could feel at home they would possibly have spoken up, for they had no sympathy with the murderers. However a family of considerable means was alleged to have become poor; a few cottagers were alleged to have found it not altogether an ill wind. At any rate they were perfectly and happily convinced that retributive justice overtook the murderer, for he never slept again.[66]

---

[65] The flexibility of the extra-legal response to wrongdoing has been discussed in Ireland "Perhaps my Mother Murdered Me" pp.239 et seq. Note also the comments of the Reverend Jenkins to the mother of an illegitimate child "I asked her how she had the face to come to the sacrament on the Sunday before", *Carmarthen Journal* 24/November/1865.

[66] D.Parry-Jones *Welsh Country Upbringing* p.32. The tombstone of the murdered Eleanor Williams of Llangyfelach, Carmarthenshire dating from 1832 similarly invokes Divine retribution against the unprosecuted murderer.

For the people of Wales the criminal law was part of a process of dispute settlement, not as yet the monopoly force of social control. The "independence" of rural Welsh jurors should be viewed in this broader context, as should the reservations which were expressed in respect of it. Such jurors negotiated, with a knowledge of the circumstances of the offender and the conditions of the community or communities in which he or she moved, the boundaries between legal and social condemnation and punishment. As the paradigm of a uniform and de-socialized conception of the Rule of Law became dominant as the nineteenth century progressed one of the reasons advanced for an expansion in summary jurisdiction has been that it represented a desire to restrict the element of waywardness which the involvement of juries necessarily carried.[67] The idea no doubt depended on the idea that Justices of the Peace were more "sound" and objective in their application of the law than were jurors. Such a belief is not, I think, necessarily true for rural Wales either: but the justification for such an assertion requires another paper![68]

---

[67] See the comments by R.Wiener in (1987) 26 *Journal of British Studies* p.88.
[68] I would simply remind readers at this point of the presence of JPs on Grand Jury panels as discussed earlier.

SIR JOHN NICHOLL OF MERTHYR MAWR THE REFORM OF THE TESTAMENTARY JURISDICTION OF THE ECCLESIASTICAL COURTS

Brian Hutton*

THIS article has its origins in research into the legislative attempts to reform the testamentary jurisdiction of the ecclesiastical courts between 1830 and 1857, and, more immediately, in a paper given to the Welsh Legal History Society at Aberystwyth in July 2001. Two Welsh lawyers, Sir John and Dr John Nicholl, father and son, played important parts in that reform process, but the present article will deal only with the contribution made by Sir John Nicholl in the 1830s.

In 1830 the ecclesiastical courts in England and Wales, and their practitioners, still enjoyed a monopoly not only over testamentary business but also in respect of matrimonial causes, church rates, tithes and defamation, a bundle of jurisdictions virtually unchanged by or since the Reformation. The courts still applied rules and followed procedures originating in the canon laws of Continental Europe, and thus stood apart from the English traditions of common law and equity.

Most of the business in these civilian courts was testamentary and most of that was non-contentious or common form, the relatively simple granting of probate to executors; but some was contentious and involved the judicial settling of disputes about the validity of wills. The courts and will registries in England and Wales were widely scattered and numerous, between 300 and 400. At diocesan level and below, in the archdeaconries and peculiars, the courts had clerical judges with no legal training; sinecurist registrars; much episcopal nepotism in appointments; no advocates, the civilian barristers; local attornies carrying out the duties of proctors, the civilian solicitors; and inadequate arrangements for the storage and production of wills. A typical 'answer', given to the Ecclesiastical Courts Commission by the diocese of Bangor in 1830, showed that neither the clerical judge nor his clerical deputy,

* The writer is most grateful to Murray McLaggan in particular, and also to the staff of the Glamorgan Record Office, for the opportunity to examine and make use of the Merthyr Mawr Papers.

both of whom were related to a former Bishop, had any 'regular legal education'; the sinecurist registrar was a lunatic whose duties were performed by a local solicitor; the court fees had not been revised since 1785; and the registry was attached to the Cathedral.[1] At provincial level, the York courts were little better provided for than the diocesan courts, and it was only in London, at Doctors' Commons, where there was a corps of trained civilian judges, advocates and proctors, that the courts exhibited anything like professional standards in handling business, although sinecurism and nepotism were similarly prevalent there. Doctors' Commons housed both the Court of Arches, the appeal court of the Province of Canterbury, and the Prerogative Court of Canterbury. The latter was the busiest testamentary court in the country, in part because the bona notabilia rule diverted lucrative business thither and away from the diocesan courts in that province, which at that time also embraced the Welsh dioceses. Nicholl was to preside over both of those courts for 25 years. The other principal civilian courts sitting at Doctors' Commons were the London Consistory Court and the High Court of Admiralty.

This was the world in which Sir John Nicholl, as he was to become, plied his trade as a civilian lawyer. He was born on 16 March 1759 at Llanmaes, Glamorganshire, into a line of minor gentry and parsons, and was educated at Cowbridge and Bristol before being elected to a Founder's Kin fellowship at St John's College, Oxford, through the exertions of an uncle.[2] Instead of entering the Church as had been envisaged, Nicholl graduated as a civilian lawyer and was admitted to Doctors' Commons as an advocate in 1785. He soon built up an extensive practice and in 1798, before he was 40, he succeeded Sir William Scott, later Lord Stowell, as King's Advocate. In that post, which carried with it a knighthood, Nicholl was chief adviser to the Crown on matters of civil law, canon law, maritime law and international law. He entered Parliament in 1802 and was in the Commons until 1832 as a Tory MP for a succession of English constituencies. Then, in 1809, in his fiftieth year, Nicholl succeeded Sir William Wynne as both Dean of the Arches, the Archbishop of Canterbury's most senior judge, and Judge of the

---

[1] See Appendix B Part II to the General Report of the Ecclesiastical Courts Commission; P.P. 1831-32 (199) xxiv.

[2] BL, Add.Ms.4053, ff.288-9, 6 Nov.1844, Dr Nicholl to Peel.

Prerogative Court.[3] Between entering Parliament and becoming Dean of the Arches, and as if to mark his successes, he purchased a country estate at Merthyr Mawr near Bridgend in 1804 and closely supervised the building of the present house, into which his family moved finally in the summer of 1810.[4] Nicholl had married Judy Birt of Wenvoe Castle in 1787 and there were five childen, three daughters and two sons. One son died in infancy, the surviving son being the John Iltid Nicholl who was to follow his father to Doctors' Commons and Westminster and later to inherit the house and estate. Sir John Nicholl built up an impressive collection of 4000 volumes at Merthyr Mawr and his fashionable portrait by Lawrence still dominates the Library there.[5] He was to be involved not only in good works in the locality but also in the establishing of King's College London, and he became a Fellow of the Royal Society and of the Society of Antiquaries.

Then, in 1812, when Nicholl was already an established figure, Tory MP, judge, knight and influential country magnate,[6] he experienced in the Commons an early attack upon the ecclesiastical courts mounted by the law reformer, Samuel Romilly, and his allies. The occasion was the harsh treatment of Mary Ann Dix in a defamation case before the Bristol Consistory Court, but the broader attack was upon the alleged inefficiency and expense of the ecclesiastical courts and the anomalous nature of the non-spiritual jurisdictions still exercised by them. Sir William Scott bore the brunt of that attack, but Nicholl, whilst ready to concede that 'a spiritual court was not the most favourable sound to the ear', argued defensively that most of the business conducted in such courts was testamentary and that the courts themselves 'were interwoven in the judicature of the country'.[7] Later, by which time he had succeeded Scott as the most senior civilian lawyer in

---

[3] Thomas, Hilary M. *Merthyr Mawr House*, (Cardiff, Glamorgan Archive Service, 1976), pp.7, 16.

[4] DNB, xl, pp.435-6; 'Memoir of the Right. Hon. Sir John Nicholl', *Legal Observer*, xvii, pp.3-4.

[5] McLaggan, Murray.'The Library at Merthyr Mawr: A Bibliomaniac Great-Grandfather', in *Bibliophily, Publishing History Occasional Papers* 2, ed.by Robin Myers and Michael Harris, (London, 1986), pp.122-3.

[6] For a brief account of Sir John Nicholl's influence in Glamorgan politics, see Grant, Raymond, *The Parliamentary History of Glamorgan*, 1542-1976, (Swansea), pp.113-5.

[7] Hansard, xxi, 23 Jan.1812, c.314.

the Commons on the government side, it was Nicholl who found himself caught up, directly or indirectly, in a sequence of criticisms of the performance of the ecclesiastical courts.

By the late 1820s those courts were coming under sustained pressure. In February 1828, in his great speech on law reform, Brougham attacked the continuing practice of prelates appointing judges to exercise what were, arguably, secular jurisdictions.[8] In June 1828, a private bill came before the Commons to secure the sinecurist interest of the then Archbishop of Canterbury, Charles Manners Sutton, in the registrarship of the Prerogative Court. Nicholl was not directly involved in such patronage, despite being judge of that court, but he witnessed the opposition of the radical MPs, Joseph Hume and Daniel Whittle Harvey, and some 50 supporters in the Commons.[9] In July 1828, Nicholl was himself the target of criticism in the Commons, again from Hume, for his alleged judicial mishandling of the petitioner's attorney and advocate in a protracted will suit, Peddle v Evans. In curious circumstances, Nicholl was defended by Stephen Lushington, then Judge of the London Consistory Court and MP for Tower Hamlets. Lushington, a much younger man, was Nicholl's political opposite but a close friend. Amid all the furore and recrimination, Nicholl's opponents complained about the secrecy and nepotism within the Prerogative Court and called for a an inquiry into the state of the courts generally.[10]

Another problem for Nicholl, in January 1829, was the crowded and unsafe condition of the Prerogative Registry at Doctors' Commons. The Registry, its staff and its profits were controlled by the sinecurist registrars not by the judge, but, nonetheless, Nicholl was expected by the Home Office to explain how matters stood.[11]

Then, in the summer of 1829, Nicholl found himself once more under attack from Hume and his allies in the Commons. At the request of Peel as Home Secretary in Wellington's administration, Nicholl introduced an innocuous Ecclesiastical Courts Bill. The Bill was intended to implement

---

[8] Ibid.,2d.ser., xviii, 7 Feb.1828, cc.151-4.

[9] Ibid.,2d.ser., xix, 5 June 1828, cc.1035-6; 16 June, 1371-3.

[10] Ibid.,2d.ser., xix,15 July 1828,cc.1694-7;17 July, cc.1749-62. Lushington took great care over preparing Nicholl's defence in the Commons, see Merthyr Mawr Papers (MMP), L.209, 21 July 1828, Lushington to Nicholl.

[11] See Appendix D of the General Report, op.cit., pp.532-3.

recommendations made by the Officers of the Courts of Justice Commission in 1823 and 1824,[12] and it sought to do little more than harmonise the fees charged by the ecclesiastical courts in London. In their efforts to get the measure through the Commons, which they eventually did, both Peel and Nicholl hinted that other reforms might be introduced on another occasion. That did not satisfy Hume or deter him from demanding that the ecclesiastical courts be brought 'under the operation of the statute law' and from reciting a litany of defects in the Prerogative Court in particular, which included allegations about Nicholl's family connections with 'no less than five individuals practising or otherwise employed in that court'.[13]

Finally, in June 1829, as Dean of the Arches, Nicholl sentenced an immoral Bedfordshire parson, Dr. Free, to be deprived of his living and to pay costs. Nicholl's decision, which was upheld by the High Court of Delegates in the following February, came only after the case had dragged on for six years in the lower ecclesiastical courts. That ineffectiveness was regarded as being as scandalous as Free's original behaviour.[14] Both Eldon[15] and the Bishop of Exeter[16] believed that Free's case influenced the decision of the Duke of Wellington to appoint the Ecclesiastical Courts Commission, as he did at the beginning of 1830, to inquire into the various jurisdictions exercised by those courts.

The forming of that Royal Commission was a sensitive and complicated exercise which Wellington himself controlled at every step. However, the choice of the Commissioners was also influenced by Peel's philosophy that gradual reform was best achieved by entrusting it to those with a vested interest in what was being scrutinised, and a remarkable balance was achieved within the sixteen chosen members between prelates, civilian

---

[12] Officers of the Courts of Justice Commission, P.P. 1823 (462) vii; 1824 (43) ix; 1824 (240), ix.

[13] Hansard, 2d.ser., xxi, 12 May 1829, cc.1318-9; 21 May, cc.1543-5; 3 June, cc.1700-01. Manchester has commented on the way in which members of the 'Jenner-Nicholl family showed remarkable enthusiasm for this branch of the law', see A.H.Manchester, 'The Reform of the Ecclesiastical Courts', *American Journal of Legal History*, x, 1966, pp.59-62.

[14] Outhwaite, R.B. *Scandal in the Church: Dr Edward Drax Free*, 1764-1843 (London, 1997), pp.95-6.

[15] Hansard, 2d.ser., xxiii, 25 March 1830, c.829.

[16] Ibid., 3d.ser., xliv, 26 July 1838, cc.611-2.

lawyers and senior common law judges. It seems that Nicholl's name was mentioned to the new Archbishop of Canterbury, William Howley, when the need for a Royal Commission was disscussed privately between Prime Minister and Archbishop on 6 July 1829.[17] Nicholl was also one of two civilians, Lushington being the other, who was subsequently consulted by the Lord Chancellor, Lord Lyndhurst, about the drafting of the Commission's broadly-based remit.[18] From the first meeting of the Commission on 4 February 1830 until its last meeting on 15 February 1832, Nicholl was heavily involved in its work, despite his age and despite the death of his wife just before Christmas 1829 and the death of his youngest daughter, Katherine, in November 1830. The Minutes of the Commission, which met on 81 occasions, reveal how busy he was.[19] He attended business meetings and interviews with witnesses on a regular basis, apart from his practice of returning to Wales during the recess. He also drafted the Commission's brief Special Report which recommended the abolition of the High Court of Delegates as the appellate court for the ecclesiastical courts and for the Admiralty Court, and which recommended the transfer of that jurisdiction to the Privy Council.

However, the greater task faced by Nicholl and his fellow Commissioners was the sifting and shaping of the evidence which had been gathered during the first year as a preparation for the drafting of the General Report during the second year. Two facts stand out. First, that the procedures and problems associated with testamentary jurisdiction dominated the Commissions's deliberations, despite the much broader range of its remit. Secondly, that all the essential reforms recommended by the Commissioners in the General Report were initially drafted either by civilian lawyers, Nicholl, Lushington, Jenner, and Robinson, or by the senior common lawyers, notably Tenterden, Tindal and Wynford. For example, at the meeting on 6 May 1831 Nicholl took the initiative and submitted to the

---

[17] Wellington Papers (WP), Southampton University Library, WP1/1030/37, 7 July 1829, Howley to Wellington.

[18] WP1/1034/1, 27 July 1829, Lyndhurst to Wellington.

[19] Church of England Record Centre, Bermondsey, Minutes of the Ecclesiastical Courts Commission, 1830-32. All references to the business of the Commission are drawn from the Minutes.

Board the heads of the General Report, and those topics were then allocated to individual lawyer Commissioners. The proposed reforms which emerged from this process can be described briefly. The testamentary jurisdiction, both contentious and non-contentious, was to be removed not only from the inferior courts but also from the diocesan courts, and was to be transferred to the two provincial courts and registries in London and York, appropriately reformed and strengthened. The grounds for transferring the contentious business to the provincial courts were that the skilled and qualified judges, advocates and proctors were concentrated there. The grounds for transferring non-contentious business to the provincial courts were to avoid the mistakes, frauds and inconvenience arising from distinctions between jurisdictions, most markedly so when probates became null and void if bona notabilia had not been detected. Similarly, all existing wills were to be transferred from the existing tiers of registries to centralised and improved registries in London and York. It was patently not true that York could provide the professional standards to match those in London, and Nicholl did not think it could, but the Commissioners felt unable to press that point when the General Report was being prepared for publication.[20]

The General Report thus sought to preserve the jurisdiction of ecclesiastical courts over testamentary business in an enlarged and centralised form, whilst acknowledging the non-spiritual nature of that jurisdiction. However, because the Report was issued in February 1832, at the beginning of the Parliamentary session in which the Reform Bills took centre stage, the responses to these findings came first from outside Parliament. Whilst it was favourably received by the Legal Observer[21] and The Times,[22] and to a lesser degree by Abraham Hayward's Law Magazine,[23] there was forceful opposition to the Report from the diocesan registrars, those professional men whose livelihoods would be put at risk by the loss of their pabulum of non-contentious probate business. In mounting what was to be a continuing anti-centralisation campaign, the registrars defended their own interests by harnessing support from others who wanted to preserve that

---

[20] General Report, op.cit., pp. 9-74.
[21] Legal Observer, iii, pp.372-3, 388-9, 402-4, 421-4.
[22] The Times, 28 August 1832.
[23] Law Magazine, vii, April 1832, pp.263-98.

CARDIFF UNIVERSITY PRIFYSGOL CAERDYDD

kind of local justice.[24] About this time there was beginning to be much unease and much debate about the phenomenon of centralisation and the need, as it was perceived, to defend local liberties.[25]

Two events in April 1833 brought Nicholl back into the fray. First, there was the issuing of the Fourth Report of the Real Property Commission, and secondly, there was the death of Sir Christopher Robinson, the Admiralty Judge.

The new Report recommended that the testamentary jurisdiction of the ecclesiastical courts should be ended, that the non-contentious business should be dealt with by registration and that the contentious business should be transferred to the Court of Chancery.[26] That Report created as much panic in Doctors' Commons as the earlier Report had done among the diocesan practitioners, and for the same reasons, the likely loss of business.[27] More than that, it presented the Government with the dilemma of how to implement conflicting recommendations from two Royal Commissions, and especially because the First Commissioner of the Real Property Commission, John Campbell, had since become a law officer in Grey's administration.

Robinson's death in April 1833 also posed a problem for Sir James Graham as First Lord of the Admiralty. Graham had already embarked upon other reforms within the Admiralty, and now, instead of finding a suitable civilian replacement for Robinson, he decided to try to consolidate the duties of the Admiralty Judge, a Crown appointment, and those of the Judge of the Prerogative Court, an archiepiscopal appointment. To bring about that scheme of consolidation, and to deal also with the awkwardness of the Real Property Commission Report, Graham needed the consent of Howley to the surrender of patronage, the willingness of Nicholl to serve as Admiralty Judge ad interim and the anticipated approval of a 'well-chosen' Commons Select Committee. By May 1833, Nicholl was approaching his mid-70s. He had left the Commons in 1832 when his son, Dr John Nicholl, was elected

---

[24] 'Memorial of the registrars of the courts of the several dioceses in the province of Canterbury, 1833'.

[25] Hoppen, K.Theodore. *The Mid-Victorian Generation, 1846-1886* (Oxford, 1998), pp.104-5.

[26] Fourth Report of the Real Property Commission, P.P.1833 (226) xxii.

[27] Law Magazine, x, August 1833, p.252.

MP for Cardiff under the patronage of the Marquess of Bute, but he was still Dean of the Arches and Judge of the Prerogative Court. Nicholl gave detailed advice to Graham about how to provide adequate judicial cover in the two courts, pending the promised legislation, but he then found himself agreeing to take on the extra duties of Admiralty Judge for the time being.[28]

When the Commons Select Committee sat in June 1833, ostensibly to inquire into the Admiralty Court, there was a contest between the London-based civilian witnesses, who had served on the Ecclesiastical Courts Commission and who wanted the testamentary business to remain in their own hands, and the common lawyers, who had served on the Real Property Commission and who offered an alternative and secular solution. Those sittings also provided a forum for the views of the disgruntled diocesan registrars. The verdict of the Committee was indecisive about one of Nicholl's concerns, what the judicial complement needed to be to deal with the combined work-load of the Prerogative Court and the Admiralty Court in normal circumstances, However, the Committee did favour the abolition of the York jurisdiction and the concentrating of all testamentary business in a reformed court and registry in London. Nicholl had given firm evidence to the Committee on that subject, putting the case strongly for such a solution and with a freedom possibly denied to him as a Commissioner.[29]

The Report of the Commons Select Committee had produced more or less the outcome desired by Graham and Nicholl. They were in regular contact throughout the remainder of 1833 and the early months of 1834, during which time Nicholl was told that some progress was being made in the drafting of bills to consolidate and regulate both the ecclesiastical courts and the Admiralty Court. Nicholl was not well during this period, was feeling the strain of presiding over both courts and was not happy at 'having to leave a remnant in each Court to the ensuing term'. He pressed Graham to arrange the early appointment of a second judge, but reluctantly agreed to continue with his extra duties when told that such a decision would fetter the discretion of Parliament.[30]

---

[28] Graham Papers, Bodleian microfilm, May 1833.
[29] Report from Commons Select Committee on Admiralty Court, P.P. 1833 (670) vii.
[30] Graham Papers, August 1833, January 1834, March 1834.

In the event, a measure to be known as 'Sir James Graham's Bill' was drawn up 'in communication with Sir John Nicholl'. It was intended to implement the combined recommendations of the Ecclesiastical Courts Commission and the Commons Select Committee by consolidating and centralising the testamentary jurisdiction in a single ecclesiastical court in London, and it was to strongly influence subsequent measures prepared by governments of both persuasions. Nothing came of the Bill immediately, however, because Graham resigned from Grey's administration in May 1834, taking the draft Bill with him,[31] and Grey himself resigned shortly afterwards.

In that same year Nicholl became Vicar General to the Archbishop of Canterbury and stood down as Dean of the Arches and Judge of the Prerogative Court in favour of his nephew, Sir Herbert Jenner. Despite those changes, neither his judicial career nor his active involvement in trying to reform the testamentary jurisdiction were at an end, because Nicholl continued as Admiralty Judge until his death in 1838, and he was consulted further by successive administrations of both persuasions about the drafting of reforming legislation.

When Peel formed his short-lived administration in December 1834, in succession to Melbourne's few months in office, one of his first acts was to contact Nicholl about reviving Graham's Bill, even before he was urged to do so by Graham himself. The main feature of the earlier Bill, a centralised court and registry to handle all testamentary business, was preserved by Peel, but what Graham admitted to Peel, and what he seems not to have admitted to Nicholl, was that such a concentration of business in London was likely to meet with fierce resistance at a diocesan level and that the full weight of the Government would be needed to carry any such measure.[32]

The country practitioners had reacted critically to the verdict of the Commons Select Committee in 1833, because it had favoured the civilians at

---

[31] Sir John Nicholl's copy of 'Sir James Graham's Bill' has survived, see MMP, L.82/1.

[32] BL, Add.Mss. 40407, ff.204-5, 24 Dec.1834, Nicholl to Peel; 40408, ff.165-6, 31 Dec.1834, Nicholl to Peel; 40318, ff.15-25, 25 Jan.1835, Graham to Peel, 31 Jan.1835, Peel to Graham, 2 Feb.1835, Graham to Peel.

Doctors' Commons,[33] and by 1835 Peel's Attorney General, Sir Frederick Pollock, was being warned that local opposition would hold up the Bill.[34] Certainly, many public petitions were aimed at it in the House of Commons.[35] Much confusion then ensued in Parliament. Peel's administration ended in April 1835. Melbourne's second administration tried without success to push through a barely altered Whig version of the Tory Bill, only to meet with the same opposition from local interests. In the same session Brougham was even floating his own reform measure in the Lords in which he perversely advocated the retention of the York courts.

Nicholl involved himself in reforming legislation for the last time in 1836. After the setback to the Whig measure in the Commons in the previous session, the newly-appointed Lord Chancellor, Cottenham, was asked by Melbourne to introduce a Bill in the Lords. Cottenham's Consolidation Bill owed much to those which had gone before. It sought to abolish the testamentary jurisdiction of all but a single ecclesiastical court and registry in London. The centralising thrust of the 1836 measure was opposed so aggressively in the Lords, especially in the form of hostile public petitions, that the matter was referred to a Lords Select Committee late in February 1836, a Committee which also armed itself with the findings and reports of the Ecclesiastical Courts Commission.[36] It was at this point that Nicholl intervened behind the scenes. He contacted Lyndhurst, the former Lord Chancellor and a member of the Select Committee, with a number of compromise suggestions which seem to have been intended to save the Bill. The most notable suggestions were that the diocesan registries should be allowed to handle non-contentious probate business of small value and that the registrars themselves should be salaried and appointed by the judge of the proposed new metropolitan court. These suggestions were passed by

[33] Following the issuing of the Commons Select Committee Report in 1833, the diocesan registrars produced a detailed defence of their position under the title 'Local Testamentary Courts', see MMP, L.109.

[34] Hansard, 3d.ser., xxvi, 12 March 1835, cc.914-16.

[35] House of Lords Record Office, Report on Public Petitions, 1835, pp.92-3, 111-12, 130-1.

[36] Hansard, 3d.ser.,xxi, 22 Feb.1836; Lords Journal, xviii, 1836, pp.32-3.

Lyndhurst to the new Lord Chancellor and within days Cottenham and Nicholl had met to discuss and revise them.[37] Nicholl's suggestions were incorporated in a recognisable form into the Report of the Lords Select Committee when it appeared at the end of March 1836, and Cottenham immediately amended his Consolidation Bill accordingly. As it happened, the Bill went no further that session because the House of Lords was in a wrecking mood.[38] Nonetheless, Nicholl's tentative efforts in 1836 to create a workable and acceptable balance in the provision of testamentary jurisdiction between central and local priorities and between the interests of metropolitan and country practitioners were influential efforts, and they were to be revived many times over and in many forms before the Probate Act of 1857 was eventually passed.

Sir John Nicholl died in harness as Judge of the Admiralty Court on 26 August 1838 and was buried in the family vault in Merthyr Mawr churchyard. The house and estate passed to his surviving son, Dr John Nicholl, advocate and MP. Later, and by an extraordinary irony, the son was asked by Peel in the 1840s to try to implement the recommended reforms of the testamentary jurisdiction to which his own father had contributed so much. An account of Dr John Nicholl's experiences as a junior minister in Peel's second administration, from 1841 to 1846, is intended to be published as a sequel to this article.

---

[37] For these exchanges between Nicholl and Cottenham in March 1836, see MMP, L.91.

[38] Lord John Russell told Melbourne on 5 June 1836, writing about the House of Lords, that '... a majority of the House are combined, not to stop or alter a measure, but to stop or alter all measures which may not be agreeable to the most powerful, or, in other words, the most violent, among their own body', see Walpole, Spencer. *The Life of Lord John Russell*, (London, 1889), i, pp.266-7.

'UN O'R BARNWYR DOETHAF ERIOED' LORD ATKIN OF ABERDOVEY *v* THE ARCHBISHOP OF WALES *et al.*

The Venerable Anthony Crockett

In the March 28, 1998 edition of Y Llan, *the Church in Wales' Welsh language fortnightly, Professor Dafydd Jenkins wrote to take issue with some adverse editorial comments on the recent Statement of the Bench of Bishops of the Church in Wales on Marriage and Divorce, in which the Bishops had reversed the instructions of their predecessors, at first prohibiting, and later strongly counselling and advising against marrying divorced people in Church, during the lifetime of a former spouse; instead, the Bishops' Statement of 1998 left the issue to the discretion of their clergy. The history of this matter goes back to the legislation which brought about disestablishment in 1920, and in it a crucial part was played by that prominent layman of the Church in Wales, and Lord of Appeal in Ordinary, Lord Atkin of Aberdovey, whom Professor Jenkins describes in his letter as* un o'r barnwyr doethaf erioed - *one of the wisest judges ever. Professor Jenkins goes on to say that if he had the time and the energy, he would like to go into considerably further detail on the subject under debate. This essay is offered as a poor substitute for that further work which Professor Jenkins, amidst all the other calls upon him, has not found time to do. I shall set out an account of the role played by Lord Atkin in a dispute which arose in 1938 and which threatened to breach the peace which held the eighteen year old Province of Wales together, and which took sixty years to settle.*

In the wake of the passing of the Matrimonial Causes Act 1937 - to say nothing of the national neurosis caused by the abdication of King Edward VIII in 1936 - the Bench of Bishops of the Church in Wales issued two pastoral letters in February 1938, on the subject of marriage and divorce. One of the letters was *ad clerum*, beginning sonorously with a reference to 'certain erroneous and strange doctrines current in our land'; the other was for public reading in Church. In both, the Bishops purported to have the authority not only to forbid clergy to solemnise the marriage of any parishioner whose earlier marriage had ended in divorce and whose former spouse was still living, but also, in effect, to excommunicate any member of the Church who re-married after divorce during the lifetime of a former spouse. Atkin and several other legal authorities, at first privately, and then publicly, disputed the Bishops' right to issue such an 'unlawful' instruction, and looked for the withdrawal of the letters. The Archbishop of Wales, Dr Charles Green, however, was not for turning, and a constitutional crisis loomed.

In order to put this matter into context, it is necessary first and briefly to visit the history of the two Acts of Parliament which finally brought about the disestablishment of the Church of England in Wales. After attempts in 1870, 1895 and 1909 had failed (this last at a time when Parliament was engaged in discussing the Bill which became the Parliament Act 1911), another Bill was introduced in 1912 - *to terminate the establishment of the Church of England in Wales and Monmouthshire, and to make provision in respect of the Temporalities thereof, and for other purposes in connection with the matters aforesaid.* Having been rejected three times in the House of Lords, it was forced through by the provisions of the 1911 Parliament Act and became the Welsh Church Act 1914. Part of its effect was eventually modified by the Welsh Church (Temporalities) Act 1919, and what is important for the purposes of this paper is the effect of this legislation on the law relating to marriage in the newly disestablished Church.

Section 22 of the 1912 Bill proposed that, while the law of marriage would be unaffected as far as members of the Church in Wales were concerned, when neither party in a marriage was a member of the Church in Wales, they 'shall not be entitled as of right to have their marriage solemnised in a Church of the Church in Wales' - a right which they had previously enjoyed as parishioners, ie inhabitants of a defined parish, irrespective of ecclesiastical allegiance. However, during the progress of the Bill through the Commons, this proposal was changed, so that Section 23 of the resulting 1914 Act provided that 'the law relating to marriage in Churches of the Church of England (including any law confirming any right to be married in such a Church) shall cease to be in force in Wales....' The effect of this was to deprive Anglican clergy in Wales of their status as 'authorised persons' by virtue of their ordination, to require church buildings to be registered for marriage, and to make necessary the presence of an authorised person to complete the civil law requirements. In other words, the Church in Wales was to enjoy none of the privileges which had existed formerly relating to marriage, and was to become just another denomination.

However, because of the international situation, the implementation of the 1914 Act was postponed for a year or for the duration of the war which began in the month before it received royal assent. This gave to those who had opposed disestablishment (one of the foremost among them being Dr Charles Green, then Archdeacon of Monmouth) the opportunity to lobby to modify some, at least, of the Act's provisions, including those which affected the law of marriage. Their efforts resulted in the Welsh Church (Temporalities) Act 1919, Section 6 of which provided that 'Nothing in this Act or in the Welsh Church Act, 1914, shall affect....the law with respect to marriages in Wales or Monmouthshire....and section twenty-three of the Welsh Church Act, 1914, is hereby repealed'. The effect of this was entirely to restore the former privileged position of the Anglican Church in Wales, regarding the rights and duties of Bishops, clergy, **and** parishioners - be they Anglicans or not - in relation to the law of marriage. It was, in Thomas Watkin's memorable phrase, a true 'vestige of establishment';[1] it was also a point which Lord Atkin clearly understood, even if Green and the Bench of Bishops were to interpret it otherwise.

Archbishop Green's interpretation is found in *The Setting of the Constitution of the Church in Wales* – 'To this extent the State continues to protect the Church and confirm her acts' - a somewhat one-sided view of the law which had the effect as much of protecting the pre-disestablishment rights of inhabitants to marry in their parish church and the rights of individual clergy to marry those legally entitled to marry, as of 'protect(ing) the Church and confirm(ing) her acts.'[2] This attitude on the part of the Archbishop is crucial to understanding the context of Atkin's disagreement

---

[1] See T.G. Watkin, 'Disestablishment Self-determination and the Constitutinoal Development of the Church in Wales', in Norman Doe (ed.), *Essays in Canon Law: A Study of the Law of the Church in Wales* (Cardiff, 1992), p. 24, at 36.

[2] C.A.H. Green, *The Setting of the Constitution of the Church in Wales* (London, 1937), p. 311

with Green and the Welsh Bishops in 1938, and the threat which it posed.

The minutes of the Bench of Bishops show that between September 1937 and January 1938, Archbishop Green, with the help of his fellow Bishops, produced the text of the *ad clerum*, intended to 'forewarn and advise the congregations committed to your charge concerning the Holy Estate of Matrimony'. Clearly, Green had the bit between his teeth, for on 22 October 1937 the Bench of Bishops discussed his proposals for two Bills in the Governing Body of the Church in Wales, the first for the formal excommunication of divorcees remarried during the lifetime of their former spouse, and the second to prohibit clergy from solemnising such marriages in Church. At that meeting the Bishops decided not to proceed with the former Bill 'but that necessary action be taken by Diocesan Bishops, as the Sacred Synod of the Province'. Reasons for this change of tactics are not given in the Bench's minutes, but this issue of excommunication is one to which we shall return, for it troubled Lord Atkin deeply. The Archbishop's Registrar was instructed to draft the proposed second Bill for the next meeting of the Bench on 10 December 1937, the minutes of which make no mention of it. However, the minutes of the meeting held on 19 January 1938, when the text of both letters was finally approved, record: 'The Registrar drew attention to the resolution contained in the minutes of October 22nd, 1937 whereby it was agreed that a Bill be introduced at the next session of the Governing Body to prohibit the solemnisation of marriage of a divorced person, whose husband or wife is still living, by any clergyman of the Church in Wales and in any cathedral or church or chapel in the Province of Wales. It was agreed that further consideration of this matter be postponed'. There is no indication of the reasons for this postponement, and it is tempting to speculate that the Registrar, having taken legal advice, as he surely would have felt bound to do, had been warned against such a Bill, the provisions of which would not have been in accordance with the law, as it affected the right of clergy to solemnise the marriage of those legally entitled to marry. Unfortunately, no such opinion is extant, and this must be conjecture.

The *ad clerum* (in English) was then issued, together with the letter (in English and in Welsh) to be read publicly 'From the pulpit at the time of the sermon, in the morning and in the afternoon or evening of one of the Sundays of February (1938)'. The *ad clerum* directed the clergy 'diligently to instruct your people in the principles of Christian marriage, which is a personal union, for better or for worse, of one man with one woman exclusively of all others on either side and continuing until they are parted by death....'

The letter to be read publicly is much simpler than the *ad clerum*, and in referring to the Matrimonial Causes Act, 1937 says: '....the Act gives to the Church freedom to decide in what circumstances she shall give permission for the use of the Marriage Service and of her Churches'. It also directed that 'where hereafter a civil marriage after divorce has taken place, both parties to the contract shall abstain from receiving Communion unless formally permitted to do so by the Bishop of the Diocese' - this was the action to 'be taken by Diocesan Bishops, as the Sacred Synod of the Province', referred to above. These two sentences were to raise profound issues of law which took sixty years to reach a resolution in the Church in Wales.

Immediately after the issue of the Bishops' letter in February 1938, Lord Atkin, who had played a key role in the legal affairs of the Church in Wales for decades, objected to the Archbishop (who as Bishop of Bangor, was Atkin's diocesan bishop) that the Bishops' action was *ultra vires*. The correspondencc is preserved in Geoffrey Lewis' biography of Lord Atkin,[3] and it illustrates the difference in understanding of the law between the head of the Church in Wales and a leading member of the judiciary. It is important to realise that Atkin had seen only the text of the letter to be read in public, as published in *The County Times*. The matter of the correspondence is not related directly to the rights of non-Christian parishioners, divorced or not, to marry, although the *ad clerum* had stated plainly that 'Marriage in Church is intended only for baptised Christians'. In his response to Atkin on 18 February 1938, Green makes this same point, which Atkin does not take up. Green says: "The 'Parishioner' in the old sense of the term disappeared on 31st March 1920: and with him any legal rights which he may have had before that date'. This is true in relation to every other aspect of church-life *except* marriage (and burial); it is an astonishing remark from one who had lived and breathed the Church Defence case before 1920 (and must therefore have been aware of the way in which the Church sought to cancel or at least to soften the effects of the 1914 Act by various means, including the Welsh Church [Temporalities] Act

---

[3] Geoffrey Lewis, *Lord Atkin* (London, 1983), appendix 6.

1919). One is at a loss to explain Green's ignorance (or ignoring) of the full effect of Section 6 of the 1919 Act. He writes to Atkin as if Section 22 of the 1912 Bill had been enacted in 1914 and was still in force. One is driven to the conclusion that the High-Church Dr Green was carried away by that spirit of anti-Erastianism which certainly characterises his *The Setting of the Constitution*. He was not going to be gainsaid by a mere layman, albeit a Lord of Appeal. What Green seems to have found in the disestablishment legislation was a one-sided freedom on the part of the Church in Wales to pick and choose which of the rights and duties of parishioners and clergy, re-instated by the 1919 Act, the Bishops would recognise and implement. If the Church had settled for the incorporation of Section 22 of the 1912 Bill in the 1919 Act, then this stance would have had been well founded in law. As it is, Green's position, in relation to the law of marriage, would seem to be quite without basis, and clearly Atkin was not going to give in to the Archbishop's assertions of superior knowledge.

Atkin's complaint was that the Matrimonial Causes Act 1937 - in which, as we shall see, he had intervened specifically to protect the rights of Church in Wales clergy - gave no freedom 'to the Church', as claimed in the Bishops' public letter. It did, however, give to individual clergy a right to decline to perform their ecclesiastical duty to solemnise the marriage of parishioners who were otherwise entitled to marry according to law, if they had been divorced and there was a former spouse still alive. In a new provision, the individual cleric was also granted a right to refuse to allow the use of his Church for such a purpose. The Act makes no mention of any freedom which 'the Church' has in this matter; indeed, it was Atkin's authoritative view there was no such freedom for the Church. There was only a free discretion granted to clergy as individuals 'as a convenience to tender consciences' (see Atkin to Green, 15.2.38, in Lewis, 1983).

Atkin was not the only prominent layman to take issue with the Bishops. The minutes of the Bench meeting of 25 April 1938 record that the Bishop of Monmouth had received two memoranda critical of the Bishops' action from his Diocesan Chancellor, Mr St.John Micklethwaite KC. The minutes record that 'Careful consideration was given to the argument of (his) memoranda but the Bishops were convinced that by their letter no change had been introduced into the law of the Church...' This is an interesting response, and Micklethwaite's initial observations do not survive. One suspects that it is slightly - and perhaps deliberately - off the point, since it appears that the objections concern the law of the land, namely the 1937 Matrimonial Causes Act, rather than 'the law of the Church'.

Atkin was certainly concerned with the legal position of the clergy, for in his correspondence in *The Western Mail* of 9 June 1938 (which made the whole dispute public knowledge), he makes a fundamental point about the duty of the clergy to obey their Bishop - '....but for a churchman, the critical point is that the bishops have given directions which are unlawful. What are the clergy to do? Their canonical oath of obedience is to obey in "things honest and lawful", and the oath cannot be invoked to justify obedience to an unlawful order, still less the giving of an unlawful order'. It would seem that Atkin's major concern was the potential consequence of the blanket sentence of excommunication which the Bishops had made, by declaration, on any member of the Church in Wales who had remarried after divorce during the lifetime of a former spouse. The only grounds on which such a person could be excommunicated, according to Atkin, were that he or she were an 'open and notorious evil liver', in the words of the Book of Common Prayer of 1662. No doubt, Atkin recalled the celebrated case of *Bannister* v *Thompson* of 1908, and the *dicta* of Lord Loreburn and Lord Halsbury when the case went to appeal in the Lords as *Thompson* v *Dibdin*.[4] Lord Loreburn had said that '...it is inconceivable that any court of law could allow as a lawful cause (for excommunication) the cohabitation of two persons whose union is directly sanctioned by Act of Parliament, and is as valid as any other marriage within this realm'. Lord Halsbury concurred, saying 'the language of the rubric is inappropriate to persons who are legally married, and whose marriage is absolutely established by Act of Parliament'.[5]

The Western Mail and South Wales News broke the news of the dispute on 9 June 1938 with the headline: **LORD ATKIN RESIGNS CHURCH OFFICES - Bishops' Divorce Ban 'Grave breach of the law' - Letter sent without consulting laity.** The article contains Atkin's letter - referred to above - giving his opinion that 'there cannot be the slightest doubt that the

---

[4] *Bannister v Thompson* [1908] P. 362;[1910] P.57;*Thompson v Dibdin* [1912] AC 533

[5] Quoted in *Opinion of Vicar General to the Archbishop of Canterbury*, 22 December 1938, preserved in National Library of Wales File LL1987/H3/8 - *Standing Liturgical Commission of the Church in Wales - papers relating to Holy Matrimony.*

innocent petitioner in divorce would not and could not be held to be a "notorious evil liver" in any court in the country. The result is that the direction of the bishops if followed by the clergy, would subject an incumbent to an action at law, probably for an injunction, certainly for damages, which might be considerable'. He also asserted that a person who had been declared excommunicate in such circumstances 'had rights which could be and were enforced with ecclesiastical law in the ecclesiastical courts'. Furthermore, he regarded such a threat of excommunication by the bishops as an 'unlawful intrusion upon the rights of the laity'.

The Western Mail confirms that it was not only Lord Atkin who had resigned all his church offices bar one, in protest at the Bishops' refusal to reconsider their action in issuing the February letter. He was joined by Sir Henry Mather Jackson Bt and Mr St.John Micklethwaite KC. The article looked forward to a lively debate at the Governing Body. 'That the matter will be thoroughly thrashed out at the Governing Body is indicated by Lord Atkin's statement that he is remaining on that body for the sole purpose of participating in the discussion of this issue'. In his letter to the newspaper, he indicates that his concern is pastoral, as well as legal: he says: 'May I add that I share the views of Mr Micklethwaite as to the disastrous effects of the bishops' attitude to divorce on the Church generally, but I content myself with stressing the complete illegality of the particular direction as to Holy Communion'.

On 10 June 1938, *The Western Mail* published a further article entitled: **IRONY OF WELSH CHURCH CONTROVERSY ON DIVORCE.** This referred to the fact that the Bishops were able to purport to ban marriages in Wales by citing a clause which Atkin himself had initiated in A.P.Herbert's Bill which became the Matrimonial Causes Act 1937. This specifically included incumbents in Wales in the terms of the new provision, namely that they could refuse the use of their churches for the marriage of divorced persons within the lifetime of a former spouse.[6]

---

[6] In his biography, *Lord Atkin*, Geoffrey Lewis refers, at p.33, to *The Church Times* of 17 June 1938, and its dismissal of the Atkin letter as 'Erastian' and 'irrelevant'. However, it seems to take refuge in rhetoric rather than counter-argument to the powerful points made by Atkin - and, no doubt, Mather Jackson and Micklethwaite.

At this point, Lord Sankey enters the fray, for the article of 10 June is sub-titled: **Viscount Sankey hopes for a way out**, and he is quoted as saying: 'I very much regret to hear of Lord Atkin's resignation. The matter is undoubtedly a difficult one upon which I do not desire to express an opinion. **I am not without hope some way out may be found**'.[7]

The minutes of the meeting of the Bench of Bishops held at the Grosvenor Hotel, London on 29 June, 1938 record Sankey's attendance and, tantalisingly, refer to 'the compromise suggested by (him)'. It appears that he had been in touch with the Bishop of Swansea and Brecon, in order to offer his help in reaching an accommodation. Discussion of 'the compromise' was postponed until the next meeting of the Bench, and the minutes simply record a decision that the Bishop of Monmouth would 'move a resolution' at the September Meeting of the Governing Body 'in similar terms to the resolution passed....on March 31, 1921'. On July 20, the Bench agreed to the wording of the September motion based on the 1921 resolution - 'The Governing Body views with grave concern the recent legislation giving widely increased facilities for Divorce, and desires to record its opinion that a loyal observance by church people of their marriage rules will help to maintain the standard of family life throughout the country'. It was also decided not to seek Counsel's opinion 'for the time being' about the assertion of Lord Atkin in his letter to *The Western Mail* concerning the vulnerability of incumbents to actions for damages if they were to follow the instructions of the Bishops. But of the Sankey 'compromise' there is no further mention.

There the matter seems to have rested, awaiting the next meeting of the Governing Body, when a motion in Lord Atkin's name was down for discussion on September 28, along with the motion of the Bishop of Monmouth. The order paper for that meeting no longer survives, but Lewis says that Atkin's resolution claimed that the Bishops' letter 'casts a slur unmerited and not justified in law upon the honour and reputation of innocent people who in the exercise of their Christian liberty have contracted such marriages'. *The Western Mail* reports that he would propose that 'the directions of the Archbishop and the bishops in relation to the rights of

---

[7] Original emphasis

divorced persons to receive Holy Communion be considered with a view to their being withdrawn'.

A constitutional crisis was thus looming, in which it is difficult to see how, without recourse to the secular courts, the issue could have been resolved, if Atkin's motion had been successful. Green had already in 1937 made clear in *The Setting of the Constitution* his view of the authority of the Bishops. He wrote: 'The plenitude of ecclesiastical authority and power was vested by Jesus the Messiah in His Twelve Apostles, and through them in their successors the Bishops. The problem whether the Clergy and Laity could or should confer authority or power upon the Bishops can never arise, because Bishops through their Consecration already possess the same in full measure. There remains another question, however, ... namely, to what degree, and in what manner, the Episcopate should associate with itself, in the exercise of its inherent rights, the subordinate Clergy and the Laity of the Church ... For the Province of Wales the answer to the question is to be found in the Constitution, and the history of its making is evidence that the rights of the Governing Body are devolved from above, not conferred from beneath.'[8] However, in spite of this, even he has to admit that 'Legally there seems to be no limit to the capacity and power of the Governing Body'.[9]

One suspects that there was no room for compromise, and that the Archbishop of Wales was not prepared to take dictation from the Governing Body, still less from a mere Lord of Appeal in Ordinary of known liberal-mindedness. Similarly, it is most likely that Atkin would have been fully aware of Green's overbearing view of episcopal authority, for he would, undoubtedly, have seen Green's *magnum opus*, and he certainly recognised the problem inherent in Green's view of the role of the episcopate within the Governing Body and, indeed, within the Church at large. In his letter to Green as early as 20 February 1938, he had said: 'I cannot expect you or the bishops to withdraw your directions much as I should desire it.'

In the event, September saw a complete anti-climax in this dispute, for international affairs intervened decisively. September 28, 1938 was a truly momentous day. In the morning, the British navy was mobilised; later in the day Chamberlain made his address to the nation about the threat to world

---

[8] See Green, *Setting of the Constitution*, pp. 192-193

[9] Ibid., p.203.

peace from 'a quarrel in a faraway country between people of whom we know nothing.' He then announced in the Commons that he would be going the next day to a four-power conference in Munich.

The Western Mail's account of the meeting of the Governing Body held at Llandrindod Wells on that day is headlined: **'CHURCH GOVERNING BODY PUTS CONTROVERSY ASIDE'**. Both Atkin's motion and that of the Bishop of Monmouth were withdrawn along with five others, on a proposal of Sir Edward Marlay Samson, in the absence of Lord Sankey, who had been recalled to Parliament. Sir Edward said: 'In view of the grave international crisis it is highly expedient that the discussions of this body should be curtailed. Our minds are concentrated on the grave prospect before us.'[10] Lord Atkin himself seconded the proposal, arguing for peace in the Church in Wales, even if there was little prospect of it in Europe. He is reported as saying that there were on the agenda items 'which at normal times would raise differences among them, but now those differences seem to fall to the background.' It seemed to him essential that men and women should be able to say that the Church had been able to put aside all controversy, that it spoke with one voice, and that it prayed for peace. The motion was carried without further comment.

There the matter ended, at least as far as the public forum was concerned, for thirteen years. However, it is clear that the Bench continued to be exercised about the admissibility to Communion of re-married divorced persons following the 1938 letter, but the minutes of the Bench seem to indicate that cases were treated individually, rather than by a blanket excommunication. In 1949, the Bench, on which two of the veterans of 1938 were still present, began drafting another pastoral letter on the same subject, finally issued in 1951. Almost incredibly, the drafts contain the same prohibitions and excommunications as the 1938 letter, but by then Lord Atkin was long dead (as was Archbishop Green), and one is left with the impression that the Bishops felt that their position in 1938 had been vindicated. However, the Bench minutes in 1950/51 make it clear that, after receiving a (now lost) Counsel's opinion, they specifically amended the language of the 1938 letter, so that they abandoned prohibition and excommunication, and instead strongly *counselled and advised* against such

---

[10] See *The Western Mail*, 29 September 1938.

marriages. They even exhibited an uncustomary sensitivity to the rights of the clergy, for they said: 'The advice and guidance on this subject which we now give is not intended to interfere with any right or duty of an incumbent under such parts of the Ecclesiastical Law as are binding by way of contract upon the Bishops, Clergy and Laity of the Church in Wales under the Constitution of the Church.' This begs the question posed by Lord Atkin's stand in 1937 as to what are these rights and duties in relation to the law of marriage. In time, this counsel and advice effectively hardened in the minds of the clergy (and of subsequent members of the Bench) into prohibition. At least, re-married divorcees were no longer to be deemed 'inadmissible to Holy Communion', as in 1938, but now they were to be 'advised' by the incumbent 'to abstain from receiving Holy Communion … unless the Bishop … directs the incumbent not to give such advice, or, if it has been given, to withdraw it.' At least one member of the Bench into the early 1970s was meticulous enough to keep a register of such advice.

The change in language between the initial drafts and the final version of the 1951 letter seems to indicate that, albeit grudgingly, the Bishops accepted that Atkin had been right in his interpretation of the law, namely that the Bishops had no right to issue prohibitions and orders to the clergy as to their use of their personal discretion in this matter. It was not, however, until 1998, sixty years after Lord Atkin's intervention, that the Bench of Bishops of the Church in Wales publicly abandoned the stance of both the 1938 and 1951 letters, and cut the Gordian knot of this vexatious subject by leaving matters to the pastoral good sense and conscience of parish clergy, as the law required. This change in policy was not without controversy, and it was a great comfort to the Bench in 1998 that this time their stand had the support of such influential lawyers as Professor Dafydd Jenkins, as indicated in his letter to the editor of *Y Llan*.

LORD MORRIS OF BORTH-Y-GEST LECTURE 2000*

LEGAL WALES: ITS MODERN ORIGINS AND ITS ROLE AFTER DEVOLUTION: NATIONAL IDENTITY, THE WELSH LANGUAGE AND PAROCHIALISM

Mr Justice Thomas[1]

Introduction

JOHN William Morris, Lord Morris of Borth-y-Gest, when speaking in favour of the bill that became the ill fated Government of Wales Act 1978, described by him as a "rather modest bill", asked that the Lords approach the bill as dealing not with a region but a nation:[2]

> When we speak of a nation we speak of something alive, vigorous and vibrant. Scholars may write learnedly on the topic of what constitutes a nation. Suffice it to say that Welsh people feel that they are a nation...

There can be no doubt today about the recognition of Welsh nationhood. But what of the law and its institutions? As is epitomised in modern times by the life of Lord Morris, the contribution of Welshmen to the development of the law outside Wales has been enormous and is well known.[3]

---

* This is the text of the lecture delivered on 25 October 2000 at Swansea University; a few corrections have been made and further references added.

[1] I am enormously indebted to Miss Elizabeth Buchanan for her very extensive research in the Public Record Office in London and in the Artemus Jones papers held at Bangor and to Miss Justine Davidge for her extensive research at the Glamorgan Records Office.

[2] Hansard HL Vol 392 col 866 (23 May 1978)

[3] An interesting summary is contained in Professor D. Seaborne Davies' *Welsh Makers of English Law*, Annual Lecture of the BBC in Wales, 1967, published by the BBC.

When Lord Bingham, the then Lord Chief Justice of England and Wales, opened the Mercantile Court of Wales and Chester in May 2000, he spoke of the establishment of the court as

> long overdue recognition of the need for the Principality of Wales to have its own indigenous institutions operating locally and meeting the needs of its citizens here. This Court is another step towards recognising Wales as a proud, distinctive and successful nation.

But how has the law and its institutions within Wales recognised national identity and what contribution can be made today by "Legal Wales" to the nation? An answer to this question must begin in Wales' modern past.[4]

1830:The abolition of the Courts of Great Session

1830 saw the abolition of the Courts of Great Sessions of Wales. This completed the absorption of the legal system of Wales into that of England begun with the Acts of Union 1536-1543 by abolishing Wales' separate legal system. Wales, in contrast to Scotland, thus lost one of the institutions that is a mark of a distinct national identity and it was subsequently seen as a significant symbolic event. Whatever final view is taken of the merits of the Courts of Great Sessions, it deprived the Welsh people of effective local courts at the start of the transformation of Wales into an industrial society; it also removed for the next 159 years the right of the Welsh people to litigate Chancery disputes in Wales.

Substituted was the English Assize system; the Royal Commissioners who reported in 1829[5] had advocated (as was contemplated by another Royal

---

[4] There has been little written on the legal history of modern Wales since the beginning of the twentieth century save for the materials to which reference is hereafter made. This should be remedied in due course by the Welsh Legal History Society; the inaugural lecture of the Society on Sir William Jones was given in May 2000 by Professor David Ibbetson, Regius Professor of Civil Law at Cambridge, in the presence of the Attorney General of England and Wales, Lord Williams of Mostyn QC.

[5] First Report of the Commissioners into the Superior Courts of Common Law p 48 (Parl Papers 1829 ix). They proposed that Flintshire and most of Denbighshire would

Commission 140 years later) the absorption of Wales and Chester into the existing English circuits. Those Commissioners thought it was too large a geographic area to be convenient and the number of cases was too small to attract a competent bar. Nonetheless a separate circuit, known as "the Welsh Circuit", was established covering Wales and Chester.[6] It was, however divided into two divisions – the North Wales Circuit (which included Chester) and the South Wales Circuit (which excluded Monmouthshire).[7]

Thus 1830 is a starting point as it is the origin of our modern unitary system of justice.

1846: The County Court and Welsh speaking judges

But if one looks at this unitary system within Wales from the point of national identity, 1846 is another starting point. 1846 was the year of the journeys through Wales of the Commissioners who produced the blue books; their report, published in 1847 concluded that in the administration of justice,[8]

> the evil of the Welsh language is obviously and fearfully great. .... It distorts the truth, favours fraud and abets perjury

---

have their Assize town at Chester, parts of Montgomeryshire at Shrewsbury, Radnor and part of Breconshire at Hereford and another part of Breconshire part at Monmouth. They proposed four new Assize districts in the rest of Wales based at Bangor, Dolgellau, Carmarthen and Neath. The Report contains very detailed arguments for the scheme proposed and mileage tables. For example, if a centre had been established at Neath, Cardiff would have been the furthest town served by that centre.

[6] s 19 and 20 of the Act for the More Effectual Administration of Justice in England and Wales 1830 (1 Wil 4 c 70).

[7] There was subsequently a considerable controversy as to whether two circuits were in fact created; see for example: *The Welsh Circuit and its Future* by Artemus Jones KC published in *The Welsh Outlook* May 1925, 121.

[8] Report of the Commissioners of Inquiry into the State of Education in Wales: Accounts and Papers, 1847, Vol 27, pt.ii, 66.

But it is not for that reason that I have chosen that year. It was the year in which local justice was restored to Wales by the creation of the County Courts. That creation also marked the beginning of acceptance of the distinct identity of Wales within the unitary legal system because of the Welsh language. During the debates on the bill to establish the County Court System, the Lord Chancellor, in a brief response to the Earl of Powys, accepted that:[9]

> it would be a great recommendation that those candidates should be appointed in Wales who were acquainted with the Welsh language; but he was afraid that if Members of the English Bar were to be appointed to these offices, some difficulty would be found in obtaining persons possessing the qualification; he would, however, take care, that they should have the preference.

Each county court judge was given a circuit; 4 of the circuits[10] were completely in Wales and one spanned Wales and the border counties; Welsh speakers were appointed as Judges of 3 of the circuits. The Report of the Judicature Act Commissioners on the County Courts published in July 1872 shows how very busy they had become by then; for example on the circuit that covered North Wales 12,281 proceedings were filed in 1868, though only 132 of them were for over £20.[11]

---

[9] Hansard 3rd Ser Vol 88 col 279-80.

[10] The boundaries of circuits 24, 29, 30 and 31 were wholly in Wales; circuit 28 also covered Shropshire. The geography of Wales was not entirely understood in London; as Judge Terrell noted in his response to the Judicature Commissioners, although Neath and Llanelli were in his circuit, Swansea was not; he had not been able to discover why. (Second Report of the Judicature Commissioners: Answers to Questions and Minutes of Evidence (1872) p 42).

[11] Second Report of the Judicature Commissioners: Answers to Questions and Minutes of Evidence (1872): p 460. The evidence of the judge of that Circuit, Richard Vaughan Williams, was that he often tried very small cases (evidence 16 May 1870 (4578)). There were some radical recommendations in the Report such as the incorporation of the County Court into the High Court and special provisions for the needs of Manchester and Liverpool, but none of these radical changes were made.

1872: The controversy over an appointment

However, shortly before the publication of that Report, political controversy had arisen[12] about the appointment of a non Welsh speaking lawyer to be the Judge of the Mid Wales County Court Circuit.[13] The need for Welsh speaking judges[14] arose because the success of the county court had meant there were many unrepresented litigants whom a judge ought to have been be able to understand without interpreters[15]. When the failure to appoint a Welsh speaking judge was raised on the floor of the House of Commons on 8 March 1872[16] by Osborne Morgan QC[17] it was made clear[18] that this was not a claim of Wales for the Welsh or any step towards home rule, but a necessary qualification for doing justice in Wales. In the course of the debate, Osborne Morgan[19] referred to a circuit story about that very distinguished Judge, Parke B, who;

> had been explaining with great lucidity the law in an ejectment case, when he was interrupted by the foreman of the jury, who called out in Welsh - Tell that old gentleman to cut his speech short – we hav'nt understood a word he has been saying, and we settled yesterday who was to have the property over a glass of claret at the Mostyn Arms.

---

[12] There is a detailed account of the controversy: 'Wales for the Welsh? The Welsh County Court Judgeships, 1868 –1900' by Mark Ellis Jones, 19 *Welsh History Review* 643 (1999).
[13] Homersham Cox. He had been a leader writer of *The Telegraph* and was a scholarly man but did not have a substantial practice.
[14] See the correspondence between Osborne Morgan and the Lord Chancellor, Lord Hatherley, in November 1871 which was printed by Order of the House of Commons in 1874 (Parliamentary Papers 1874).
[15] Mr Osborne Morgan thought that in the High Court the fact that there would be bilingual professional men would ensure that the case of a Welsh speaking litigant was properly understood.
[16] 8 March 1872 Hansard 3rd Ser Vol ccix col 1648
[17] He was elected the Liberal MP for Denbighshire in 1868; he became a QC in 1869 and took a prominent role in Welsh matters; he held office under Gladstone in 1880 and 1886. He died in 1897.
[18] By Mr Richard who had become Liberal MP for Merthyr in1868: Hansard 3rd Ser Vol ccix 1665.
[19] Hansard 3rd Ser, Vol ccix col 1649

The House passed a resolution:

> in the opinion of this House, it is desirable, in the interests of the due administration of justice, that the Judge of a County Court District in which the Welsh language is generally spoken, should so far as the limits of selection allow, be able to speak and understand that language.

The controversy died down[20] and the Judge concerned survived for a time.[21] It did not arise again until 1892 as a result of an appointment made by Lord Halsbury, the Lord Chancellor,[22] to the same mid Wales circuit.

The organisation of the High Court

Before turning to those events in 1892, another issue had arisen about the administration of justice in Wales. The introduction of the English assize system to Wales had meant that judges visited each county irrespective of whether there was any judicial business; the Judicature Commissioners in their first report in 1869 considered[23] that this led to a great waste of judicial strength and recommended the holding of assizes in certain central towns. This was a debate that continued until the report of the Royal Commission under Lord Beeching 100 years later in 1969; Wales[24] was often at the centre

---

[20] A debate on 8 March 1875 (Hansard 3rd Ser, vol. ccxxii col 1394) demonstrates how important the language was; Morgan Lloyd QC (who had been elected a Liberal MP for Anglesey Boroughs in 1874) explained that there were too many acquittals in Wales because a considerable portion of the jury did not understand the judge and therefore gave the defendant the benefit of the doubt.

[21] In 1884, he attributed to the Welsh a propensity to perjury after hearing a disputed right of way case at Llanidloes and was transferred to Kent.

[22] He had practised in Cardiff as a member of the Welsh Circuit.

[23] See First Report of the Judicature Commissioners p 16; their Fifth and Final Report in 1874 again recommended reform of the circuit system.

[24]The legislative provisions that followed confirmed the continuation of a separate circuit for Wales and Chester known as "The North and South Wales Circuit" by Order in Council made on 5 February 1876. Paragraph 4 of the Order provided:

> "The North and South Wales Circuit shall be divided into two divisions, the North Wales Division and the South Wales Division…"

of the debate not only because it had the most towns with the least business,[25] but because national identity and the language were important factors.[26]

In pressing for reform the Judges' Council recognised by their resolution of 11 December 1883[27] not only the problems caused by the existing circuit system, but also the distinct national identity of Wales:

> We attach importance to disposing of Welsh business in Wales, instead of concentrating the business for N Wales at Chester, both because there are real local peculiarities by which Wales is distinguished from England, of which the prevalence in many places in Wales of the Welsh language is most prominent and because we have reason to believe that the population attaches much importance to the local administration of justice. Nothing can be worse than the present arrangement. Of the 12 Welsh towns at which Assizes are now held, Cardiff and Swansea are the only ones where there is any considerable amount of business. Several such as Cardigan, Haverfordwest, Presteign and Mold afford hardly any business at all and others are most inconveniently situated. .... "

However objections to reform of the system flowed in from the great and the good across Wales; for example the Lord Lieutenant of Radnorshire in a letter[28] to Fry LJ pointed out how bad the railway system was in Wales and then alluded to the risk of:

> exposing the witnesses to all the temptations of a strange town which would certainly be the case if the Assizes were removed to Swansea or Carmarthen.

It continued to be known as the "Welsh Circuit" and its two divisions were known as the "North Wales Circuit" (or sometimes the "North Wales and Chester Circuit") and the "South Wales Circuit".

[25] On the Winter Assize, towns on a circuit could be grouped under the Winter Assize Act 1876. This was done for the Welsh Circuit. As a result for that Assize, Montgomery, Merioneth, Denbigh and Flint had an Assize at Ruthin, Anglesey and Caernarfon at Caernarfon, Pembrokeshire, Cardiganshire and Carmarthenshire at Carmarthen and Brecon and Radnor at Brecon. Glamorgan had its own Assize.

[26] The judges played a significant role in the debate. One proposal by the Master of the Rolls, Lindley, in 1883 was that crime continued to be dealt with locally but civil work be grouped in larger towns such as Swansea or Cardiff. It was sent to the Lord Chancellor with the note by Sir Muir MacKenzie, the Permanent Secretary (PRO/LCO 1/5):
"This looks so exactly like what is wanted that I sent it at once for you to see".

[27] PRO/LCO 1/5

[28] PRO LCO 1/6

Although this parochialism became a serious obstacle to any attempt at rationalisation, the view of the judges about the distinct identity of Wales was supported by numerous letters and resolutions from Quarter Sessions or Grand Juries that objected to the trial of Welsh defendants at Chester. It was criticised[29] as the:

> unfairness of trying Welsh prisoners before an English Judge and an English Jury in an English City

and pointed[30] out that within Wales

> the prisoners and the Welsh speaking witnesses would have the advantage of a jury who would understand the evidence as given…

The judges pursued attempts at reform and these were finally embodied in resolutions of the Judges' Council in 1892;[31] it was, for judges, a radical agenda but was rejected by the Lord Chancellor.[32]

---

[29] See the letter from Edward Swetenham QC MP to the Home Secretary dated 5 October 1886 (PRO LCO 1/7)

[30] Resolution of the Grand Jury of Montgomeryshire on 13 January 1887; the Grand Juries of the other counties passed similar resolutions as did the North Wales division of the Circuit. (PRO LCO 1/8)

[31] The Judges proposed a Royal Commission, but when the Lord Chancellor refused, they established with his agreement, a committee. After a three day debate, the Judges' Council, they passed 100 resolutions of the Judges Council in June 1892. These covered a wide spectrum of reform including proposals which varied from the establishment of a Commercial Court and a Court of Criminal Appeal to ordering costs to be paid at once to prevent unnecessary applications for summary judgment. With regard to the administration of justice, they recommended that whilst judges should visit each county to try criminal business 3 times a year, areas should be grouped for civil cases which should only be tried at 16 centres, instead of the 56 assize towns; on the Welsh Circuit these were to be Glamorgan, Caernarfon and Chester. In view of the very powerful lobby made by the counties, the proposals for a judge to visit each county was inevitable. Although the judges implemented some of the reforms themselves (such as establishing the Commercial Court in 1895), grouping towns for civil cases required legislation and the Lord Chancellor decided against it. The resolutions are printed in the Law Journal for 13 August 1892 p 526; the radicalism of the proposals can be seen from an article in The Times of 9 and 10 August 1892 written by "a member of the bench". It begins:

1892: The National Institutions (Wales) Bills and further controversy over the appointment of a County Court Judge who was not Welsh speaking

1892 saw, however, the re-awakening of the controversy over the appointment of county court judges who were not bilingual. This occurred in very different circumstances to the 1870s. First there was a general dissatisfaction at the standard of appointments; an editorial in the *Law Times* expressed it thus:[33]

> "..the Profession has become thoroughly reconciled to the fact that any and every qualification except learning and experience justify a selection to the bench of the inferior courts.."

Second, and much more significant, was the change in the membership of the representation in the House of Commons from Wales; in consequence the Westminster Parliament had passed in 1881 the first piece of legislation which treated Wales as a national unit[34] – The Wales Sunday Closing Act.[35] That was followed in 1889 by the Welsh Intermediate Education Act[36] with

---

> "For the first time probably in the history of this country, the entire body of Judges of the land have approached the Crown with a report on the defects of the present administration of justice, and with a scheme for their improvement. …No similar document has ever been presented to an English Government. The occasion is unique.
>
> ……….
>
> The Circuit system ….. fell into grave confusion….. The chief persons concerned in maintaining the ambulatory pilgrimages of the judges into each county town are the local hotel keepers and lodging house keepers, a knot of tradesmen in each place and their constitutional representative, the borough member."

[32] In March 1893; see the Memorandum by Lord Wright appended to the interim report of the Hanworth Committee on State of Business in the High Court (Cmd 4471), 1933.

[33] 10 October 1891

[34] See K.O. Morgan: *Wales in British Politics* p 43; Monmouthshire was not included.

[35] In 1873, there was published the first official abstract of an Act of Parliament in Welsh – the Metalliferous Mines Regulation Act 1872 – see paragraph 203 of the Departmental Committee on Welsh in Education and Life (1927).

[36] This extended to Wales and Monmouthshire and was the result of the Welsh national educational movement (see K.O. Morgan, supra, 98-101).

its recognition of Welsh nationhood.[37]

In 1891 Alfred Thomas, the future Lord Pontypridd, introduced the first home rule measure for Wales – the National Institutions (Wales) Bill. Although like most succeeding bills until the 1970s, it never got beyond its first reading, the interest of the bill relates to its treatment of the legal system.[38] This bill only dealt with the administration of justice in relation to the Welsh language and the appointment of JPs.[39]

On 10 February 1892, Alfred Thomas introduced his second home rule bill;[40] but this contained a provision that the Welsh National Council to be created under the bill should submit a list of the names of county court judges to the Lord Chancellor from which appointments were to be made.[41] This change seems to have come about because of the controversy Lord Halsbury had re-ignited by his appointment to the mid Wales County Court Circuit of Judge Beresford who could not speak Welsh; nine days after the first reading of Alfred Thomas' bill, Lloyd George (a supporter of that bill) moved a resolution in the House attacking the appointment of Judge Beresford. Again the debate was concerned with the importance of a knowledge of Welsh to the administration of justice in Wales; Alfred Thomas quoted a letter from Judge Gwilym Williams:[42]

---

[37] The Aberdare Committee (The Report of the Committee on Intermediate and Higher Education in Wales) had reported in 1881:
"The first thing to be noted is that Wales has a distinct nationality of its own... The existence, therefore, of a distinct Welsh nationality is in our opinion a reason for securing within the limits of Wales itself a system of intermediate and higher education in harmony with the distinctive peculiarities of the country."

[38] The first reading was on 15 July 1891 (Bill No 411) (Hansard 3rd Ser. Vol 355 col. 1327). For a detailed account see: Alfred Thomas: 'Welsh Home Rule', printed in *The Welsh Review* (April 1892) 549; Chappell: *Wake up Wales* (Cardiff Western Mail & Echo 1943) p 23-28; 'Alfred Thomas' National Institutions (Wales) Bills of 1892' by J Graham Jones 15 *Welsh History Review* 218

[39] Clause 6; the power was to be transferred to the Secretary for Wales; the bill also provided that the Secretary for Wales could order proceedings to be conducted in Welsh (clause 9).

[40] (Bill 115) Hansard 4th Ser Vol 1, col 170

[41] Clause 26 (12)

[42] Hansard 4th Ser Vol 1, 850. Judge Gwilym Williams was the owner of the Miskin estate and a barrister. He was appointed a stipendiary magistrate for Pontypridd and

> The case, I think, to which you refer is that of a man who had failed to make himself understood to the Registrar, and on whom an order was made and a judgment summons issued, and on being heard before me I discovered his utter ignorance of English, and that he was not indebted to his creditor, the result being that I struck out the case. I am of opinion that the mistake arose from the man's ignorance of English and my knowledge of Welsh prevented a further miscarriage of justice.

In 1893, Beresford was moved and replaced by a fluent Welsh speaker; the principle was established that in four of the five County Court circuits in Wales the judges had to be bilingual; a Parliamentary Sub-Committee could record in 1920:[43]

> We have been assured that for some time past it has been the invariable practice to select for appointment to Welsh County Court judgeships barristers able to speak the Welsh language.

This was an important recognition of language in the national identity of Wales.

---

the Rhondda in 1872 when bilingual judges were sought. He was appointed a Judge of the County Court in Glamorgan in 1885 where he continued until he died in 1906. He was Chairman of Glamorgan QS from 1894 until his death; a statue to him is in front of the Law Courts at Cardiff. He was a great *Eisteddfodwr*.

[43] Paragraph 18 of the Report of Lord Stuart of Wortley's Committee on the Judiciary, Appendix V to the Report printed as: *Devolution Conference: Letter from Mr Speaker to the Prime Minister* (Cmd 692) In 1935, Judge Sir Thomas Artemus Jones KC in response to a question from Sir Claud Schuster accepted that there had been no difficulty in appointing bilingual judges in the county court for many years (Evidence to the Peel Commission, 1935, 2559- 2565). Sir Claud Schuster's Memorandum of 18 May 1944 (PRO LCO2/3214) on a separate Welsh Judiciary noted in respect of the five Welsh County Court Circuits that:

> "For many years it has been the practice of successive Lord Chancellors to appoint to the Judgeships of Circuits 28, 29, 30 and 31, Judges who are conversant with the Welsh language. It has not been thought necessary to follow this rule invariably as respects circuit No 24, where it is thought that the great majority of the population are monoglot English speakers."

Whether the position was quite as clear as this is uncertain: cf an account given by J. Eaton: Judge John Bryn Roberts (Cardiff, 1989) at p 54.

The law, commerce and national institutions

But what of commerce in Wales, which by this time had been transformed by industrialisation? The great expansion of the industrial economy of Glamorgan had been met by sending two High Court Judges to each Assize from 1872 where a significant amount of Commercial business was heard until the establishment of the Commercial Court in London in 1895.[44]

From at least 1882, Manchester and Liverpool had been seeking special treatment and permanent sittings of the High Court to deal with civil business; the impetus to this was spurred by the Gorrell Committee on the relations between the High Court and the County Court which was appointed in July 1908 and reported in February 1909[45]; it attributed the decline of civil business to dissatisfaction with the arrangements for dealing with High Court business away from London. In May 1909, most of the Chambers of Commerce in the UK presented a memorial[46] noting the fact that the provinces were neglected and seeking a means:

> whereby litigation (and especially commercial litigation) arising in the provinces, shall be dealt with efficiently and expeditiously and at reasonable cost.

Liverpool pressed their needs in a determined manner and in June 1909 provision was made for a High Court Judge to stay until the conclusion of all civil business[47] and this was subsequently developed so that special arrangements were made for hearing commercial cases.

In 1913,[48] a Royal Commission was appointed under Viscount St Aldwyn to examine delay in the courts;[49] their principal recommendation

---

Sir Claud Schuster was keenly interested in this matter; for example, when it was suggested by a witness before the Peel Commission that the County Court Judge for Glamorgan (Circuit No 24) should be Welsh speaking, Sir Claud asked that the information be provided directly to him (5042).

[44] Details were given in my Lecture to the Cardiff Business Club in January 1999.

[45] 19 February 1909

[46] PRO LCO 2/242

[47] On 5 May 1909 a powerful delegation led by Sir William Holland visited the Lord Chancellor (PRO LCO 2/242); the change was made by Order in Council of 28 June 1909.

was the implementation of proposals along the lines advocated by the Judges in 1892.[50] The interest in the commission is in the evidence of Sir David Brynmor-Jones KC[51], the member for Swansea.[52] He told the Commission that, if there was a mercantile dispute in Wales, then the parties would take it to the Commercial Court in London, whereas 20 years before it would have been tried at Cardiff or Swansea. They did so in cases of that kind as expense did not matter. He said that there had been no request for a system akin to that in Liverpool or Manchester; that was only being discussed.

At Cardiff, there was by this time a practising bar[53] and solicitors with large mercantile practices; a bar was being developed at Swansea. It was also

---

[48] On 1 July 1909 a Joint Select Committee of the House of Lords and House of Commons had been appointed to examine delay in the Courts (HC 1909 VIII); the evidence before the Select Committee pointed to the waste of judicial time in Wales because of the Assize system. The lack of business in Wales featured, particularly in the evidence of the President of the Law Society (William Winterbotham) on 26 October and 2 December 1909. He put forward proposals suggesting grouping of all business under which, although there were to be 5 centres in Wales, cases from Flint and Denbigh were to go to Chester. The Select Committee reported on 2 December 1909 that extra judges be appointed and reforms be made.

[49] Cd 7177

[50] A number of witnesses from Wales gave evidence; on Monmouthshire, the Deputy Mayor of Monmouth, (Sambrook) Mr Moxon (solicitor) and Sir Henry Mather Jackson (Lord Lieutenant and Chairman of QS); on Anglesey, Thornton Jones (solicitor); on Brecon, the Hon. Robert Devereux (Chairman of QS); on Cardiganshire J E Lloyd (Solicitor); on Flint, Tilby (clerk to the Council); on Merionethshire, Sir Osmond Williams (Lord Lieutenant and Chairman of QS); on Montgomeryshire, Richard Lloyd (Chairman of QS); on Pembrokeshire, Edward Marlay Samson (barrister – see below) and on Radnor, J. Corrie Carter (barrister and Chairman of QS). They did not take any specific evidence on Chester.

[51] He was called to the Bar in 1876 and became a County Court Judge in 1885 first for the Mid-Wales circuit and then for the Gloucester circuit. He resigned in 1892 and became an MP first for Stroud and then for Swansea from 1895-1914; he was appointed Recorder of Merthyr in 1910 and Cardiff in 1914. He was a member of the Welsh Land Commission and his interest in the legal history of Wales is evident from *The Welsh People* which he wrote with Sir John Rhys. His brother was Viriamu Jones FRS, the first Principal of the University College at Cardiff. He died in 1921. At the time he gave his evidence he was chairman of the Welsh Liberal MPs in Parliament.

[52] Minutes of Evidence, 15 April 1913 questions 2115 – 2126

[53] A very brief account of the growth of the bar is given in *The Welsh People* by Sir John Rhys and Sir David Brynmor-Jones at p 392-4.

perceived that it would be sensible if Monmouthshire was joined with Glamorgan for the purpose of civil sittings. But the economic advantage to Wales of having a court to try its mercantile disputes in Wales was not raised. Why was this? Why did not Wales assert its position, as Manchester and Liverpool had done?

The records of the Cardiff Chamber of Commerce,[54] the City of Cardiff and the Cardiff and Bristol Channel Shipowners Association show that the only requests were requests for the appointment of a county court judge experienced in admiralty cases[55] and a separate assize for Cardiff. On 25 March 1914, Lord Crichton Stuart and the Recorder led a delegation from the city to the Lord Chancellor seeking a separate assize for Cardiff. However even this modest request was defeated by the parochialism evident in the strong opposition from several other Glamorgan towns, including Swansea, Neath and Merthyr.[56] The First World War brought an end to the request;[57] it was briefly revived in the late 1920s, but by then the commercial position of Cardiff was in decline. In the result, Wales had failed to take steps to establish an indigenous institution to cater for its commercial needs at the height of its prosperity.

What happened is in contrast not only to Liverpool and Manchester, but also to the development of the other institutions in Wales. For example, the period before the first World War saw the establishment of the National Library and Museum, the Welsh Department of the Board of Education and a separate insurance commission for Wales. That is not to say that there was inactivity by the lawyers; far from it. First and foremost was the establishment of the Law School in Aberystwyth in 1901; then there was an

---

[54] The Records of the Chamber of Commerce show that a new Chamber of Arbitration was established in 1908 to deal with shipping and other commercial disputes.
[55] Letter from Cardiff Chamber of Commerce 27 October 1909 sent on the death of Judge Owen (records of Cardiff Chamber of Commerce). According to the evidence given by his predecessor in 1869, the County Court tried a number of collision and salvage cases.
[56] See the correspondence in PRO LCO 2/690 and in the reports of the Council and Committees 1913-14 at the Glamofgan Record Office; Swansea was strongly opposed and many other areas of West Glamorgan were influenced by its attitude.
[57] See letter of 13 January 1928 from the City of Cardiff to the Lord Chancellor's Department (PRO LCO 2/690)

outpouring of learning – for example the collection by Judge Ivor Bowen KC[58] of the Statutes of Wales in 1908 and numerous articles by W Llewellyn Williams KC[59] and Sir David Brynmor-Jones. When land reform was debated, there were calls for the establishment of a land court for Wales modelled on the county court.[60]

Although these distinguished lawyers did not achieve the creation of any new legal institutions, they had a vision of the revival of the Court of Great Session which was by then viewed as a great loss to Wales; for example Judge Ivor Bowen observed that Wales had until 1830:[61]

> a law system adapted to its special needs and circumstances, expeditious, cheap and in several marked respects excelling the English system.

That vision became important after the First World War.

---

[58] He worked in a bank in London and was made secretary of the London *Cymru Fydd* Society on its formation in 1887. He was called to the bar in 1889 and took silk in 1912, was Recorder of Merthyr 1914-5 and of Swansea 1915-18; he was a County Court Judge of the Mid Wales Circuit 1918 – 1933. He was Treasurer of Grays Inn in 1923. He died in 1934

[59] When at Oxford, he was one of the founders of *Cymdeithas Dafydd ap Gwilym* and an ardent member of *Cymru Fydd* He then became a journalist in South Wales (being editor of the Barry South Wales Star and Swansea South Wales Post, both of which he tried to run on nationalist lines – see K.O Morgan, supra, p 110). In January 1897 he was called the bar. He was Liberal MP for Carmarthen Boroughs 1906 –1918, but never gained office (see K.O. Morgan Wales 1880-1980 p 139). He broke with Lloyd George in 1916 over conscription (K.O. Morgan: *Wales 1880-1980* p 164-5). He contested a bitterly fought by-election in Cardiganshire in 1921, when he was defeated by Ernest Evans (see K.O. Morgan: *Modern Wales, Politics, Places and People* 243-6). He took silk in 1912, leader of the South Wales Division of the Circuit, Recorder of Swansea in 1914 and was Recorder of Cardiff from 1915 until his death in 1922.

[60] See Second Reading Debate on Land Tenure (Wales and Monmouthshire) Bill, 19 May 1897 Hansard 4th Ser, Vol xlix, 817 at 819. For the background see K.O. Morgan, supra, 123–129 and 174-7. W. Llewellyn Williams opposed this: see K.O. Morgan: *Wales 1880-1980* p. 84-5.

[61] His views on the loss were trenchant; he commented in his preface to his *Statutes of Wales*, (1908) p cix-cx:

> "It must be noted here that the abolition of the Welsh Court of Great Sessions was not brought about at the instance of the main body of the Welsh people, or of Welsh suitors, but at the instance of the landed gentry of Wales. The wishes of the humble Welsh suitors were not so much regarded as the ambition of the

1920: The consideration of a separate High Court for Wales

Sir Brynmor-Jones in his evidence to the St Aldwyn Commission had also alluded to, but not urged, a revival of the Court of Great Sessions and to Wales making its own judicial arrangements;[62] E.T. John's Government of Wales Bill of 1914 (of which Sir David Brynmor-Jones was one of the supporters) made provision for the power to create a separate High Court for Wales[63]. However, in 1919 and 1920, the issue was seriously considered in the context of a conference under the chairmanship of the Speaker which considered home rule "all round" through the creation of legislatures for each of the four nations.[64] In December 1919 the Conference appointed a Sub-

---

nobility and the landed proprietors of that time to make Wales a part of the judicial system of England."

There was a considerable danger in the alteration, for it was a change from a fairly efficient method of judicature which had grown after three centuries of useful working into a national institution easily capable of being reformed, to the acknowledged defects and notorious costliness of the English system….

The long establishment of this separate jurisdiction shows that Wales had until 1830, as Scotland still has, a provincial judicature which distinguished it from any other part of the United Kingdom."

There are similar passages in the writings of W Llewellyn Williams K.C.- see for example his lecture to the Cymrodorion in 1911 in the presence of Lloyd George, printed in *Y Cymmrodor* Vol XXVI and separately as *An account of the King's Court of Great Sessions in Wales* (1916). For a different view, see Sir Claud Schuster's memorandum of 18 May 1944 (PRO LCO/2 3214).

[62] Minutes of Evidence 15 April 1913 (2007, 2048, 2102). His evidence contains a detailed historical account. He was fiercely opposed to grouping and advanced the argument that any substantial alteration of the circuit system in Wales would be a breach of the legislative bargain between the Welsh people and the central government made when the separate Welsh judicature was suppressed (2000-2006).

[63] Bill no 115; read for the first time on 11 March 1914 (Hansard 5th Ser Vol lix 1235); clause 18 proposed that a separate division of the High Court should be constituted to exercise the jurisdiction of the High Court in Wales. The other courts were to continue until the Welsh legislature decided otherwise, save that the judges of the other courts were to be appointed by the chief minister of the Crown in Wales known as the Lord President (clause 9). For the context, see K.O.Morgan, supra, 259 and Chappell, supra, 73. There is no explanation as to why the Bill was not read a second time; it was suggested by Lord Prys Davies in *Turning a dream into reality* (Annual Lecture of the Welsh Political Archive) that it was postponed whilst he looked for wider political support.

[64] For the background: see Sir Reginald Coupland: *Welsh and Scottish Nationalism: A Study* p 313-331 (London, 1954)

Committee on the Judiciary which reported in April 1920.[65] It recommended that in any scheme of devolution for the UK the judicial system in Scotland with its own separate law and courts should remain unchanged. But what of Wales?

A strong argument was mounted and led by Llewellyn Williams, by then the Recorder of Cardiff, for the re-establishment of a separate judiciary for Wales by restoring "to Wales something of the judicial independence she lost in 1830". It was urged that Wales should have a Chancellor, Court of Appeal, High Court and Law Officers of its own; the High Court in Wales was to have full criminal and civil jurisdiction and be merged with the county court; the bar was to be distinct from the bar of England.[66]

The Sub-Committee took evidence on this from two very eminent judges with strong Welsh connections – Bankes LJ[67] and Sankey J.[68] Both were very cautious in expressing any view about the desirability of such a proposal, but commented on the practical implications.[69] Bankes LJ considered that the existence of the County Court, the Courts of Quarter

---

[65] The Report of Lord Stuart of Wortley's Committee on the Judiciary, Appendix V to the Report printed as: *Devolution Conference: Letter from Mr Speaker to the Prime Minister* (Cmd 692)

[66] Letter of Judge Rowlands to Schuster 29 February 1920 (PRO LCO 2 /507); W Llewellyn Williams KC produced a detailed memorandum, but I have not so far been able to trace a copy.

[67] He was one of the great commercial judges of the twentieth century; when he sat in a division of the Court of Appeal with Atkin and Scrutton LJJ, it was one of the most influential courts in the development of Commercial law. He was born in Flintshire and subsequently was Chairman of Flintshire Quarter Sessions for 33 years. With Atkin and Sankey he drew up the Constitution of the Church in Wales; he was Chairman of its Representative Body for many years. He also understood the separate national identity of Wales; for example, in his evidence to the St Aldwyn Commission, he made clear that transferring defendants from Flint to Chester should not take place as that was "taking a Welshman into England". (3747)

[68] He was called to the bar in 1892 and practised at Cardiff where his family lived; he moved to London in 1907 and took silk in 1909. He was appointed to the High Court in 1914 and to the Court of Appeal in 1928. In 1919 he chaired a Commission on the Coal Industry and recommended nationalisation (for its effect on Wales see: John Davies, *A History of Wales,* 530-5). He was Lord Chancellor from 1929 until 1935. Among his achievements was the establishment of the Law Reform Committee as a permanent body to consider law reform.

[69] PRO LCO 2/507; the précis of the evidence differs in emphasis to the summary of

Sessions and local Justices provided effective local justice; outside the industrial areas of South Wales, the volume of business was small; there might be difficulty in attracting the right men for an independent judiciary. He thought that the only way it could be done was to abolish the distinction between the High Court, the County Court and possibly Quarter Sessions; eight judges would be needed, five of whom would be the existing 5 county court judges. He commented:

> "Whether the Commercial Community of South Wales where the bulk of the important civil business comes from, desires a Welsh Judiciary with an exclusive jurisdiction, should be ascertained before any extension of the Judiciary is attempted"

Sankey J was concerned that the establishment of a separate system might seriously damage Welsh international credit and was against disturbing the system. Although he shared Bankes LJ's view that it was probably advisable to fuse the High Court and the County Court for civil matters, there were practicable difficulties such as finding a means of dealing with small cases; in Admiralty cases, foreigners might not understand the actions of a new court. Both considered civil appeals should be dealt with in Wales with a court comprised of judges who had not heard the case along the lines of the old Exchequer Chamber; they differed as to whether criminal appeals should be heard in England or Wales.

The Lord Chancellor's Department was not directly informed of the establishment of the Sub-Committee, but as soon as the very powerful Permanent Secretary who held that post from 1915 to 1944, Sir Claud Schuster, learnt of it, he took a great interest. He sought from Judge Rowlands[70] in South Wales his views as to what actuated the wish for severance, beyond vague national sentiment. Judge Rowlands told him that not only did Welshman want for Wales what Scotland and Ireland had, but there were also practical problems. Litigants wanted a system where cases could be tried in Wales with as little expense as possible by judges who understood local conditions. There was no Chancery court in Wales.

---

their views expressed in the Report of the sub committee.

[70] He had been called to the Bar in 1892; he was appointed Judge of the County Courts for Glamorgan in 1918. He died in 1935.

Businessmen in London always had a judge available and there was no reason why the same should not be true in Wales.

In his evidence to the Sub-Committee, Sir Claud vigorously opposed the proposal to create a separate judiciary for Wales in any scheme of devolution. With an impressive array of figures, he demonstrated that two thirds of the High Court civil business in Wales was from Glamorgan and Monmouth; although there was every opportunity in the appropriate case for local trials, litigants in Glamorgan preferred trial in London. His most powerful point was that the Welsh courts had been a burden on the general fund; if the courts of Wales were severed from those of England, "the result would be to relieve England of a considerable charge and impose that charge upon Wales". He expressed the view:

> It is difficult to imagine any system in which the Welsh atmosphere and Welsh ideas could be fostered better than by the present system. The Bench of the Supreme Court comprises two Lord Justices (Bankes and Atkin) and 3 puisne Judges (A.T. Lawrence, Bailhache and Sankey) who are Welsh either by race or association. All the Bar practising on both circuits is Welsh. All five County Court Judges are Welsh and four of them are Welsh speakers. Presumably the Registrars of the County Courts are Welsh, and the proceedings in the Court are conducted in the Welsh language when occasion calls for it.

He argued that the proposals for a separate judiciary would inflict a very grave injury on the interests of the Principality and its inhabitants - cost, the need for a central registry, the difficulty for the North if this was located in the South, the lack of a sufficient number of capable barristers from which a Welsh High Court could be appointed and the risk of inconsistent decisions, particularly in commercial matters between London and Cardiff. The chief injury would be on the individual Welshman; the history of the English and Scottish bars showed that however strongly national sentiment might operate, there would always be the "tendency for the aspiring lawyer to come to where the biggest prizes are offered"; the loss to England would be very serious, as had there been a separation, the English bench would not have gained judges such as Sir Samuel Evans, one of the great Admiralty judges in history.[71]

---

[71] He was the son of a Skewen grocer. He was first a solicitor at Neath and then called to the Bar in 1891 and practised on the South Wales Circuit. He was MP for Mid Glamorgan from 1890-1910. He was appointed Solicitor General in 1908 and

Judgments of the Welsh Courts would not command the respect paid to British justice and the effect upon Welsh commerce would be considerable.

His arguments prevailed. The Sub-Committee expressed the view that there should be no separation under the proposed scheme of devolution, unless the proposed Welsh legislature decided otherwise. For political reasons, the overall proposal for devolution foundered.[72] The report and the evidence were forgotten.[73]

The triumph of parochialism

The failure of these aspirations did not address the problems of the administration of justice in Wales. In his evidence, Sir Claud Schuster had suggested that much improvement could be achieved by restricting the towns visited by the High Court to Caernarfon, Ruthin, Chester, Carmarthen, Cardiff and Swansea; if the position of Wales was to be marked from that of England, there was no objection to the transfer of Chester to the Northern Circuit and Monmouth to the Welsh Circuit. This might seem very rational, but what happened?

In 1919, the Lord Chancellor, Lord Birkenhead, and the Lord Chief Justice, Lord Reading, had agreed on a proposal for the appointment of two more judges and improving the use of judicial time by abolishing visits to 10 towns where there was little or no business. 8 of these were in Wales. When the proposal was submitted to the cabinet in 1920, the need for additional

---

President of the Probate Divorce and Admiralty Division in 1910. His great work was as Admiralty Judge during the First World War where he logically developed the law of Prize and applied it to the new conditions.

[72] See K.O. Morgan, supra, 291-2; John Davies, supra, p.541-3.

[73] On 10 February 1922, Sir Robert Thomas presented a further Government of Wales Bill (Bill no 17); it provided for the continuation of existing judicial institutions. It was withdrawn on 8 May 1922 (Hansard 5th Ser Vol 153 col 382) in favour of a Government of Scotland and Wales Bill; this further bill followed the scheme proposed by the Speakers Conference, including the report of the sub-committee on the judiciary. On 26 May 1922 (Hansard ibid col 1642). Sir Robert Thomas said that he had first proposed a Welsh Secretary of State; that he had then been advised by the Prime Minister (Lloyd George) to propose a full scheme of devolution and had then worked on the bills which had been drafted with the assistance of Herbert Lewis (Parliamentary Secretary to the Board of Education) and Sir Alfred Mond (Minister of Health).

judges was accepted, but as the Prime Minister, Lloyd George, was hostile to the idea of abolishing the assizes, including those at Beaumaris, Lord Birkenhead dropped that part of his plan.[74]

However, pressure from the Treasury in 1922 led to the establishment of the first of four committees or commissions that sat in the inter war years to examine the operation of the Assize system. Wales featured extensively in all of them for the same reason it had in the 1880s and 1890s. But it also featured because of the continued division of the circuit into two parts, the position of Monmouth and Chester and the Welsh language.

It is convenient to look at the first three issues together because they exhibit the undoubted triumph of parochialism over national identity. Four of the fifteen members of the first of the Committees established by Lord Birkenhead in 1922 under the Chairmanship of Rigby Swift J were Welsh.[75] It recommended,[76] by majority, the grouping of business at the towns suggested by Sir Claud Schuster, and also the union of the two divisions of the circuit. The minority, who favoured making no change, was led by the leader of the South Wales Circuit. This minority view won the support of the small circuit towns affected;[77] it is not unfair to summarise the view of each assize town affected as being delighted to be one of the centres for grouping, but if their town could not be the centre, they were opposed. Sir Marlay Sampson[78], one of the Welsh members of this Committee, had anticipated this opposition. He suggested that Monmouth should be brought into the Welsh Circuit and Chester transferred out, as "the recognition of Wales and Monmouthshire as a Unit for the purpose of the Circuit would be in accord with Welsh National sentiment and would tend to reduce local hostility to

---

[74] Correspondence and memoranda in PRO LCO 2/556

[75] Sir Ellis Griffith KC, Thomas Artemus Jones KC, Sir Edward Marlay Sampson KC and Roland E.L.Vaughan Williams KC.

[76] Cmd 1831. The expenses of the committee were £38.1.8.

[77] In a letter to Schuster dated 13 February 1925, the Hon. Stephen Coleridge, the Clerk of Assize of the South Wales Circuit, reported that Roland Vaughan Williams views' as leader had appealed to the "trade union instincts" of the bar at a mess of the South Wales Circuit; he expected the bar to get the counties to follow the same line. (PRO LCO 2/690)

[78] He was called to the Bar in 1892 and joined the South Wales Circuit in 1894 with chambers in Swansea; he took silk in 1919. He became Chairman of Haverfordwest QS and Pembrokeshire QS; he was Recorder of Swansea 1919-1923 and appointed

such proposed changes"[79]. We will not know if national sentiment would have blunted hostility for his proposal was never adopted, but it seems highly unlikely because parochialism was more evident than national identity. For example, the bar of the South feared competition and the adverse effect it might have on their obtaining recorderships.[80] As the leader of the South Wales Circuit[81] explained in 1935 from the bar's viewpoint:

> the present arrangement suits everybody

even when it was pointed out to him that the salaries paid to the circuit officials were so low that they did not attract professional people without independent means.[82]

The system of visiting each small town was indefensible; one judge started his evidence in 1935;[83]

> I have been going round South Wales – the usual sort of holiday with a few hours work at rare intervals!

Stipendiary Magistrate at Swansea in 1923. He was also Chancellor of St David's and Swansea and Brecon. He had given evidence to the St Aldwyn Commission. He died in 1949.

[79] Memorandum in PRO LCO 2/523.

[80] The North Wales Division only had 2 Recorderships - Chester and Birkenhead; South Wales had 4 - Cardiff, Swansea, Carmarthen and Merthyr. There was also a difference between the South where the work was largely done by the local bar and Chester and the North where the work was generally done by practitioners in London. (See the memorandum by Francis Williams, the Junior to the North, published in the appendix to the Minutes of Evidence of the Peel Commission).

[81] Roland Vaughan Williams KC. He was the son of Vaughan Williams LJ; he was called to the bar in 1893 and took silk in 1913. He became successively Recorder of Carmarthen and Swansea; he was Recorder of Cardiff from 1930-1945. He was a member of the Anglo-German-Mixed Arbitral Tribunal 1920-28. He died in 1949.

[82] Evidence to the Peel Commission of Roland Vaughan Williams KC (4839- 4847).

[83] McKinnon J in his evidence to the Peel Commission (appendix to the Minutes of Evidence); he had said the same 10 years earlier in his charge to the Grand Jury in January 1925 (PRO LCO2/690). Mcardie J was one of those who favoured the status quo. So too did Lord Atkin in his evidence to the Peel Commission (3442-3445). As Sir Claud Schuster observed " I am afraid that the Judges really do like, or some of them, their progress through the little towns." (letter to Coleridge 20 July 1925).

But Judges went on visiting these towns, not (for the most part) because they enjoyed the holiday, but because any change to the system was met by a stream of protest to Parliament[84] from the town affected and vociferous opposition from the profession.

But what was more significant was that the opportunity of creating a rational system was lost.[85] For example, in 1925, Aberystwyth offered to build new law courts with a view to it becoming a centre for mid Wales, given the fact that it had the Welsh law school; this appealed to some with nationalist sentiments;[86] furthermore, as it would have been a centre covering parts of both the Northern and Southern divisions of the Circuit, it would have forced the union of the Circuit[87]. However, the neighbouring towns and districts opposed this vociferously and the proposal was lost. Much the same happened in the other three committees in the 1930s;[88] the opposition was the same parochialism, reform was defeated and Wales suffered.

---

[84] Lord Hailsham's description as recorded by Artemus Jones (Written statement of evidence to the Peel Commission 22 March 1935)

[85] There were suggestions canvassed in the discussions in the Rigby Swift Committee and thereafter that consideration be given to centres other than the traditional assize towns – Bangor, Wrexham, Colwyn Bay, Rhyl, Llandrindod and Aberystwyth.

[86] Letter Artemus Jones to Schuster 27 February 1925 (PRO LCO 2/690). He reported that Ernest Evans MP (see below) had made clear his view of treating the matter as an issue for Wales and not the bar of the circuit. Artemus Jones' views were repeated in an article in the Welsh Gazette on 26 March 1925 which was based on an his paper in the *Welsh Outlook* in May 1925; the article bemoaned the death of W. Llewellyn Williams and the lack of vision:

> "It is idle to denounce the [Rigby Swift] Committee as animated by a desire to rob Dolgellau or Ruthin or Lampeter or Presteign of the glory of its Assizes, or as inflicting a grevious hardship upon the poor litigant dwelling on the uplands of Cardigan or Merioneth or Denbigh or Cardigan or Radnor. Dolgellau is, no doubt, a very important place and so likewise is Lampeter. … It is equally true that Wales is more important than any of them."

Aberystwyth was proposed in a memorandum by the Hon. Stephen Coleridge, Clerk of Assizes of the South Wales Circuit, in a memorandum to Sir Claud Schuster on 11 December 1924. (PRO LCO2/ 690). Aberystwyth was seen as a good centre in the evidence to the Peel Commission: see for example, McKinnon J (Appendix) and Artemus Jones (2603).

[87] See letter 27 March 1925, Coleridge to Sir Claud Schuster (PRO LCO 2/690).

[88] In 1932, the Committee established by Lord Sankey, by then the Lord Chancellor, under the chairmanship of the Master of the Rolls, Lord Hanworth, dealt with the

The Welsh language and the institutions of justice

However, on the fourth issue in which Wales featured in these reports of the inter war years – the Welsh language - the position was quite different.

Since the final controversy over the County Court judges in 1892, the departments in Whitehall had adopted a more pragmatic approach to the use of Welsh in the Courts. For example, in 1911,[89] as a result of pressure from W Llewellyn Williams, HM Treasury, no doubt with the sympathy of the then Chancellor, agreed that the cost of interpreters would be defrayed out of public funds for all civil cases[90] at Assizes in Wales and Monmouthshire.[91] It was a partial recognition of the distinct status of Welsh, for the usual practice was for parties to defray the expense of interpreters.[92]

The formalities of taking the oath were generally[93] dealt with by handing the so called "monoglot Welshman" a card on which there was a Welsh

---

Circuits its second interim report (Cmd 4471). A Royal Commission followed under the Chairmanship of Earl Peel which recommended much the same (Cmd 5056). Finally in 1936, the Circuit Towns Committee under Finlay J made similar, but less radical proposals (Cmd 5252).

[89] Letter from the Treasury to the Lord Chancellor, 13 December 1911 (PRO LCO 2/4420.

[90] In criminal cases, the court had had power since 1858 to make an allowance for an interpreter and to charge it to the county authorities: see a letter to Sir K Muir McKenzie, Permanent Secretary at the Lord Chancellor's Department, 3 August 1911(PRO LCO 2/4420).

[91]Litigants in South Wales, unlike North Wales, never got the benefit of this practice; see the exchange of correspondence between Sir Claud Schuster and John Morgan, Clerk of Assize of the South Wales Circuit, in July 1942 (PRO LCO 2/ 4420). By 1927, the practice seems to have been abandoned as para. 201 of the Report of the Departmental Committee on Welsh in Education and Life, referred to below, records that the parties had to pay for interpreters in civil cases at Assizes.

[92] The correspondence deals with the position at Quarter Sessions and the Magistrates Courts (see PRO LCO2/4418); the consensus was that there was not so much of a problem and where there were costs, these should be borne by the local authorities. In the County Courts the Treasury had paid interpreters' fees in those rare cases where the Judge had not understood Welsh or a court official could not interpret.

[93] This practice was questioned by Daniel Lleufer Thomas in 1923– see below. It was not always followed; for example, in the Pontardawe Magistrates Court, the witness had the oath dictated to him by an interpreter in Welsh and repeated it after him (see letter from J.W.N. Thorpe, Clerk to the Swansea Justices on 18 June 1923). (PRO LCO 2/4420)

translation which he could then read out without the need for the oath to be translated, or, if he could not read, the oath was administered in Welsh by the interpreter.[94] In the County Court, as the Judges were generally bilingual, cases were tried in Welsh.[95] So too in the Magistrates' Courts in much of North and West Wales,[96] though not at Quarter Sessions or Assizes.[97]

But none of this was statutory and the strict position was governed by the language clause of the Act of Union.[98] During the premiership of Lloyd George[99] no change was made. However on 21 February 1923, Daniel Lleufer Thomas,[100] then the Stipendiary magistrate for Pontypridd and the

---

94 This was the practice at the Assizes; see correspondence in July 1923 between Sir Claud Schuster and Sir Ernley Blackwell (PRO LCO 2/4420).

95 See for example the evidence to the Peel Commission: Ithel Davies (5003); Moelwyn Hughes (5018); see also paragraph 202 of the Report of the Departmental Committee on Welsh in Education and Life, 1927 (see below)

96 See an undated memorandum by Professor Hughes Parry and Sir T. Artemus Jones KC submitted in relation to Clerks to the Justices (Artemus Jones' papers, Bangor). The Clerk to the Justices also often acted as interpreter; the memorandum deplored the practice of using a policeman as interpreter.

97 This was the conclusion of the Departmental Committee on Welsh in Education and Life (1927).

98 There was some controversy in the 1930s as to whether the clause had been repealed and replaced by a provision in a 1731 Act (6 Geo ii c 14. ss. 1-3) and by the 1746 Act (20 Geo 2 c 42) which declared that where England was mentioned in an Act of Parliament it should be deemed to include Wales and the town of Berwick upon Tweed; see the memorandum of Artemus Jones to Sir Claud Schuster 24 March 1936(PRO LCO 2/4418) and the memorandum by Professor David Hughes Parry sent to Sir Claud Schuster in January 1939. (PRO LCO 2/4419). For a discussion of the effect, see Andrews and Henshaw: *The Welsh Language in the Courts* (1984) p 1-2.

99 In 1942, the Home Secretary asked a delegation from the Welsh National Party why no change was made; he was told that it had been raised during the premiership of Lloyd George, but not pressed as it became mixed up with the question of Home Rule for Wales (PRO LCO 2/4419)

100 Sir Daniel Lleufer Thomas was one of the original members of the *Cymdeithas Dafydd ap Gwilym* and at the first meeting of the *Cymru Fydd* Society in London proposed a motion for home rule. He was called to the bar in 1889 and joined the South Wales Circuit; he was secretary to the Welsh Land Commission and from 1897-1909 he practised at the Bar at Swansea. He played an important part in the establishment of the National Library and many other aspects of Welsh life. From 1909 to 1933 he was the stipendiary magistrate for Pontypridd and Rhondda and sat frequently as a deputy county court judge. He became incapacitated in 1932 and died in 1940.

Rhondda, gave a decision that the oath could only be taken in Welsh through an interpreter, clearly intending to initiate the need for a change to the law.[101] Parliamentary questions followed,[102] but nothing else.

In 1927, the Departmental Committee on Welsh in Education and Life[103], undoubtedly at the instigation of Lleufer Thomas as one of its members, went beyond the strict remit of its terms of reference. It called for the repeal of the Language Clause of the Act of Union and provision for oaths to be taken in Welsh in a manner of equal statutory authority with the English forms and for interpreters at the expense of the state.[104] Consideration was given to trying to alter the report to delete these recommendations, but the view of the President of the Board of Education expressed to the Lord Chancellor was that:

> Any alteration in the Report of this kind would be sure to leak out and the matter would then excite a great deal more attention and controversy than it would if the Report is published as it stands. I hope, therefore, that you will be willing to let matters take their own course[105]

---

[101] I am grateful to Lord Prys Davies for his considerable assistance with this important event; a more detailed account and the action taken by Lleufer Thomas is at pp 220-2 of Lord Prys Davies' chapter entitled 'The Legal Status of the Welsh Language in the Twentieth Century' in *Let's do our best for our Ancient Tongue: the Welsh Language in Twentieth Century* (published in 2000 shortly after this lecture was given)

[102] Although the Home Secretary stated in February 1923 in answer to Major William Cope MP that the ruling was correct in law (Hansard 3rd ser. Vol 209, col 1648), Sir Claud Schuster questioned this; he stated that if the law was as had been stated, the Lord Chancellor was of the view the law ought to be amended: see the correspondence in May 1923 between Sir Claud Schuster and Sir Ernley Blackwell, Legal Assistant Under Secretary of State at the Home Office. Sir Claud was in favour of the pragmatic approach of allowing the then current practice to continue (PRO LCO 2/4420).

[103] The Departmental Committee had been appointed by Baldwin on 23 March 1925 and was chaired by the Bishop of St David's; paragraphs 196-203 set out the Committee's view on the current status of the use of Welsh in legal proceedings.

[104] Recommendations 70-72. Daniel Lleufer Thomas played a prominent role in securing the inclusion of there recommendations which set out the views he had expressed in letters he had written to the *Western Mail* after his decision of 21 February 1923.

[105] Letter dated 18 July 1927 (PRO LCO 2/4418).

However, although questions were again raised in Parliament,[106] nothing happened until the Royal Commission was appointed in 1934 under the chairmanship of Earl Peel.

That Commission had been appointed to examine speeding up the work of the courts; the towns at which courts should be held in Wales were high on the agenda. At its third meeting,[107] one of the Commissioners, Clement Davies KC, MP[108] spoke of the need for radical reform of the system and made the point that there would be strong efforts to keep Wales separate because of the language difficulty. He told his fellow Commissioners he wanted Sir Thomas Artemus Jones KC, by then the County Court Judge for North Wales, to give evidence.[109]

Artemus Jones[110] was a man of considerable vision; that is not only because he was instrumental in ensuring that a very eminent new silk, John William Morris, became in due course chairman of Caernarfon Quarter

---

[106] The matter was raised on 14 and 23 February 1928. For the background, see the memorandum of Sir Ernley Blackwell to Sir Claud Schuster sent under cover of a letter dated 12 April 1929 and other correspondence between the Board of Education and the Lord Chancellor's Department (PRO LCO 2/4418). Sir Ernley saw in the report's recommendations the danger of "ardent" Welshmen who were perfectly capable of using English insisting on taking the oath and then giving evidence in Welsh. See further Lord Prys Davies, supra, at pp 222.

[107] 10 January 1935; minutes in LCO 2/1614

[108] For an account of his life see: Lord Hooson QC: 'Clement Davies: An Underestimated Welshman and Politician', 1997 *Transactions of the Cymmrodorion Society* Vol 4 N.S. 168; see especially p 183-4 for his belief in the need for a Welsh Parliament where the Welsh language would have the same standing as English.

[109] Letter Clement Davies to Artemus Jones 11 January 1935 (Artemus Jones Bangor Papers).

[110] He was born in Denbigh and left school before the age of 16. He became a reporter on a local paper. He was called to the bar in 1901, joined "the Welsh Circuit (Northern Division)" in 1902. He took silk in 1919 and became Leader of the North Wales Circuit and Deputy Chairman of Caernarfonshire Quarter Sessions. He was appointed County Court Judge for North Wales in 1930. He had contested parliamentary seats for the Liberals (and was selected in 1913 to fight Merthyr against Keir Hardie). He served on the Anglo-Mexican Claims Commission 1928-29. He died in 1943. Some of his lectures and essays are collected together and published under the title *Without My Wig* (Brython Press Liverpool 1944). He wrote a number of articles on the judicial system in Wales which were published in *The Welsh Outlook.*

Sessions,[111] but he had a deep understanding of the law in Wales, its language and what was practicable.

Artemus Jones' evidence, particularly that skilfully led by Clement Davies, pointed out how the Welsh circuit differed from all other circuits because regard had to be paid to national feeling[112] and to the Welsh language; it was a time when over 800,000 spoke Welsh as their first language and 97,000 could speak only Welsh.[113] It was suggested that all Welsh speaking parts should be brought together into a single circuit, including Monmouthshire and excluding Chester. Another Welsh speaking county court Judge, Judge H.W. Samuel KC,[114] similarly guided by Clement Davies agreed. They thus revived the proposal of Marlay Sampson put forward in 1921, but underpinned his view of national sentiment with the role of the Welsh language as delineating national identity.[115]

But the evidence went further.[116] Artemus Jones pointed out the

---

[111] See the correspondence in 1939 between Artemus Jones and J.W. Morris KC (Artemus Jones papers at Bangor). As J.W. Morris explained, he satisfied the resident requirement as his father had "a small house at Borth-y-Gest, Portmadoc, where he goes between about Easter and about October and for many years I have been going there during Easter, Whitsuntide and the Long Vacations".

[112] Clement Davies led other witnesses in the same way; see for example Ernest Evans MP (5288-5299)

[113] Figures from 1931 census; in 1891 30 per cent of the population were monoglot Welsh speakers and 54 per cent spoke Welsh.

[114] He was called to the bar and practised at Swansea; he took silk in 1931. He was Labour MP for Swansea West 1923-4 and 1929-31. He was Recorder of Merthyr 1930-1933. He was appointed County Court Judge of the Mid Wales Circuit (No. 28) in 1933 and was also Chairman of Radnorshire QS. He died in 1953.

[115] The evidence was that on the right bank of the Usk a considerable amount of Welsh was spoken. Lord Atkin thought that Wales ought to be one unit, though with only the part of Monmouthshire on the right bank of the Usk added to it. (3463). However, the Town Clerk of Newport wrote to the Commission to say that this was "misleading and inaccurate"; no person since 1870 (whether litigant or witness), had asked to give evidence in Welsh at the Monmouth Assizes. (PRO LCO2/1612, Part 3.)

[116] There was an opposite view: Roland Vaughan Williams KC said:

> "With all respect I do not think that the promotion of the Welsh language is a matter which has to be considered except in so far as the Welsh language requires an interpreter in the Courts. But I should very much deprecate going on the wider lines of nationality when you are considering a strictly juridical problem."

grievances that existed because Welsh was not treated on a basis of equality with English; that there was "the studied disregard" of the Welsh language by the High Court; that there were the difficulties that were encountered with trials at Quarter Sessions.[117] The dilemma of empanelling Welsh jurors who did not understand English had been highlighted by a decision of the Privy Council which had quashed a conviction in India because one of the jurors had not understood the language of the trial.[118]

The publication of the evidence of these two distinguished Welsh judges had an immediate effect.[119] A National Committee was formed, a National Petition prepared calling for English and Welsh to be placed on an equal footing in the courts, that there be a Welsh Circuit including Monmouthshire, that the judges and officials should be bilingual and the jurisdiction of the County Court should be extended in Wales. This was presented to the Peel Commission and impressive evidence given in support;[120] the Welsh Parliamentary Party (the body comprising all the members of Parliament

---

[117] For example, at trial at Caernarfonshire Quarter Sessions of a monoglot Welshman in September 1933 all the jurors took the oath in Welsh, all the witnesses were Welsh speaking and the advocates and Chairman (The Rt Hon David Lloyd George MP) bilingual. The trial could not proceed in Welsh because the shorthand writer was a monoglot Englishman. Furthermore the record for the Court of Appeal had to be in English (This was also true in the County Courts where a Judge conducting a trial in Welsh had to make his note in English in case there was an appeal). This problem was resolved by the Lord Chief Justice insisting that the evidence be translated into English and recorded in English: see the letter from Sir Claud Schuster to Sylvester, 6 March 1936 (PRO LCO/2 4418).

[118] *Lal* v *The King–Emperor* [1934] WN 207. In contrast, the Court of Criminal Appeal had refused to admit evidence from two Welsh speaking jurors who had sat on a jury at Merioneth Quarter Sessions to the effect that they had not understood English sufficiently to follow the evidence (*R* v *Thomas* [1933] 2 KB 489. This decision was criticised by Lord Atkin in the Privy Council in *Lal*.

[119] See the Minutes of Evidence of the Peel Commission, Day 25 (28 June 1935)

[120] When it was presented to the Commission on 28 June 1935, the Chairman asked how they related the recommendation that English and Welsh be placed on an equal footing with an enquiry into the despatch of business in the King's Bench Division. The answer was that in Wales the business at common law would be more satisfactorily carried out and the Welsh would look up to the administration of the law with even greater respect than they presently did (4998). The discussion before the Commission was comprehensive and addressed difficult topics such as to the language to be used where one party wanted English and the other Welsh and what

who represented constituencies in Wales and Monmouthshire), though ardently advocating the parochial view that a Judge needed to visit each of the existing towns, broadly supported the Petition.[121]

These requests linking the administration of justice with national identity and the Welsh language were considered in the Peel Commission's report published in January 1936; as to national identity, it recommended that there be one Welsh Circuit without divisions; that it might be desirable that it include Monmouthshire and exclude Chester.[122] These recommendations were subsequently considered by yet another committee – the Circuit Towns Committee in 1936. Although it supported the ending of the division of the Welsh Circuit, it recommended against any other significant change. The one Welsh Member, Morgan Jones MP,[123] who had led the delegation that had presented the National Petition on the language signed the report reluctantly;[124] he had favoured the proposals for a Welsh Circuit with

---

was to happen before the Court of Appeal which would be English speaking (See the minutes of evidence of 28 June 1935).

[121] See the evidence of Ernest Evans MP (a barrister who practised on the South Wales Circuit – see below) and Sir William Jenkins MP, 5 July 1935. There was also support from well known solicitors such as Cyril Jones in Wrexham and William George of Cricieth; the evidence of William George was particularly critical of the High Court's treatment of Welsh. The Advisory Board of Law of the University of Wales (which had considered the matter at the request of the Court of the University of Wales) also supported this as well as the inclusion of the whole of Wales and Monmouthshire in one circuit, though it advocated that there be no change to the circuit towns.

[122] Para 136. The minutes of 26 May 1935 (PRO LCO 2/1614) show that they were much more committed to the transfer of Monmouthshire at an earlier stage. However, such a transfer was strongly opposed by the Monmouthshire and Newport Councils; the latter saw it as involving a loss of prestige to Newport and an addition to the prestige of its keenest competitor, Cardiff. They were supported by the Bar mess of the South Wales division of the Circuit (see the evidence of its leader, Roland Vaughan Williams KC). A leader of the North Wales Bar (Ralph Sutton KC) was fiercely opposed to the transfer of Chester which he described as a centre for Welsh work, not only from the point of view of the bar but also of Welsh litigants (4790); he was supported by Roland Vaughan Williams KC (4836)

[123] He was a teacher born in Glamorgan. He was Labour MP for Caerphilly from 1921 until his death in 1939. He was Parliamentary Secretary to the Board of Education 1924 and 1929-31. He was Chairman of the Public Accounts Committee 1931-38.

[124] His dissent stated (Cmd 5262):

"In signing the Report, I desire to say that I would have liked to have seen a re-

Monmouthshire and without Chester, but concluded that the evidence given to them was against it.[125] That evidence included for example representatives from the Chester and North Wales Law Society who produced statistics which showed it was very convenient for the people of North Wales to have their cases tried at Chester; that a formidable number of Welsh bodies met at Chester; that a Welsh speaking litigant or prisoner was at no disadvantage in Chester because he could always have an interpreter.[126] The result was that, although in 1945 the two divisions of the Welsh Circuit were amalgamated and the Welsh Circuit re-named the "Wales and Chester Circuit", the boundaries were essentially unchanged[127] and Monmouthshire was not brought within the Circuit.

More significant, however, for the longer term were the Peel Commission's recommendations that court officials should be bilingual and

---

arrangement effected in relation to Chester and Newport. With the recommendation for the amalgamation of the North and South Wales Circuits, I would have preferred to see Chester attached to either the Oxford or Northern circuit and Newport transferred to the Welsh circuit. But I confess that the evidence given was wholly against that idea. In the circumstances, I have felt bound to acquiesce in the retention of the present arrangements."

125 The main oral witnesses were the Town Clerk of Chester and Mr Trevor Roberts (of Caernarfon) on behalf of the Chester and North Wales Law Society, R.M. Montgomery KC, Recorder of Chester (1926-48) and Leader of the North Wales and Chester Circuit and Roland Vaughan Williams KC, leader of the South Wales Circuit (evidence 28 May 1936); Sir Henry Mather Jackson, the Mayor of Monmouth, the Governor of Cardiff Prison, St John Micklethwait KC (Oxford Circuit), H.S. Lynne (on behalf of the Monmouthshire Law Society), Alderman Moxon of Newport, Alderman Harries of the Monmouthshire County Council (19 June 1936) and Judge Austin Jones (3 July 1936) (see PRO LCO2/1168-1170)

126 They dismissed the claims of Wrexham which had made a powerful case as an alternative centre; see PRO LCO/2 1168 (see the letters from the Town Clerk of Wrexham dated 18 April 1936 and 23 May 1936 and from the Wrexham Leader dated 20 May 1936); Wrexham's claims were fiercely opposed by the other towns in Denbighshire and Flintshire.

127 Commissions of Assize had always been issued by the Lord Chancellor's Department referring to it as the "Wales and Chester Circuit" (see the letter R. Rieu to the Lord Chief Justice 7 March 1945 PRO LCO 2/4461). The Lord Chief Justice approved of the name; "It has the merit of being the old style &, I think, it is more accurate & dignified than N.& S. Wales Circuit". (letter to Rieu of 8 March 1945, PRO/LCO2/4461)

their hope that in time a bilingual High Court Judge would be appointed.[128]

Whilst these recommendations were being considered, further problems emerged; for example, as a consequence of the Privy Council decision that a verdict would be quashed if a juror could not understand the language of the trial, jurors who could not understand the English oath were asked to step aside.[129] Then in October 1936 Saunders Lewis and two colleagues were tried at the Caernarfon Assizes for arson at the RAF bombing school on the Lleyn peninsula; the jury disagreed, the trial was moved to the Old Bailey by the Lord Chief Justice where convictions were duly obtained.[130]

There can be no doubt that this trial brought about a realisation of the need for change or as was put "recent events have undoubtedly been a shock". Prosecuting counsel in the trial, Wintringham Stable QC, the future Stable J, wrote a memorandum[131] to the Attorney General pointing out "how few Englishmen appreciate the fact that there is in Wales a strong national consciousness" and making clear that there was a grievance that ought to be addressed. His analysis was perceptive, but I do not think the same can be said for his solution. He urged a change in the way in which the assizes were conducted:

> "The Kings' Commission is read only in English and often to an audience who do not understand what it is about. No mention of Wales is made and in the entire ceremonial the existence of such a place as Wales is ignored. Emphasis is laid on

---

[128] Para. 133-4. In a separate memorandum published with the Report (Cmd 5065), Clement Davies went further and said that all Chairmen of Quarter Sessions and Recorders in Wales should be bilingual and capable of conducting trials in Welsh. In 1938, s. 1 of the Administration of Justice Act 1938 provided that the Lord Chancellor was to take into account representations made in respect of the appointment of Chairmen of Quarter Sessions as to the ability to speak Welsh

[129] At the request of David Lloyd George MP, Artemus Jones had considered the wider implications of these decisions and the question which had arisen at Caernarfon Quarter Sessions in 1933; on 24 March 1936, he submitted a detailed memorandum to Lloyd George with a copy to Sir Claud Schuster; it met with a very sympathetic response from Schuster (PRO LCO 2/4419).

[130] For the background see: John Davies, supra, p 591-593; K.O. Morgan: *Wales 1880 –1980* p 253-6; Dafydd Jenkins: *A Nation on Trial: Penyberth, 1936.*

[131] 14 January 1937 (PRO LCO 2/1227); I am indebted to His Honour Dewi Watkin Powell for his assistance in identifying the author of this document. Stable had taken silk in 1935 and was appointed a High Court Judge in 1938; he retired in 1968. He was Chairman of Montgomery QS from 1944. He died in 1977.

> the fact that the Lord Chief Justice is Lord Chief Justice of England. In the course of the proceedings, a good deal is heard about the law of England."

He went on to suggest that "the whole thing could be put right by a little imagination involving a few trifling alterations".[132]

But the contribution of others was more significant. Efforts went on to try and secure legislation; in 1937, Ernest Evans,[133] supported by Clement Davies, introduced a bill to enable Welsh to be used in the courts as of right and to prevent the removal of cases from Wales; it failed on the second reading.[134] At the Cardiff Eisteddfod in August 1938, the better known Welsh National Petition[135] was launched; in 1941 it was presented to Parliament. Behind the scenes Artemus Jones assisted by Professor David Hughes Parry[136] maintained a close dialogue[137] with a sympathetic Sir Claud Schuster; his view, as expressed to the Attorney General, was that there was

---

[132] He expressed strong opposition to the creation of a separate Welsh judiciary. He also went on to make practical suggestions as to the increased role of the Crown in Wales

[133] He was educated at Aberystwyth and Cambridge where he was President of the Union. He was called to the bar in 1910 and practised on the South Wales Circuit, taking silk in 1937. He was Private Secretary to Lloyd George 1918-1920 and Liberal MP for Cardiganshire 1921-1923 (after defeating W. Llewellyn Williams) and for the University of Wales 1924-1942. He succeeded Artemus Jones as County Court Judge of the North Wales Circuit (No.29) in 1942 and retired in 1957. He was also Chairman of Anglesey QS and Cardiganshire QS. He died in 1965.

[134] Bill No 23 of 1937. The second reading was on 26 February 1937. In moving the second reading, Ernest Evans said:

> "All I will add, in conclusion, is that the Welsh people are deeply conscious of their own distinctive nationality and are proud of it. They feel that the existing legislation casts a slur upon their nationhood and they appeal to the British Parliament to remove that reproach."

The bill was strongly opposed by the Attorney General, Sir Donald Somervell, though in a letter to the Lord Chancellor on 1 June 1942 (PRO LCO 2/4419), he said he had at the time supported the repeal of the Welsh language clause of the Act of Union.

[135] Amongst its patrons were Lloyd George, Viscount Sankey, the Archbishop of Wales, Clement Davies, Aneurin Bevan, Morgan Jones and a large number of other Welsh MPs. See the Hughes Parry Report (Cmnd 2785) para 40; Andrews and Henshaw: *The Welsh Language in the Courts*, Aberystwyth 1984; J Graham Jones: 'The National Petition on the Legal status of the Welsh Language 1938-42', 15 *Welsh History Review* 92

[136] He had become Professor of English Law in London in 1930, a post in which he held until 1959; he was Director of the Institute of Advance Legal Studies 1947-59.

a real grievance that had to be remedied.[138] They had the strong support of David Lloyd George MP.[139] However, it was the supervening effect of war that was the final catalyst that brought the increasingly effective campaign for change to a conclusion; for example, in wartime Britain, when allied courts existed where the Dutch and Norwegians were tried in their own language, could this be denied to the Welsh?[140] In the early summer of 1942,[141] a bill was drafted and passed in October 1942. But the wartime

---

He held a large number of very distinguished academic positions including the Hamlyn Lectureship; he was Deputy Chairman of Caernarfonshire QS 1950-1966. In 1965 he chaired the Committee that produced the report on The Legal Status of the Welsh Language (see below). He died in 1973.

[137] After the memorandum of 24 March 1936, Artemus Jones had kept in close contact with Schuster. In January 1939, Hughes Parry, after consultation with Artemus Jones, produced a succinct and powerful memorandum which he sent to Schuster on 26 January 1939 seeking "a measure of official recognition" for the Welsh language and setting out what he described as the National and the Legal reasons for change; referring to those whose native language was Welsh:

> "These (many of them steeped in the culture of their own race) feel a sense of indignity and humiliation when they are debarred from expressing themselves in their mother tongue on their native soil. They are aggrieved in that they are treated as foreigners in the Law Courts of their own King."

This memorandum was discussed at a meeting on 30 January 1939: see note of meeting between Sir Claud Schuster, Artemus Jones and Professor David Hughes Parry (PRO LCO2/4419). For a more detailed account see Lord Prys Davies, supra, pp 227-232.

[138] Letter Sir Claud Schuster to Sir Donald Somervell, A-G, 2 February 1939 commenting on a memorandum from Sir John Stainton (Second Parliamentary Counsel to the Treasury) which argued for the *status quo* of treating Welsh like any other foreign language.(PRO LCO 2/4419); see also Sir Claud Schuster's Memorandum to the Lord Chancellor of 10 February 1942 (PRO LCO 2/4419).

[139] He also played a crucial role in securing the passage of the 1942 Act: see Lord Prys-Davies, supra, at pp 231-2.

[140] See for example the memorandum of a meeting between the Home Secretary and a deputation of the Welsh Parliamentary Party on 4 February 1942 and the memorandum of a further meeting on 18 March 1942. (PRO LCO 2/4419). Moreover the War Cabinet had laid down a policy that not only was an effort to be made to include representatives of Wales on committees, but also to permit soldiers to send and receive letters in Welsh. (PRO LCO 2/4419).

[141] A first draft was prepared by Viscount Simon, the Lord Chancellor, (who described himself as half Welsh) on 28 May 1942 after seeing a delegation of Welsh MPs on 14

conditions that had brought about its enactment were used to justify its limited scope.[142] It did not place Welsh on an equal footing with English,[143] but it did repeal the language clause and did provide for subordinate legislation prescribing forms of oaths in Welsh and for the payment of interpreters at the expense of the state.

Those prescribed form of oaths[144] still have statutory force. Sir Claud Schuster stipulated that they should "approximate more closely to the common speech of the people than to classical Welsh".[145] He entrusted this

---

May 1942. (PRO LCO 2/4419). In commenting on the draft, Sir Granville Ram, Parliamentary Counsel, concluded by stating:

> "I hope we shall not reach the point at which all statutes must be bilingual, the Welsh and English texts being of equal validity!"

[142] It only permitted Welsh to be used by a party or witness "who considers that he would otherwise be at any disadvantage by reason of his natural language of communication being Welsh". There was strong opposition from some even to this limited measure. For example, the Associated Law Societies of Wales passed a resolution on 11 April 1942 which stated:

> "That this Association desires to protest most strongly against a matter of this kind being brought forward in time of war."

This was sent to Sir Claud Schuster on 28 April 1942 (PRP LCO 2/4419) with a protest at the revolutionary and far reaching change proposed.

[143] Equality was what the Welsh Parliamentary Party had sought; a statement of their seven main proposals was discussed with Schuster and Maxwell on 18 March 1942 (PRO LCO 2/4419; these included:

> "1. The Welsh language shall be placed on a basis of equality with the English Language in all courts of law in Wales. ….
>
> 3.All formal documents used or required for any proceedings in any Court of Law in Wales.. shall be printed or issued in the Welsh as well as the English language.
>
> 4. All litigants shall have the right to have their case, if they so desire, conducted in any court in Wales … in the Welsh Language. …
>
> 6. Whilst not pressing at this juncture for a translation into Welsh of the present statutes, it is urged that all new enactments shall be translated into and published in Welsh, and the Welsh version shall have equal authority with the English".

[144] The Welsh Courts Oaths and Interpreters Rules 1943 (1943 SI 683). When the Lord Chief Justice, Viscount Caldecotte, was asked to approve the Order, he commented in a letter to Sir Claud Schuster of 12 April 1943 (PRO LCO 2/4422):

> "It is of course a foreign language to me and, to tell you the truth, I do not know that I feel very sympathetic to this plan for keeping alive what, like Erse and Gaelic, is really a dying language."

[145] Letter dated 25 November 1942 (PRO LCO 2/4422). He may have been influenced

task to Louis Jones, Registrar of the Wrexham County Court, who assembled a small team comprising his wife (a fellow in Welsh of the University of Wales) his former articled clerk, J. Iorwerth Williams who had a first class degree in Welsh[146] and Professor Ifor Williams FBA,[147] Professor of Welsh at Bangor. The new forms were then approved by three Judges – Judges Samuel, Clark Williams[148] and Ernest Evans[149]. This team was the necessary and powerful combination of linguists and lawyers of high distinction. An illustration of their approach can be found in their consideration of the word felony; consideration was given to the use of the term *"Drwg-weithred"* (evil deed), but Louis Jones thought that this was inadequate for a word that had borne a distinct legal meaning for centuries; he therefore adopted at the suggestion of Professor Williams a Welsh form of *"ffeloni"* which met with approval from the three judges. He explained to the Lord Chancellor's Department:[150]

---

to this view by a letter from the Welsh speaking Clerk of Assize, John Morgan who pointed out the problems that had arisen in his experience. In his letter of 9 November 1942, one of the illustrations he used was the following:

"The advent of industry seems to have caught the Welsh language napping. English words, pronounced in a Welsh way, are constantly used in industry by all concerned, not concurrently or even promiscuously with, but to the exclusion of, the Welsh equivalents. Instances are: truck, tram (called dram), rails, sprags, haulier, rider, repairer, fireman, manager, tin, steel, ingots, shearer, annealer, etc etc. To one who has made Welsh his special study there are Welsh equivalents, but if these words were put to a witness in approved Welsh on the spur of the moment (or to me) there would, I fear, be a little flustering even among those of us who are fluent, although not scholarly, in Welsh."

[146] He was a solicitor in Oswestry and a Clements Inn Prizeman and Scott Scholar.

[147] Sir Ifor Williams (as he became in 1947) was Professor of Welsh Language and Literature at Bangor 1929-1947. He became FBA in 1938 and was Chairman of the Board of Celtic Studies 1941-1958. He died in 1965.

[148] Sir George Clark Williams (as he became when made a baronet in 1955) qualified as a solicitor and practised at Llanelli until 1908. He was called to the bar in 1909 and joined the South Wales Circuit. He took silk in 1934. He was County Court Judge for Glamorgan (Circuit No.30) from 1935-1948. He was Lord-Lieutenant of Carmarthenshire 1949-1953. He was a Life Governor of the University of Wales, Aberystwyth and Vice-President of the University of Wales, Swansea. He died in 1958.

[149] The MP who had tried to introduce the bill in 1937 about the use of Welsh and the removal of cases from Wales.

[150] Letter to Sir George Coldstream 12 January 1943 (PRO LCO 2/4422)

> The fact that the English word is borrowed from the French justifies borrowing it for the purpose of the Welsh language also. Welsh people use *ffelwn* for a whitlow and it is interesting to note that the following is given in the pocket Oxford Dictionary: "Felon: One who has committed a felony; small abscess, especially near the nail.

The changes of the 1960s: The Welsh Language Act 1967 and the Beeching Commission

There was little change thereafter as regards the status of the language or the courts in Wales until the 1960s. However the changes that occurred then, govern our position today on these matters.

First the Welsh language. I can deal more briefly with this as the position is well known. The decisions in the 1960s the Ammanford Election case[151] and *Merthyr Tydfil Justices*[152] case made clear the limited scope of the 1942 Act; in the last of these Widgery J stated that the only benefit which the 1942 Act gave was to enable an individual to use Welsh if he was at a disadvantage in expression if he was required to use English. That apart,

> the language difficulties which arise in Wales can be dealt with in exactly the same way as language difficulties at the Central Criminal Court where the accused is a Pole.

In July 1963,[153] Professor Hughes Parry, by then Sir David Hughes Parry QC was appointed to chair a committee to examine the legal status of the language and the Report in October 1965[154] recommended the principle of equal validity with the objective of raising the status of Welsh to one of equality with English. The Welsh Language Act 1967 saw the implementation of this principle, subject to qualifications, with respect to the

---

[151] *Evans* v *Thomas* [1962] 2 QB 350.
[152] *R* v *Merthyr Tydfil Justices* ex p *Jenkins* [1967] 1 All ER 636; see Andrews and Henshaw p 14-15; Robyn Léwis *Cyfiawnder Dwyiethiog* (1998), Gomer, p 67-71.
[153] For the background to the appointment: see Lord Prys Davies, supra, pp 236-239.
[154] Legal Status of the Welsh Language (Cmnd 2785), October 1965. The other members were Professor Glanmor Williams (Professor of History at Swansea) and D.W. Jones-Williams M.C.

administration of justice.[155] The basic principle has been re-enacted in the Welsh Language Act 1993 in terms that both languages must be treated on the basis of equality in the administration of justice; the 1993 Act governs our position today.[156]

As to the administration of justice in Wales,[157] little had been done. Lord Evershed's Committee on Civil Procedure (1949-53)[158] revisited the 1892 resolutions of the judges, but did not recommend any real change; its view was London centric:

> England is a small country and London is accessible from its remotest parts. The bar is organised in the four Inns of Court, the barristers practising in the Supreme Court having for the most part their chambers in the [Inns].

Radical change came under the Royal Commission chaired by Lord Beeching which was appointed in 1966. Unlike the previous committees and

---

155 It also recommended that all the chairmen of QS (or one of their deputies) should be Welsh speaking and they concurred with the view expressed to them that it was highly desirable that the County Court Judges and Magistrates for West, Mid and North Wales should be Welsh speaking (para 200-1). "In Cardiff, Swansea and Glamorgan while a bilingual judge might not be necessary, it would be very desirable that he should be conversant with both languages". They also urged the use of language courses (para 196-199).

156 In 1973, Edmund Davies LJ made a report to the Lord Chancellor on the operation of the Welsh Language Act 1967; it is summarised at Hansard HL Vol 343 col 534 (12 June 1973), but the full report has never been published; he commented that the capacity of some judges to preside over trials would be improved by courses "recently arranged by the University College of Aberystwyth". There is a very useful discussion of the effects of and reaction to the Act in Andrews and Henshaw at p 28-70, including a valuable survey made in 1981. The position in relation to public administration was brought up to date in 1995 by the Report under the Chairmanship of Lord Prys Davies: *The Report of the Panel for Official Welsh.* For some information on the extent of use of Welsh in the courts, see p 20 of my paper on *The Legal Implications of Welsh Devolution* delivered at the first conference of UK Judges in April 1999 and published in *Devolution in Wales: Public Law and the National Assembly* (ed Miers, Cardiff 1999) published by the Wales Public Law and Human Rights Assn.

157 An Interdepartmental Committee under Streatfield J (Cmnd 1289) reported in December 1960 and made some recommendations to improve criminal justice; Sir David Hughes Parry QC was a member.

158 Interim Report 1949 (Cmd 7764); Second Interim Report 1951 (Cmd 8176); Third Interim Report 1952 (Cmd 8167); Final Report 1953 (Cmd 8878).

commissions, it had no Welsh member; this was raised by Emlyn Hooson QC in a parliamentary question. As was acknowledged by the Lord Chancellor's Department in a note prepared to supplement the answer to be given, it was appreciated that Wales would be affected as, of the 29 Assize towns with a population of under 50,000 and likely to be affected, 11 were in the 13 Welsh counties; the only member who had even the slightest connection with Wales was Sir Andrew Wheatley, but that was no more than being an assistant solicitor with the Pembrokeshire County Council for two years in the 1930s.[159]

A substantial body of written evidence was submitted to it from Wales, including a very powerful submission from the bar of the circuit;[160] however, the only oral evidence from Wales came from Lord Merthyr and Arthian Davies LJ; the latter said he thought that the Commissioners knew more about Wales than he did as he had not been to Wales for 6 years; he thought it much more businesslike to send Flintshire cases to Chester; that "the frightful outcry" he had caused by doing this was an example of local obstruction. Two of the Commissioners did make a visit to Cardiff in June 1967; the lack of understanding can be illustrated by an observation about the Welsh language:[161]

> The translation facilities available are deemed quite adequate, and it was my impression that the future structure [of the Courts] need not seriously take into account the language factor.

---

[159] The Prime Minister's Office blamed the Welsh Office for this omission, as it had had an opportunity to make representations before the composition of the Commission was agreed. The Prime Minister was against any change once the membership had been announced (see letter to T.S.Legg at the Lord Chancellor's Department dated 10 November 1966) (PRO LCO7/224). The Lord Chancellor was also against any change.

[160] A detailed historical account was contributed by Professor Hywel Moseley (later Judge Moseley, the first judge who sat permanently in Wales to exercise a Chancery jurisdiction since the abolition of the Courts of Great Session); the remainder was drafted by a committee which included Mars Jones (later Mars Jones J), Ronald Waterhouse (later Waterhouse J), Michael Evans (later Judge Michael Evans) and Dewi Watkin Powell (later Judge Watkin Powell).

[161] Report of the visit to Cardiff on 7 June 1967 (PR0 LCO7/280)

A draft report was prepared by October 1967; it proposed the division of England and Wales into regions with Wales being partitioned between the Northern and the Western Regions of England; only two of the Commissioners objected, including Sir Andrew Wheatley.[162]

A visit was made to Chester and North Wales in February 1968; although the note of that visit concluded[163] with the view that Wales or Wales with Chester should be made a region of its own, it was not to be much of a region; fixed dates for civil cases would be made available only in Liverpool and Bristol. The majority considered there were two solutions to what they called the "Welsh problem":[164]

> The first, which would follow the principles underlying the Commission's recommendations for the rest of the country, would mean attaching north and south Wales to two different regions having administrative centres outside the Principality. The Welsh could continue to be tried in Wales if they wished because High Court judges would visit, say Caernarfon in the north and Cardiff in the south, and second tier judges would operate on circuits in courts within Wales. They would have the option of a fixed date at a court centre outside Wales or they could choose to take their chance locally...... The second and far less satisfactory solution was to regard Wales as a region in itself and Cardiff as a centre serving the whole region, however inconvenient and difficult this might be for the Welsh in the north. This was not a solution that the Commission could properly recommend both because it ran counter to the logical basis of the system that was being recommended for the rest of the country and because it would be costly in judge-power and court staff. The best course would probably be to present the arguments for both alternatives in the Report and let the politicians fight it out.

Their strong inclination therefore was to ignore the national identity of Wales in the administration of justice; in January 1969, members of the Commission met representatives of the circuit to put their views on partitioning Wales to them. It was only then they appreciated the outcry that this would cause. Subsequently strong political pressure was brought to bear; Elwyn Jones, Edmund Davies, Mars Jones, Tasker Watkins, Emlyn

---

[162] See letters of 21 October 1967 and 22 October 1967 (PRO LCO7/230)
[163] PRO LCO7/344
[164] Meeting 30 April 1968 (PRO LCO7/238)

Hooson and Dewi Watkin Powell all played an important role.[165] When the Commissioners signed their report on 4 September 1969, they concluded that, although the Wales and Chester Circuit provided an area which was:

> far from ideal for administrative purposes, ... we have, not without reluctance because of the resulting disadvantages, accepted the evidence put to us that the special circumstances in Wales are such that the Circuit should be treated as a single unit and that it should be administered from Cardiff.

However it did recommend the transfer of Monmouthshire to the Circuit[166] and the retention of a small part of Cheshire to make up the necessary case load and population[167]. The report proposed court centres, apart from the major towns of Cardiff, Swansea and Chester/Mold, at Bangor,[168] Newtown, Dolgellau, Carmarthen, Haverfordwest, Newport and Merthyr. Although it recommended the transfer of control of the courts to the central government,

---

[165] See: Mars Jones J: 'Beeching – Before and after on the Wales and Chester Circuit' 4 *Cambrian Law Review* 81. I am also grateful to Lord Hooson QC and His Honour Dewi Watkin Powell for their assistance in this respect, as these representations are largely undocumented. For example, there were frequent meetings between Elwyn Jones, Edmund Davies and Emlyn Hooson to agree the strategy. Dewi Watkin Powell and Gwynfor Evans MP made representations at a meeting with Derek Oulton, the Secretary to the Commission, and Gwynfor Evans subsequently saw him twice. Derek Oulton, subsequently a Permanent Secretary, became sympathetic to the position of Wales.

[166]Local support was obtained and the bar and solicitors assured that they would in no way be prejudiced by the change.

[167] Very strong pressure was applied to keep Chester within the Circuit, as the view was taken that a strong local bar would not be viable for North Wales without Cheshire; the support of Cheshire was obtained as it wished to prevent its absorption into Liverpool and/or Manchester.

[168] At a meeting with representatives from Wales, the view was expressed by those representing Wales which rejected Caernarfon in favour of Bangor:

> "Bangor is more accessible both to Anglesey and the mainland and is the obvious centre. The courts at Caernarfon would in any case have to be substantially adapted or rebuilt and it would be better to spend the money on buildings at Bangor. There would be an outcry on historical grounds but we were assured that good sense would win the day."

it did recommend local committees to deal with local issues.[169]

The Lord Chancellor accepted these proposals in January 1971, except for the creation of new courts at Bangor. He also included more of Cheshire, but the national identity of the circuit was essentially preserved and augmented. The subsequent legislation implementing this governs the position today.

However the Commission did nothing to remedy the lack of specialist courts in Wales.[170] Any thought of the creation of indigenous institutions in Wales would have been completely alien to their thinking, despite the fact that in May 1969 the Royal Commission on the Constitution had been appointed and it was to examine devolution.[171]

Devolution and its consequences

I have alluded briefly to the ill fated 1978 Government of Wales Act,[172] but that and the origins of the 1998 Act are outside the scope of this lecture, not

---

[169] Para 3326: Mars Jones J set up two such committees for Wales – one for the North and one for the South: see his article in the *Cambrian Law Review* at p 90. He also appointed a liaison judge for the Welsh Language; the first appointee was Judge Dewi Watkin Powell. He was succeeded on his retirement in 1993 by Judge Roderick Evans QC, the present Recorder of Cardiff. The terms of reference for the Liaison Judge included organising courses to assist judges in carrying out functions under the Welsh Language Act, liasing with the Circuit Administrator in recruiting and training interpreters, liasing with the Magistrates and assisting generally in the implementation of the policy of the Welsh Language Act.

[170] Including a powerful memorandum from Hywel ap Robert seeking a Chancery Court in Wales.

[171] For the political background and the role of Elystan Morgan MP (later Judge Lord Elystan Morgan) see: John Davies, supra 671. Initially the Royal Commission was chaired by Lord Crowther and, after his death by the Scottish Judge, Lord Kilbrandon; The Report and evidence are published as Cmnd 5460; Sir Alun Talfan Davies QC was a member. There is a very valuable account of the history of Welsh devolution and a review of the Kilbrandon proposals by Professor Sir David Williams QC presented to the UK Committee on Comparative Law in Cardiff in 1974 and published in *Cambrian Law Review* 80.

[172] See John Davies, supra, 674-8.

least because Legal Wales, with a few noted exceptions, largely passed these by and the form of devolution has not touched on justice within Wales. Since the Speakers Conference in 1920, although the two Home Rule bills in 1955[173] and 1965[174] proposed the creation of a separate judicature for Wales and Sir Claud Schuster considered again in 1944 the question of a separate judicature for Wales in relation to a wartime request by the Welsh Parliamentary party for a Secretary of State,[175] the recent debate on devolution has not concerned the administration of justice.

But devolution has nonetheless had a profound effect on Legal Wales and it is to that I now turn.

---

[173] The Bill (Parliamentary Papers 1954-5) was drafted by Eryl Hall Williams (a lecturer at the LSE) and Dewi Watkin Powell. It proposed the establishment of a Supreme Court of Judicature of Wales as a division of the Supreme Court of England and Wales; there was to be a High Court in Wales (comprising of three judges) and a Court of Appeal in Wales (comprising two justices of appeal and a chief justice). The bill was introduced by S.O. Davies, the Labour MP for Merthyr. It was debated on 4 March 1955 (H.C Vol 357, col 2439). In seconding the bill, Cledwyn Hughes (then MP for Anglesey) said that there was a real need for a Welsh judicature and pointed to the long assize lists at Glamorgan Assizes with cases being transferred from one town to another. He said the proposal was not new as it was tantamount to the resurrection of the Court of Great Sessions. For the background see: *The Labour Party in Wales 1900-2000* edited by Tanner, Williams and Hopkin (Cardiff 2000).

[174] The bill (Parliamentary Papers 1967-8) proposed transferring the jurisdiction of the High Court in Wales to a court to be known as Her Majesty's Court of Great Sessions for Wales. This Court would sit in four to six permanent Great Session Houses (the location of which was unspecified); there was also to be a Court of Appeal for Wales, presided over by a Chief Justice of Wales. It also proposed there be an Attorney General for Wales and the unification of both parts of the legal profession in Wales. The Bill was introduced into the House of Lords by Lord Ogmore and failed on its second reading (HL Vol 288 col 702); he said that Wales had had its own courts and he felt it would be of great advantage to have the same again.

[175] This resulted from a Memorandum from the 36 members of the Welsh Parliamentary Party to the Prime Minister dated 28 October 1943. It sought recognition of the nationality of Wales and the creation of a Secretary of State with powers similar to the Scottish Secretary. Sir Claud was asked to comment, as precise parity would, in the view of the Ministerial Committee considering the request, involve a separate judicial system. Sir Claud's reasons for the rejection of this consequence are set out in his memorandum of 18 May 1944 (PRO LCO 2/3214)

(i) Legal Wales and the government of Wales

There has undoubtedly been an immense strengthening of the profession in Wales over the last 10 years; devolution has increased that strength and will continue to do so. There are now based in Wales law firms that can provide the highest level of expertise and they have extended their practice successfully into England; the Bar is gradually beginning to focus itself on Cardiff, rather than on London. It was as long ago as December 1967 that the Lord Chancellor decided that Silks need not have chambers in London; still too many do not see Cardiff as the centre on which they can base a full and successful practice extending across England and Wales. The last 10 years have also seen the establishment of specialist courts in Wales, indigenous institutions which are beginning to remedy the problems evident a century before.

However, one of the most striking products of the legacy of the past 150 years has been the lack of a public law tradition within Wales and within the profession in particular. In retrospect that was inevitable, given the London centric nature of judicial review and the lack of any indigenous institutions. In 1999 the Lord Chancellor took a significant step to remedy this by enabling public law cases involving the Assembly and other public bodies in Wales to be heard in Cardiff and this arrangement was formalised by the creation in August 2000 of the Administrative Court in Wales. Parallel with this was the creation of the office of the Counsel General, an institution essential to the development of Wales and the appointment of Winston Roddick QC to that office.

Despite these measures and the creation of these important indigenous institutions, it will take time to remedy the problems caused by our earlier history. For example, very few public law cases have been initiated in Wales. It has not been easy to get the parties, even when both are Welsh, to have their cases heard in Wales. There has been very little by way of innovative or creative thinking put into practice by the profession within Wales as regards the use of the Human Rights Convention; it is striking that although it has been in force as regards the powers of the National Assembly for over 15 months, no single issue has been raised in Wales. Although Wales has produced public lawyers of the highest distinction, there was no court or institution within Wales to form a focus for public law.

Therefore the first contribution that Legal Wales must make to Wales after devolution is to ensure that public law work is done by practitioners within Wales; this formidable task has been begun very successfully by the Wales Public Law Association.[176]

But the lack of public law tradition has had a wider and more unfortunate effect; it was a factor that contributed to Wales, unlike Scotland, not enjoying the benefit of a constitutional convention prior to the creation of the National Assembly.[177]

Although the fundamental aspects of a constitution are a matter of political decision, there is a contribution that lawyers can make utilising their analytical and legal skills in trying to analyse any problems that exist and providing options for political decisions. For example, although it is a matter for political decision what powers are conferred on the Assembly, there are many ways in which this can be done. There is a general interest, for example, in seeing that there is a uniform approach to the conferring of those powers and to making the structure of the powers more readily comprehensible. There is, I think, an appreciation, that there is a need to consider technical, but nonetheless important, questions as to how the primary legislation of the Westminster Parliament is drafted so that it confers powers on the Assembly in a way which the Assembly can operate and which the public can understand. The time must surely have come[178] for Legal

---

[176] Formed in July 1999 following on a Conference on the Legal Effects of Devolution organised by the Bar, the Law Society and Cardiff University and held at Cardiff Law School in April 1999. Later that year a Wales Commercial Law Association and a Welsh Personal Injuries Law Association were formed. All these Associations are inclusive and have as members judges, solicitors, barristers and academic lawyers.

[177] Professor Sir David Williams urged the creation of a Constitutional Commission in the 1993 Lord Morris Lecture, in a paper given at the Cambridge Conference in early 1998 (*Constitutional Reform in the United Kingdom* (1998) ed Beatson: 'Devolution the Welsh Perspective') and in a paper given to a conference in Cardiff in 1999 (in *Devolution in Wales: Public Law and the National Assembly*, ed Miers, Cardiff 1999, published by the Wales Public Law Association). He returned to this subject in the inaugural lecture of Centre of Welsh Legal Affairs at Aberystwyth in May 2000.

[178] The debate in a workshop sponsored by the Wales and Chester Circuit under the leadership of Christopher Pitchford QC (now Pitchford J) and Patrick Harrington QC at the Bar Millennium Conference on 14 October 2000 showed how detached the bar in Wales had become, but also how keen it was to remedy that detachment.

Wales to make a proper contribution to this important work and to the initiatives and plans announced by the Assembly and the Government in Wales.[179]

(ii) The Welsh Language

Although the 1967 and 1993 Welsh Language Acts have been an enormous achievement, there remain important questions about the use of Welsh in the administration of justice and, now after devolution, in the preparation of legislation. The principle of equality is established, but, how is that to be translated into practice?[180]

In the first place there are, what I might describe as technical matters. Where there has to be translation, how is this best done? We need to be sure that simultaneous translation is in fact the best where absolute precision in the question and answer is necessary. We also need to ensure that the vocabulary of Welsh is adapted and enriched; I very much hope that the initiative currently being taken by the National Assembly and the Court Service to fund a project for the production of a vocabulary will be successful. We have our own indigenous example to follow in the pioneering efforts in which one of the leading Welsh scholars of his generation worked with a number of different lawyers to produce the first official forms of Welsh oaths in 1943. What of juries? The issue raised by a juror who cannot

---

[179] A very important contribution was made by Lord Prys Davies in his lecture at the Llanelli Eisteddfod August 2000: *The National Assembly: a Year of Laying the Foundations*. So too has the work of Dr Richard Rawlings of the London School of Economics: see in particular 'The New Model Wales': published with a number of other papers by lawyers in *Devolution in Wales: Public Law and the National Assembly* ed Miers, Cardiff 1999, published by the Wales Public Law Association).

[180] In September 1999, a new body, the Lord Chancellor's Standing Committee on the Welsh Language, was established as a permanent body to ensure uniform application of policy throughout all courts and tribunals in the implementation of the Acts. Its first report was published in April 2001. The Court Service established a Welsh Language Unit at Llangefni County Court in 1994 under Mrs Mildred Hughes MBE. It published its Welsh Language Scheme at the Eisteddfod in Llanelli in August 2000.

understand English or whose first language is Welsh remains unresolved.[181] As far as I have been able to determine, no such issue has arisen since 1953 when a judge at Dolgellau asked jurors, who would not read the oath in English and wished to take the oath in Welsh, to stand aside, as he thought that indicated an inability to understand English[182]. The issue may appear academic, but I doubt it. We must resolve it.[183]

But beyond these technical questions, there are more fundamental questions which Legal Wales needs to address.[184] Now that the National

---

[181] At the meeting with Sir Claud Schuster in January 1939, referred to above, Artemus Jones described the position in these terms (PRO LC0 2/4419):

> "Since Lord Atkin's judgment [*Lal* v *The King-Emperor*] it had been the custom in Cardiganshire that if a juror, when given the oath in English, said he could not understand it, he was told to stand down and treat it as disqualified non-jury service. He said that this was also done in some other counties but not in all. The only alternative which he could see to this practice would be that an instruction should be given to the persons who make up the jury list to omit those who can only speak Welsh."

[182] This caused considerable controversy; it was raised in Parliament. The Attorney General in his answer wished to question whether the Judge had acted correctly, but the Lord Chancellor refused to countenance this (see PRO LCO 2/5273). One of the jurors could read, write and speak English, but he had understood that the 1942 Act had given him the right to take the oath in Welsh. I am indebted to Lord Prys Davies for his assistance on this point.

[183] As a result of Edmund Davies LJ's confidential report in 1973, the Lord Chancellor in a statement made on 12 June 1973 announced that simultaneous translation would be made available as the best means of enabling the principle of equal validity to be recognised in jury trials whilst maintaining the principle of the random selection of jurors. (HL Vol 343 col 532-39). Edmund Davies LJ was (according to the summary of his report set out in Hansard) of the opinion that untranslated Welsh trials would debar 75 per cent of the population of Wales from jury service in a particular case and would be a radical departure from the random selection which was a foundation of the constitution. A practice note issued by the Presiding Judges of the Circuit in August 1976 implemented this policy. However s.10 of the Juries Act 1974 (as amended) makes a person ineligible to serve on a jury if he does not have a sufficient understanding of English. See also Robyn Léwis, supra, at p 23 and 79-81.

[184] The question as to how far language impacted on the judicial system in Wales was raised by the delegation that presented the Petition to the Peel Commission in 1935. The argument was advanced that a separate judicial system for Wales was needed to give the language its rightful place in the administration of justice in Wales. In his May 1944 memorandum, Sir Claud Schuster answered this by saying that this would create a grave injustice to the monoglot English speakers in Wales, would be

Assembly is passing legislation in a bilingual format[185], do our universities need to teach legal courses in Welsh? Do we need materials in Welsh so that the argument on the texts can proceed as easily in Welsh as in English? How can this happen when so much of the primary material is in English? In this our Universities – their Welsh departments and their law departments- have a vital role. The departments within the Universities need to co-operate, as do the Universities themselves. How is this best done?

These are difficult questions and the solutions will not be realised in the short term. I think we must look at a timescale[186] to be measured in terms of half a generation or more; certainly that has been the experience in parts of Canada as I have recently learnt.[187] But these are issues that must be addressed by Legal Wales and addressed in a way that is inclusive of the whole of the Welsh people.

(iii) The legal system and its institutions

It is evident from the story I have outlined that it has been the lack of indigenous institutions that has been the principal difficulty in developing the legal system within Wales to serve the needs of Wales. The new institutions are in their infancy. There are developments yet to be made; the ability of the new institutions has yet to be tested in relation to bilingual Assembly legislation or in a judicial review of a significant decision of the Assembly.[188]

---

impossible because of the lack of a sufficient number of Welsh speaking appointees and there would be very grave problems on appeals.

185 The Hughes Parry Report rejected bilingualism in the administration of justice as impracticable in so far is it involved conducting trials wholly in Welsh (where desired) and keeping records in English and Welsh; it considered that there were overwhelming financial and practical difficulties – see para 169-170 of the Report.

186 In a reading delivered to the Middle Temple in 1937, Artemus Jones observed:

> "In the distant future, I believe that the ultimate solution of this problem in Wales will be on the lines of bilingualism as in the case of South Africa and Quebec."

187 See: *Bilingual Law Making and Justice: A Report on the lessons for Wales from the Canadian experience of bilingualism.* (Office of the Counsel General to the National Assembly for Wales, March 2001)

188 As Sir David Williams pointed out in his 1993 Lord Morris lecture, it would presumably be politically unacceptable to entrust such power of judicial review to the High Court in London. As a result of the Lord Chancellor's decision following the

I see no reason at present why these developments cannot continue and the new indigenous institutions flourish within the unitary system we share with England.[189] Wales and the legal profession in Wales does derive very substantial benefits from that unitary system; for example, it would be much more difficult for Cardiff with what I might term its "export orientated" law firms to succeed in becoming one of the principal legal centres in the United Kingdom outside that unitary system. It is for these reasons I presently see that our goal should be to develop and nurture our indigenous institutions within that unitary system. How is this best done?

To that end, we have embarked with the magistracy, the tribunals (which have been left too long outside the legal fold) and others concerned with the administration of justice on an overall strategy for Wales to try and improve access to justice across Wales. Will this be acceptable to the people of Wales? What else should we do? How do we strengthen the profession and ensure that the profession based in Wales does Wales' legal work in Wales to the benefit of Wales as a whole?

There is no doubt that outside of Cardiff and Swansea, the court system across Wales faces the legacy of parochialism and the lack of national identity and a national focus; there is a ready example which explains the current problems in Montgomeryshire.

Quarter Sessions in Montgomeryshire used to take place alternatively at Welshpool and Newtown; this was because[190] the Earls of Powys were often

---

first Conference of UK Judges on 9 April 1999 (see LCD Press release of 9 April 1999 and the Forward by the Lord Chancellor to *Devolution in Wales: Public Law and the National Assembly* (ed Miers)), judicial review of any such decision will take place in Cardiff; the decision was implemented in the Practice Direction on Devolution Issues (June 1999). If these arrangements do not stand the test, then as Sir David predicted in 1993,

> "the pressure would surely be towards a Welsh or localised judicial system with ultimate authority vested in the judicial House of Lords. Scotland in 1979 had its judiciary in place, as did Northern Ireland in 1921. Wales would need to fashion its own judiciary and legal system from scratch."

Since 1993, steps have been taken to build institutions of justice and repatriate proceedings from London.

[189] The Court of Appeal Civil Division sat for the first time in Cardiff in October 1999; further sittings have taken place in May and October 2000.

[190] As recounted to John Morgan, by then Clerk of Assize of the Wales and Chester Circuit, by Clement Davies; see his letter to Sir Albert Napier the Permanent

chairman of Quarter Sessions; as Welshpool was near Powys Castle where the Earl spent his winter months, Quarter Sessions in the winter took place at Welshpool. In the summer the Earl moved to a mansion in Newtown and so the summer Quarter Sessions were held at Newtown. Assizes followed a similar pattern because a High Sheriff in 1835 organised a petition and other evidence which persuaded the Privy Council to ordain that whilst Welshspool was the town for the Winter Assize, the Summer Assizes were at Newtown on condition there was a proper court. This was done and that High Sheriff's family made a building available at a peppercorn rent in Newtown, while the Council provided and maintained the premises at Welshpool.[191]

By the 1940s that Newtown building had become a cinema but was used as an Assize court each summer. As Clement Davies observed to the Permanent Secretary of the Lord Chancellor's Department in 1948:

> It just appals me to think that there may be taking place a trial for life from 10am until 6pm and then at half past six in come the crowd to laugh at some funny picture.

He therefore proposed that the Assizes cease to sit at Newtown to the delight of the Lord Chancellor's Department:

> The fact that the Member of Parliament advocates the suppression of one of the Assize towns in his own constituency seems to provide admirable opportunity, from the political point of view, of suppressing an inconvenient Assize town if that is what the judges think ought to be done.

The Permanent Secretary therefore wrote to the Montgomeryshire County Council in April 1948 proposing the closure of Newtown. However the great grandson of the Sheriff who had been instrumental in getting the Summer Assize moved from Welshpool to Newtown intervened and found another building in Newtown, the Church House, which had been used for Quarter Sessions and could, in his view, be easily adapted for use as an Assize Court.

Secretary in the Lord Chancellor's Department dated 19 February 1948 (PRO LCO2/4786).

[191] As recounted by Capt. E. W. Minton Beddoes, High Sheriff of Montgomery in 1948. (Letter to the Lord Chancellor dated 9 May 1948, PRO LCO 2/4786)

He showed the visiting Judge around; that judge reported to the Lord Chief Justice that it would make an admirable court.[192] Thus spurred into action the Montgomeryshire County Council instructed that county architect to examine the plan to convert Church House. He prepared plans; the cost was to be £652 17s 4d. On 25 February 1949 the Council wrote to the Permanent Secretary to say they would not spend this sum;[193] on St. David's Day the Permanent Secretary replied that an Order in Council would be made discontinuing Newtown as an Assize town.[194]

The question of a court in Newtown came back for consideration by the Beeching Commission; they concluded Mid Wales must have a centre and the obvious candidate town was Newtown; it, however had no suitable courts and Welshpool would have to serve temporarily. The Lord Chancellor endorsed this in 1971. Nothing happened. Today, in part as a direct legacy of the parochialism and rivalry between these towns that goes back to a fateful decision made over 50 years ago, there are no satisfactory court buildings in Montgomeryshire.

That is but one illustration of the parochialism that has bedevilled creating a rational system for access to justice in Wales. This is in large part due, so far as my researches have gone, to the triumph of parochialism over national identity.

---

[192] In May 1948 Lord Goddard, the then Lord Chief Justice, stated that if the local authorities were willing to provide a proper court at Newtown, they would consider holding the Assizes there; it was suggested that the most satisfactory thing would be to tell the local authorities to submit plans to the Department showing exactly what they proposed and to make it clear that unless a better building was provided, then Assizes would no longer be held there. (PRO LCO2/4786)

[193] This is in contrast to Newport who obtained the transfer from Monmouth to Newport by agreeing in 1935 to build two new courts at their proposed civic centre without any cost to the county. Letter to the Peel Commission 18 November 1935 (PRO LCO2/1612).

[194] See the correspondence in PRO LCO 2/4786

A first task for Legal Wales

But parochialism has another aspect. I have spoken of the contribution that Legal Wales can make to the creation of a national identity, to the development of the National Assembly, to fostering the development of the language, to providing better access to justice, and to contributing towards the economy. But any inward looking view can always be parochial in itself; the great contribution of Welsh lawyers, such as Lord Morris, had been a contribution to developing the general law but that has largely taken place outside their native land.

There is no reason why in focusing the energies of Legal Wales in strengthening Wales, we should be introspective. For example, in developing a system of access to justice for a nation with the demography of Wales, we can as a nation be at the forefront in the use of technology. Some steps along that road can be seen first in the work of the Court Service with the Dyfed Powys Police in developing their computer network to link the courts and the criminal justice agencies. It can also be seen in the work of the Court Service and judiciary with the video conferencing network being developed with the University of Wales and the Law Society. There is no reason why Legal Wales cannot be similarly innovative and outward looking in the development of our own linguistic heritage. I am confident that can also be done, particularly in the field of legislative drafting where we are no longer bound by the history of Whitehall, but are free to draw on the experience of other nations and develop our own ideas and policy in conjunction with the wider world. In our analysis of and debate on the new constitutional arrangements for Wales, we can only gain by adopting the same outward looking approach.

If we can adopt this approach, then the national identity for Wales and its strong linguistic heritage should enable the people of Wales to enjoy a better legal and constitutional system than the forces of parochialism might suggest. We will have justified Lord Morris' attributes of vigour and vibrancy that make a nation.

As a demonstration of that vigour and vibrancy and to initiate what I hope will be an independent contribution to improving the subordinate law making powers of the Assembly, to the future of the Welsh language and to the institutions of justice in Wales, this University has agreed that part of the endowment provided by Lord Morris for this lecture can be used in accordance with Lord Morris' wish for a series of three seminars. Each will be conducted under Chatham House rules and each will produce a report.

The first of these will be on the subordinate law making powers of the Assembly. We are enormously indebted to Professor Sir David Williams QC, one of the pre-eminent public lawyers of his generation, for agreeing to chair such a seminar to be held on 19 January 2001. I have no doubt that the seminar will provide a keen focus of debate among those with a technical understanding of legislation that can analyse some of the problems that have arisen and provide ideas for their solution.[195]

The second of the seminars, in March 2001, will examine the long term issues relating to the Welsh language and its role in the courts and legislation. There is no one more fitted to chair that than the present Recorder of Cardiff, Judge Roderick Evans QC.[196]

The third, later in 2001, will examine the longer term issues relating to the legal profession and the courts in Wales and their contribution to the Welsh economy; Cardiff has been transformed into a leading civil litigation centre under Judge Graham Jones, the designated Civil Judge for South and West Wales; his energies have been harnessed to chair the third seminar.

I hope in these practical ways we can begin to contribute to making Wales, as Lord Bingham, the first Lord Chief Justice to acknowledge he was Lord Chief Justice of England and Wales,[197] observed, a distinctive and successful nation.

---

[195] The papers delivered at the seminar and the report have been published under the title *The Law Making Powers of the National Assembly for Wales* by the *Wales Law Journal* and the Law Society (2001)

[196] The papers delivered at the seminar and the report are published in [2001] 1 *Wales Law Journal* pp 9-52.

[197] He adopted this title in early 1998; it was first used officially at the opening of the new Civil Justice Centre at Swansea.

A VOICE FOR WALES
THE NATIONAL ASSEMBLY FOR WALES

David Lambert

In his contribution to this series of essays, Mr Justice Thomas asks how the law has recognised national identity. This essay considers to what extent, by reference to its existing functions, that identity has been recognised in creating the National Assembly for Wales.

To have an identity the Assembly should be able to have the capacity to make comprehensive policy and executive decisions by reference to powers which are understandable both to Assembly Members and to the public at large. Everyone should be clearly aware of what powers the Assembly possesses and what powers are possessed by other executive bodies, particularly central government.

In July 1997, the Secretary of State for Wales presented to Parliament a White Paper,[1] "A Voice for Wales - the Government's proposals for a Welsh Assembly". It set out proposals for an Assembly for Wales on which, as the Prime Minister in his preface to the Paper said, "the people of Wales will have the opportunity to vote in a referendum in the autumn. The Assembly will be a new voice for Wales, enabling many more matters that affect Wales to be decided in Wales. It will give Wales an exciting new role within the United Kingdom".

The White Paper set out "the case for an Assembly" explaining that the Welsh Office was directly responsible for a wide range of public services in Wales with an annual budget of £7 billion. The Welsh Office together with health authorities and quangos through whom the Welsh Office ran some of the services, were not directly accountable to the people of Wales. This was a democratic deficit which the Government was proposing to address by creating a National Assembly for Wales. Those controlling the spending and setting the standards for public services in Wales should be answerable to the people they serve. The Paper considered that an elected body would be more responsive to the needs of Wales.

---

[1] 1 Cm.3718

The Assembly would set policies and standards for the services for which the Secretary of State for Wales was currently responsible and in doing so it would make its own subordinate legislation within the statutory framework laid down by enabling Acts of Parliament. To achieve these objectives, the Assembly would be a modern inclusive institution gaining the trust of the people of Wales by conducting its affairs openly and properly.

The following principles would apply to the Assembly:

1. it would observe high standards for the conduct of its own business;
2. it would be staffed by politically impartial civil servants;
3. it would have regard to the interests of local authorities, business, unions and the voluntary sector and work in partnership with them;
4. it would reflect the diversity of Wales in promoting sustainable development and providing equal opportunities for all;
5. it would treat the Welsh and English languages on the basis of equality.

The Assembly is working by these principles. The policies of the Assembly Cabinet are regularly scrutinised by its subject committees and its successes are chronicled in the pages of the Institute of Welsh Affairs quarterly review of Assembly progress and in the Assembly's first annual report available at www.wales.gov.uk. This website also refers to the many pieces of subordinate legislation so far made by the Assembly.

However there is still a fundamental problem which arises from the perception of the Assembly in the eyes of the people of Wales.

The National Assembly has now been exercising its functions for 18 months. The end of its first full calendar year was celebrated in December by two cartoons in the *Western Mail*. In the first a child is saying to his father "Dad, all my friends say there's no such thing. Tell me the truth. Does the National Assembly really exist?" The second has an Assembly Minister saying "The TV want us to make a 30 second review of the Assembly's achievements." Another Minister replies "30 seconds - that's ridiculous, we'll just speak slowly".

What has brought about this apparent disillusionment with the institution? This essay considers one possible aspect - the nature of the executive powers of the Assembly. The Prime Minister had referred in the

White Paper's preface to "enabling many more matters that affect Wales to be decided in Wales". The White Paper explained that these matters were currently the responsibility of the Secretary of State for Wales and that they would be listed in the Bill that established the Assembly. The White Paper listed these responsibilities by subject area, setting out in an Annex the more detailed powers and duties of the Secretary of State for Wales". Under nine general subject area headings, sub-headings explain the particular subject matters which are the Secretary of State for Wales' responsibility.

The White Paper explained that "the Bill will contain the power to transfer the Secretary of State's responsibility to the Assembly by Order in Council." There was no intention to transfer to the Assembly "responsibility for functions which currently operate on a common basis throughout the United Kingdom. These include foreign affairs, defence, taxation ... social security and taxation".

The Paper promised that the transfer of functions to the Assembly will enable it "to set policies which can drive the Welsh economy forward and make a difference to the quality of life in Wales".

"The Government wishes to ... spread economic prosperity throughout Wales ...It believes that an Assembly with members representing all parts of Wales, responsive to its needs, can provide the necessary leadership. A directly-elected Assembly, firmly embedded in the United Kingdom and in touch with the communities it serves, will liberate the energy of the Welsh people to make a real difference".

It is questionable whether the manner in which the functions of the Assembly as currently expressed can fulfil these objectives. It is in this context that the First Partnership Agreement of the National Assembly for Wales[2] states: "We will, before the end of the Assembly's first term, establish an independent Commission into the powers ... of the National Assembly in order to ensure that it is able to operate in the best interests of the people of Wales. This review should investigate ... the relevant competencies devolved. The review shall publish its recommendations in the first year of the second term of the National Assembly in order to enable

---

[2] Entered into by the Labour and Liberal Democrat parties in the National Assembly in September 2000.

adequate reflection on the Assembly's first complete term. Whilst recognising that this Partnership Agreement will have expired on completion of this review, we will ensure that arrangements are put in place in advance to ensure that the Assembly as a whole has the opportunity to press the UK Government to bring forward any appropriate primary legislation, necessary to ensure that its recommendations can be fully implemented".

What are "the relevant competencies devolved" and why has it been necessary to propose the establishment of a Commission? Following the publication of the White Paper in 1997, the referendum carried out under the Referendums (Scotland and Wales) Act 1997[3] gave a vote, albeit by a very narrow majority[4] in favour of the Wales Assembly. Both the White Paper and the subsequent Government of Wales Act 1998[5] held out the possibility of the Assembly having general executive powers over subject areas. Indications included:

(i) a list of subject fields in Schedule 2 to the Act "in which functions are to be transferred by the First Order in Council"

(ii) a very wide power in section 34 of the Act enabling the Assembly:- "to do anything it considers appropriate to support

  (a) museums, art galleries or libraries in Wales; buildings of historical or architectural interest, or other places of historic interest in Wales;

  (b) the Welsh language; or

  (c) the arts, crafts, sport or other cultural or recreational activities in Wales."

(iii) section 56(3) of the Act - "the Assembly First Secretary shall allocate accountability in the fields in which the Assembly has functions to members of the executive committee" and

(iv) section 57(1) of the Act - "the Assembly shall establish committees with responsibilities in the fields in which the Assembly has functions".

---

[3] 1997 c.61

[4] 50% of the electorate voted, of whom 50.3% voted in favour of the proposal

[5] 1998 ch.38

The current guide issued by the National Assembly[6] reflects the subject area approach.

The powers and responsibilities of the Assembly

The Assembly has the power to develop and implement policy in a range of areas:

- agriculture
- ancient monument and historic buildings
- culture
- economic development
- education and training
- the environment
- health and health services
- highways
- housing
- industry
- local government
- social services
- sport and leisure
- tourism
- town and country planning
- transport and roads
- the Welsh language.

The expectation of a subject area competence was not fulfilled in the first Order in Council[7] transferring functions from Government Ministers to the National Assembly. Made under section 22 of the Government of Wales Act, it reflected the Government's policy decision that only the Ministerial functions of the Secretary of State for Wales should be transferred to the

---

[6] Assembly information booklet "A basic introduction to the Assembly, how it is elected and what it does" - May 2000

[7] The National Assembly for Wales (Transfer of Functions) Order 1999. SI 1999/672

Assembly. For administrative reasons those functions had not been exercised by reference to complete subject areas and there was no need for this from a legal point of view because the functions were statutorily vested in "the Secretary of State". Which Secretary of State would exercise them could usually be a matter for administrative decision.[8] The Secretary of State for Wales exercised functions in Education Acts, for example, but he was not responsible for all Ministerial functions relating to Education in Wales. Some functions were exercised solely by the Secretary of State for Education and Employment, for example matters relating to teachers' pay and some functions were exercised by both Secretaries of State acting together. Some functions were exercised with the consent of the Treasury.

This kaleidoscopic picture was mirrored over all the subject areas which were to be the basis of this first Transfer of Functions Order. Nowhere was there a comprehensive document setting out all the specific functions of the Secretary of State for Wales; there was no need for one. The result of the first Transfer Order is that the general powers given to the Assembly in section 34 of the Government of Wales Act relating to culture, sport, the Welsh language and historic buildings are not replicated in any of the other powers exercisable by the Assembly. Neither does the Assembly necessarily have all Ministerial functions exercisable in relation to Wales in any particular Act. Of the 350 Acts of Parliament listed in the Order less than a third transfer all Ministerial powers contained in them to the Assembly. An average page of the Order contains some 10 Acts which are set out chronologically and not by subject area of which perhaps:-

(a) all Ministerial powers in three Acts are transferred to the Assembly to be solely exercisable by the Assembly;

[8] While Transfer of Functions Orders were made under the Ministers of the Crown Acts 1964 and 1975, this was only necessary where a transfer of property, for example hospitals, was involved. Ministerial responsibility for social services in Wales was transferred by letter from the Secretary of State for Social Services to the Secretary of State for Wales in 1979.

(b) some Ministerial powers[9] in another three Acts are transferred, leaving the remainder to be exercised by Government Ministers;
(c) some Ministerial powers in the remainder of the Acts are transferred but those powers are required to be exercisable by the Assembly with the consent of, or after consultation with Government Ministers or Departments or are exercisable "concurrently" by the Assembly and by a Government Minister. The concept of "concurrently" is not defined in the Order. It presumably enables either the Assembly or a Government Minister or both to exercise the same powers in relation to Wales.

Some Acts within subject areas are not referred to in the Order at all and no Ministerial powers under these Acts are transferred to the Assembly.[10]

Looking at the Transfer of Functions Order it is soon apparent that the Assembly has considerable difficulties in proposing and executing comprehensive policies in many of the areas listed in Schedule 2 to the Government of Wales Act. In the example given in footnote 8 about the Agricultural Market Act 1983, a transfer of Ministerial powers by reference to a paragraph of a subsection of a section (section 6(3)(b)) and a subparagraph of one paragraph of a Schedule (paragraph 4(4) of Schedule 1) does not give the Assembly an overall competence in the subject matter of the Act. This has the consequence of lowering the standing of the Assembly in the eyes of the public of Wales. It is perhaps not without some significance that the two cartoons were published in the Western Mail not in 1999, but at the end of 2000 when the Assembly had been exercising its powers for 18 months.[11] One of the reasons for this is that Acts of Parliament passed since

---

[9] An example is the Agricultural Marketing Act 1983 (c.3). The powers transferred are those "exercisable by the Secretary of State... ...Sections 1,5, 6(3)(b) and (4) and paragraph 4(4) of Schedule 1".

[10] This became apparent to the Assembly when it was attempting to exercise functions in relation to the pay and conditions of teachers. The relevant Act was not listed in the Transfer Order and the Assembly had no power.

[11] The Assembly began exercising the functions contained in the first Transfer of Functions Order on July 1st 1999.

the creation of the Assembly continue the precedent set by the first Transfer of Functions Order. Thus:

(a) no Act gives a general competence to the Assembly to make policy decisions. Section 34 of the 1998 Act shows that it is possible to give such a competence to the Assembly by reference to the subject matter of the Act. The concept is also accepted in the Scotland Act 1998, where Schedule 5 to the Act defines many of the restrictions on the competencies of the Scottish Parliament and Executive by reference to the subject matter of an Act.[12] It is equally possible to define subject areas of parts of Acts, if it is required to limit the competency of the Assembly to a part of a particular Act;[13]
(b) some Acts give competence to the Assembly section by section with no competence being given in the case of certain sections. Thus of the twenty eight sections in Part I of the Local Government Act 1999, the functions in sections 1 (1) (d) and (e) and sections 14, 16 to 18, 24 and 27 are not exercisable by the Assembly but by the Secretary of State in relation to Wales;
(c) in some Acts it is necessary to search through the whole of the Act to ascertain whether the Assembly is given any functions. A search is necessary because there is neither a self-contained section which deals with Wales and the Assembly's powers nor a side-heading to a particular section indicating a reference to the Assembly. An example of this is the Welfare Reform and Pensions Act 1999 which without any prior or general indication gives functions to the Assembly in section 60(6) of the Act;
(d) the first order giving competence to the Assembly to implement EU Directions by means of subordinate legislation gives very limited powers to the Assembly as distinct to those given to central government in the same instrument. Thus the Assembly can implement directions which relate to the processing and marketing

---

[12] An example is the exclusion of the competence in relation to "the subject matter of the Misuse of Drugs Act 1971".
[13] An example is the exclusion of competence in relation to "Part V of the Criminal Law (Consolidation) (Scotland) Act 1985".

of forestry products and which relate to informational and educational materials dealing with the feeding of infants and young children.[14] This is not exactly a heavy responsibility for a devolved body.

It is very difficult for the Assembly to continue to function effectively in the face of these statutory problems.

The Presiding Officer of the National Assembly has recognised that "the current basis of the Assembly's powers displays no constitutional logic, but was based entirely on the political processes of the gradual acquisition of powers within the Office of the Secretary of State for Wales. Devolving secondary legislation as a category makes no constitutional sense, because it is itself legislatively various".[15]

The Assembly itself has called for the following matters to be implemented:[16]

(a) detailed explanations of the procedure through which the Assembly can influence the content of the government's legislative programme;
(b) Parliamentary Bills which impact on the functions and responsibilities of the Assembly should be drafted in such a way as to permit the Assembly maximum flexibility in implementing their provisions and developing policy in the areas concerned;
(c) remission of relevant Bills introduced into Parliament to the appropriate Assembly subject committees for consideration as to the provisions they should make for Wales and how the Assembly might use the powers in the Bill;
(d) Assembly Ministers to make statements prior to the conclusion of Bills which concern the powers of the Assembly detailing the extent to which representations made by the Assembly have been reflected in amendments made during the passage of the Bills through Parliament;

---

[14] The European Communities (Designation) (No.3) Order 1999. SI 1999/2788/
[15] Speech at University College, Aberystwyth, April 2000.
[16] Assembly resolution of 19th December 2000 tabled by the Coalition Cabinet.

(e) consultation between the Assembly Cabinet and the Assembly as to which Wales-only Bills should be requested in each Parliamentary Session.

The components of the Assembly resolution place a tremendous amount of work on an Assembly and Executive whose resources are already stretched.

In introducing this motion for debate, Andrew Davies, the Business Manager of the Assembly Cabinet, referred to the "excellent track record" of the Assembly in influencing primary legislation. Certainly this is shown in the acceptance by Parliament of the Assembly's requirement to establish a Children's Commissioner in Wales.[17] Other influences by the Assembly on legislation passed by Parliament since July 1999 are not so easy to find. Implementation of the various heads of the Assembly's resolution would certainly help. There are problems however.

(a) There is no procedure currently set out in either the Government of Wales Act or the Assembly's Standing Orders for transmitting the comments of the Assembly to Government Departments about the nature of functions which the Assembly should exercise under forthcoming Bills. The Act requires the Secretary of State for Wales to appear before the Assembly after the annual Queen's Speech.[18] The Secretary of State can then be questioned on these proposals. The Standing Orders[19] provide for there to be a debate with the Secretary of State on the proposals, but that is all. Whether the Secretary of State transmits the views of the Assembly to his Government-colleagues or how the Assembly analyses the proposed legislation with the aim of setting out reasoned arguments for greater scope to be given to the Assembly to exercise functions under proposed legislation is not a matter considered by the Act or the Standing Orders. The result is that, so far there has been no such analysis and no reasoned views given to the Secretary of State.

---

[17] Section 72 of the Care Standards Act 2000 and the additions made to the Act by the current Children's Commissioner for Wales Bill.

[18] Section 76 of the Government of Wales Act.

[19] Standing Order 6.5.

(b) There is no overall agreement between Government Departments that Bills giving powers to the Assembly should be drafted in such a way as to permit the Assembly maximum flexibility. To achieve such agreement, principles would need to be set out in Concordats between the Assembly and each Government Department. There are no such principles, a situation amply illustrated by the specific and parsimonious powers given to the Assembly under the Local Government Acts 1999 and 2000. To achieve a maximum flexibility in implementing the provisions in primary legislation and in developing policy by reference to subject areas, the Assembly will need to have wide subordinate legislative powers given in a Bill which would probably be wider and more comprehensive than those given in the Bill to central government Ministers as regards England. Such powers in a Bill should also enable the Assembly to amend Acts set out in the first Transfer of Functions Order transferring Ministerial powers to the Assembly. Thus in any future Bill on clean air in the environment, not only should the Assembly have flexible powers to implement the subject matter of the Bill, but the Bill should also give the Assembly, if necessary with Parliamentary approval, power to amend any existing relevant environmental legislation which is set out in the Transfer Order and which at present only transfers some powers within Acts to the Assembly. Thus the reference to the Clean Air Act 1993 in the Order which reserves functions in five sections and a subsection of the Act to central government in relation to Wales would be able to be amended so that, unless the integrity of England and Wales is fundamentally affected, all the Ministerial powers in the Act, unless otherwise amended by the Bill, would be exercisable by the Assembly, thus bringing the concept of allowing the Assembly to have general policy making capabilities in relation to clean air both under the new powers in the Bill and under existing powers in the Clean Air Act. It should perhaps be noted that the exercise of Ministerial powers in existing legislation relating to clean air in Scotland is a matter solely within the jurisdiction of the Scottish Executive, there being no relevant exceptions in Schedule 5 to the Scotland Act. A current problem in achieving the goal of comprehensive powers is that wide Ministerial powers in Bills to amend existing legislation are known as Henry VIII powers in recognition of the powers taken by Henry VIII under the Supremacy Acts of 1535 and 1536 to disestablish the Roman Catholic Church. Government Departments are no strangers to the exercise of this legislation[20] but some seem to exhibit a marked reluctance to agree to the Assembly exercising such powers, possibly because the Assembly is not part of central government. However, if devolution means that Ministerial powers are exercisable by the Assembly in relation to Wales then it is difficult to justify an outright refusal to contemplate the Assembly exercising a particular type of Ministerial power. There is no evidence to show that the Assembly would abuse this power and many Henry VIII powers are given to Government Ministers for the better and more comprehensive exercise of powers under an Act. This is what the Assembly seeks. If there is concern, then any such power could be exercisable by the Assembly with Parliamentary consent or both with such consent and the consent of a Minister.[21]

(c) Analysis of Bills before Parliament might be achieved by implementing the third part of the Assembly's resolution of December 2000. The initial proposal was to remit five of the most important Bills in the session 2000-2001[22] to the relevant subject committees for consideration. The problem here is that if subject committees are to fulfil the remit of the Assembly and report as to the manner in which the Bills should make provision for Wales and how the Assembly might use the powers in the Bills, considerable

---

[20] Two of the more extensive examples are Part I of the Deregulation and Contracting Out Act 1994 and the Pollution Prevention and control Act 1999.
[21] The Standing Orders of the Assembly already contemplate such procedures for certain Assembly subordinate legislation - see Standing Order 23, sections 1 and 2.
[22] The Bills were the Children's Commissioner for Wales and Health and Social Care, sent to the Health and Social Services Committee: Homes to the Local Government and Housing Committee: Regulatory Reform to the Economic Development Committee; and Special Educational Needs and Disability to the Education and Lifelong Learning Committee: all this legislation has now been enacted.

prior briefing material needs to be prepared for committees explaining the complexity of the ways in which Bills currently give powers to the Assembly, and they will need to meet many more times than the one slot that was all that was available to them; in relation to the considerable powers of these particular 5 Bills.

(d) The lack of any formal machinery for making representations by the Assembly to Government Departments may militate against the implementation of this part of the December resolution. If it is difficult to make representations then there will be little for Assembly Ministers to report to the Assembly about the extent to which representations which they have made have been reflected in amendments made during the passage of Bills through Parliament. One of the problems that backbench MPs and members of the House of Lords have had in proposing amendments to Bills in the last two sessions of Parliament to enable the Assembly to have sufficiently loose and flexible powers to create its own policy is that they have not been aware of what amendments the Assembly would wish to have. There is seemingly no channel of communication between Assembly Members and members of either House in relation to this fundamental matter.

(e) Again as regards the implementation of the December resolution requesting consultation between the Assembly Cabinet and the Assembly as to possible Wales-only Bills, there is no prescribed procedure in the Assembly's Standing Orders. Besides the Children's Commissioner proposals which were very much carried forward as a result of the Waterhouse report on children in care in North Wales,[23] few proposals for Wales-only legislation have been considered by the Assembly.[24] There are no Wales-only bills currently proposed in the 2001-2002 Parliamentary session.

---

[23] *Lost in Care*, published February 2000. HC 201,1999-2000.

[24] The assembly cabinet has suggested bills, making St David's Day a bank holiday in Wales and provisions for Wales-only legislation giving the Assembly wide powers in the fields of health and education.

The Assembly and all those who would wish to see it have more flexible provisions in legislation including greater and more general empowerment to make subordinate legislation would be considerably helped in making proposals for the achievement of these objectives if:

(a) the Assembly's functions were clearly set out in Bills when they are published following their first reading in Parliament. Functions of the Assembly in an Act could be given in their totality in a separate Part of the legislation applicable solely to Wales and to the Assembly. There is one example and, at present, one example only of this. The Learning and Skills Act 2000 assigns two separate Parts in the Act to Wales and the Assembly. This gives a clear indication of the Assembly's powers;
(b) for bills going through Parliament, explanatory notes should be prepared by the sponsoring government departments clearly indicating in tabular form the functions and particularly the subordinate legislative functions, which would be exercised by the Assembly under the Bill. So far this has been carried out in relation to one Bill only, the Transport Bill, at the insistence of the House of Lords Select Committee on Delegated Legislation;[25]
(c) the House of Commons Select Committee on Welsh Affairs could carry out more reviews of proposed legislation following the precedent created by their report on the Transport Bill in which they considered the extent of the functions proposed to be given to the Assembly.[26]

These are sentiments which have been fully supported in a strongly argued paper presented by the Law Society to the Assembly Review Group, which is currently reviewing Assembly procedures. These measures would be of assistance to Members of both Houses and to Assembly Members in being able to ascertain the extent of the powers proposed to be given to the Assembly and whether further powers could be given.

---

[25] 20th Report 1999-2000 HL Paper 73 and 37th Report 1999-2000 HL Paper 137.
[26] 15th Report 1999-2000 of the Committee on Welsh Affairs. HC.

Finally, there should be a dialogue not only between the Assembly Cabinet and the various Government Departments at the time that Bill policy is being formulated, but also the establishment of a dialogue between Assembly Members and Members of each House. Without such a dialogue there will be no informed analysis of the powers proposed to be given to the Assembly in forthcoming legislation, or how the powers could be amended to achieve more flexibility and how amendments might be drafted to persuade the Government during the passage of the Bills through Parliament to incorporate the amendments in the final legislation.

The Learning and Skills Act 2000 is an example of an evolutionary approach adopted by government departments and Parliament. It is a sign that both may be starting to be more relaxed about devolution. The devolution settlement as reflected in the Government of Wales Act enables legislation to be drafted in wide terms for the Assembly. Those wide terms will begin to appear as the Assembly continues to show that it is able to exercise its functions for the benefit of Wales. One thing is certain and that is that the continued devolution of powers to the Assembly is irreversible.

CARDIFF UNIVERSITY * PRIFYSGOL CAERDYDD *